Living Thirteen Years in Latin America

H. LYNN BECK

Pen Culture Solutions
1-888-727-7204 (USA)
1-800-950-458 (Australia)
support@penculturesolutions.com

Contents

Dedication

I want to thank my siblings: Leslie, Shannon, Shelli, and Sheri, for helping recall stories from our deep past. I also want to thank my cousins: Kathy, Dan, and Brian for adding to these stories about Grandpa and Grandma Tyler.

Chapter 1

The Decision to Join the Peace Corps

One Saturday I left my dormitory room at the University of Nebraska at Lincoln. I was bored, so I decided to walk around campus. I was in front of the student union when I saw a sign positioned to catch the attention of students entering the building. A Peace Corps representative was interviewing in a basement room.

My curiosity was tickled. I entered the student union and found the interviewing room. It was a small room with a small table and two chairs: one occupied by the Peace Corps interviewer and the other by a student. The interviewer had placed four chairs against the wall, with two people already sitting in these chairs. I occupied a third chair.

When it was my turn to talk to the representative, I gave him a condensed version of my background. He was enthusiastic, especially about my farming experience. He said the Peace Corps had unfilled positions in agriculture and that my skills would be useful in several programs. His excitement made me excited. I was an ordinary Nebraska farm boy. I felt satisfaction that the Peace Corps might need my skills.

During the summer, I felt compelled to be at home to help on the family farm. This included every weekend during the spring and fall farming season, and to any university vacation. My frustration was that I wanted to gain experience doing other things. I had friends who worked in plant nurseries, and for university professors' laboratories—all offering skills that might be useful one day, but I could not disappoint my family. I always needed to return to the family farm. My dissatisfaction grew each year. Another ten years working on the farm was not going to make me more valuable to anyone, nor would it satisfy my need to learn new things.

At the end of my conversation with the Peace Corps representative, I signed up to become a Peace Corps volunteer. As the semester's work intensified, I forgot about my chance encounter with the Peace Corps representative. I told no one about what I had done, and the memory quickly faded.

The semester ended, and I returned for another summer on the farm. I was less than enthusiastic, but it was my duty. The farm generated the revenue that paid my university fees, and I made more money from farming than I could have made from any regular job. There was no doubt about that.

As soon as I arrived on the farm, a letter arrived from the Peace Corps. They invited me to train for their program in El Salvador. My assignment, if I accepted it, would involve teaching peasants to read and write and to help the same peasants produce and market vegetables. I was thrilled. I felt needed, even if I knew nothing about producing vegetables, or teaching people to read and write.

Days later, I still had not told anyone. I wanted to make my decision without anyone telling me why it was my duty to stay on the farm and help the family. I did not need people attempting to influence my decision by making me feel guilty. This was a major decision, and I needed to make it on my own.

I did not need a map to locate El Salvador. I knew precisely where it was, thanks to my sixth-grade teacher. I went to our encyclopedia to learn more about the country. It was extremely poor, heavily populated, and mountainous, with a large Indigenous population. The encyclopedia showed photographs of beautiful, perfectly formed volcanoes. While I viewed the photographs, I reread the Peace Corps invitation. They needed me and I needed them.

I tried to imagine what it would be like to be a Peace Corps volunteer in El Salvador. Would I have running water or electricity? What kind of food would I eat? Would I be able to do what they asked of me? Would I be able to learn to speak Spanish? Could I stay away from home for the length of the Peace Corps contract: twenty-seven months. It consisted of three months training plus twenty-four months of service.

I had no idea what I wanted, but I did know that I did not want to return to the university and that I did not want to continue my life without making drastic changes. If I were not attending the university, I would have to be on the farm, working. My family expected it of me. In my mind, the consequences of not returning to the farm were unthinkable. I was trapped, except … I could join the Peace Corps. It was only five years old and everyone in the country knew of it and had a favorable opinion of it. If I left for the Peace Corps, I felt that I could leave the farm without anyone being angry with me.

I checked the box, accepting the assignment, and mailed the return envelope. I had made my decision. Now, I had to digest what I had just done and prepare for the inevitable drama. Little did I know how checking that box would influence the rest of my life. The farm boy who would leave to join the Peace Corps would disappear and an adventurer would replace him, one who always needed to see and work in another country.

After a week of self-reflection, I told my mother. She went silent on me. That was what she did when she was not happy. She won most arguments using this technique. When Mom went silent, you stayed out of her way. Most people figured it was not worth it to try to convince her to change her view, and Mom always won, but she did not win this time. I had made my decision. She played her trump card, but it did not work. Before accepting final defeat, she reminded me that I still had to tell Dad. She expected he would put his foot down and I would return with my head down and again do what they told me.

It was Sunday, and Dad was driving to inspect a farm we owned, located five miles north of our home. I thought this would be a suitable time to tell him. It had rained the night before, and rain took the pressure off farmers and put them in a good mood. In addition, Sundays were not as hectic as the other days. We tried to work only four or five hours on Sunday, mostly irrigating. Dad wanted to see how much rain had fallen on that farm so he could better allocate laborers on Monday.

Dad grabbed his pipe with one hand and while he drove with his knees, he dipped it into his tobacco pouch. He packed the tobacco into his pipe with his thumb, struck a match with his thumbnail, and lit the tobacco with its flame. He drew four or five quick puffs to pull the fire deep into the tobacco, and he tamped the tobacco again with his calloused thumb. The aroma of the tobacco filled the pickup and provided a more relaxed environment. This gave me that extra confidence I needed.

I took a deep breath and said, "Dad, I've decided to join the Peace Corps." I braced for his attack. There was none.

After three or four long puffs on his pipe, he said, "I know. Where are you going?" When I told him, he said, "When will you leave?" I told him. There was no more conversation, only the sound of his drawing on his pipe. The smoke had a calming effect on two people deep in thought.

The rest of the trip was silent, but strangely, it was not tense. It was peaceful. Dad and I had a deep connection that I did not understand. Years later, I learned that during the worst part of the Great Depression, Dad had bought a used Harley-Davidson motorcycle. A friend also had bought one, and they drove through twenty-seven states during the winter. He told me that he was never as cold as when he was in the desert at night. He and his friend tried to keep warm by finding and confiscating old wooden fence posts. They used gasoline from their cycles to start fires to stay warm. That was his attempt at finding adventure.

He told me that he had sold corn for pennies a bushel to finance his trip. This showed me that his adventure had great meaning to him. The trip, paid for with cheap corn, made the trip a very costly one. His posture, and the hint of a smile on a face that seldom smiled, told me that he did not regret his decision made so many years ago. Dad was also an adventurer.

For years, I did not understand how Dad knew that I had applied for the Peace Corps. Now, I know. The application form required three letters of recommendation; one of these was from my hometown banker. He was also my father's banker. This banker and Dad had known each other for decades. When they spoke, it was not always about the weather and loans. I am certain the banker mentioned my request for a letter of recommendation, thinking that Dad already knew. I find it revealing that Dad did not share this information with

Mom or ask me about it. I can only surmise that he wanted me to have the same chance to make my decision, as he had so many years ago about his great adventure.

After I told Mom and Dad, word spread quickly throughout the neighborhood. Everyone asked me when I was leaving, where I was going, and what I would be doing. It was exciting, but it also became tiresome. I tired of answering the same questions dozens of times, but it was comforting that the community cared so much.

I tried to imagine what things I would need while on my assignment and started to buy them, but there was one problem: it all had to fit into one small trunk. Since most people in Central America were much smaller than the typical American, I needed to buy enough clothes for twenty-seven months, because I would not likely be able to buy any clothes in my size, especially shoes, once I arrived in El Salvador.

We had a family dinner the last weekend before I left. Grandma and Grandpa Tyler and my uncles, aunts, and cousins were all there. These family dinners were always boisterous, with children running about playing. The women took turns yelling at the children to stop and be good. The men were in a corner, telling stories and laughing. Grandma hurried about with her apron on, baking things and making coffee, while Mom or an aunt set the table. Everyone was talking. The men, of which I was not yet a member, stood by a bar improvised from a card table and made themselves drinks while antagonizing me for not being old enough to drink.

Grandpa sat in his easy chair in a corner—his health had limited his mobility for many years. He had his old, deaf hunting dog, Rex, by his side. Rex never left Grandpa's side except for his short visits outside for his necessities. Family members paid their respects, one at a time. It was an honor to have a short conversation with Grandpa. He was not very talkative, but he always listened, and he enjoyed those days as much as the rest of us.

Time passed, and the day arrived for me to leave. It was a weekday, and we left home at four o'clock, which on the farm was the middle of the afternoon. It was strange seeing Dad clean and dressed up. Usually, "dressed up" for Dad was a clean pair of newer overalls, but today he was wearing dress slacks and had shaved and used shaving lotion. I felt guilty taking him from the fields before quitting time, but I felt that Mom did not have to force him from the fields to see me off. Dad felt a bit of envy about my upcoming adventure.

Everyone piled into the car. It was a forty-five-minute drive from the farm to Grand Island. No one spoke during the trip, which created an uncomfortable silence. We arrived at the airport, I checked in, and then I waited with my family for the airline to call my flight. The wait, like the drive to the airport, was clumsy and seemed never to end. It was an exceedingly small airport, so when the airline called the flight, an airline employee yelled at us over the counter and told us that we had better go to gate two; the plane was boarding passengers.

I hugged everyone and then walked through the gate onto the tarmac, out to the plane, and up the stairs. I took a windowless back seat in the plane, which was an old two-engine turboprop plane. I knew it would be twenty-seven months before I would see my family again. The Peace Corps did not allow trainees and volunteers to return home during those months, except for family emergencies. A dozen other passengers boarded the plane. No one sat near me, which was fine by me. I looked down when the flight attendant asked if I wanted anything. I only shook my head. I did not want her to see my tears or hear my shaky voice.

I flew to Lincoln, then to Omaha, back to Lincoln, and finally to Kansas City. I arrived at ten thirty that night. I spent the night roaming the empty airport, sitting in random chairs, and worrying about what was about to unfold. With eight hours to spend in an empty airport, my imagination took over and made me question my decision. I was scared. I was glad no one was there to see me pace back and forth. The next morning, my flight left at six o'clock for Chicago and then went on to Philadelphia. I was already exhausted.

After doing paperwork things in Philadelphia, we flew to San Juan, Puerto Rico where we boarded buses and headed along the north coast to Arecibo, which lies in the northwestern part of Puerto Rico.

We started training. We studied Spanish and had other community development classes for ten hours each day. After three weeks of training, the staff notified us that we had a field trip in our near future.

August 7, 1967, Puerto Rico—First Field Trip

One night, we had a meeting for all trainees going to El Salvador. The staff gave each of us a packet. Inside the packet was a highway map of Puerto Rico with an X marking a spot on a road—a different spot for each trainee. Our assignment was to make our way from Arecibo to that point on the highway, find a Puerto Rican family to house and feed us for four days and three nights, and learn as much as possible about the community. For our needs, the Peace Corps gave us four dollars a day for occasional expenditures and transportation to and from that location. We could not use any of our own money for any purpose. We were to speak only Spanish. The violation of any of these rules would result in our being terminated from the program and returned to the US. Within this period, someone from the Peace Corps would visit us on site. They would interview people in the area to learn if we had violated any of these rules and to evaluate our performance.

After the meeting, I went to one of the open classrooms and sat. I was frightened. I had received three weeks of Spanish classes, yet I could not converse in Spanish, and my level of understanding Spanish conversation was minimal—almost zero. My level of confidence could not have been lower. I did not want to be deselected.

The next morning everyone was up early, except for a few stragglers. The stragglers had nothing to worry about because they already knew how to speak Spanish. We had to be in the vans and ready to roll by 7:30 a.m. By 7:35, we were packed and stacked in the back. We needed one more van than we had. They compensated the lack of van seating by adding two or three more trainees to each of our vans. We were like cattle in a cattle truck.

A carpenter had made benches from wooden planks and covered them with foam. There was one plank on each side of the van, and another located just behind the front seat. Everyone tried to avoid the plank behind the front seat. That meant riding backward up and down the mountain; these riders tended to develop motion sickness.

The trip from our rain forest mountain camp to the city of Arecibo was a long and winding one. There were curves that, when taken too fast, threw the riders on one side of the van into the passengers riding on the other side of the van. In those days, there were no seat belts. We were unsecured ballast.

As we descended the mountain, the other trainees sang songs. I did not sing—ever. My mood was one of pure fright. The Peace Corps was transporting me into the unknown. My colleagues were all at least two years older than I was and had university degrees; most had graduated from well-known universities. Many had spent a summer backpacking through Europe, and they had had at least two years of a foreign language in high school, with additional training in college. Even though I had had two years at the university, I never again attempted to take a language course after my first fiasco. Mentally, I had never left the farm. Now, I was so far out of my comfort zone that I did not know if I could find my way back. I felt inferior to the other trainees.

They dropped us at an American restaurant in the center of Arecibo. From there, we were supposed to find our way to our separate destinations. The limited money they gave us ensured that we would not take taxis anywhere. Most trainees were nervous and divided into small groups, filling the restaurant. I stayed by myself at the counter and ordered a Coke. That was a treat, and it was so very cold, just the way I liked it. I sipped it slowly and worried about my next step.

It was eleven in the morning, and most of us were still hanging around the restaurant. I had consumed all the Coke I could afford. I had to move, or I would not reach my destination during daylight, which would result in my immediate deselection. I asked the English-speaking waiter where I should go to start my journey. After thinking and asking another waiter, he explained that it was a mile or so to a particular street in a residential neighborhood. The spot I was seeking consisted of a couple of cars parked along the street, where they waited for people to fill their cars. The drivers serviced a couple of rural villages, one being where I needed to go. I did not understand why there was no central bus system. In Arecibo, the city had decentralized the buses and taxis. Why the cars going to those villages decided to park on that street must have been an interesting story.

I decided to avoid the expense and complication of finding a bus that would take me from the restaurant to where the cars were waiting; I would walk and carry my duffel bag. I fretted the entire time. I approached what I thought was the correct street and looked for a car. Looking for a parked car in a residential area was not reassuring to me. I expected to see cars parked everywhere, but there were three cars parked—which one would take me to the X on my map, and which ones belonged to a specific house?

Finally, I saw a parked car with a couple of people hanging around and conversing. I mentally rehearsed my Spanish, but I did not know which person to approach. Finally, one walked around to the driver's door and reached inside to grab a cigarette. I approached him and asked if he drove to my destination. There was confusion, and the other person joined in, attempting to understand me. Eventually, the driver said yes. I thought I understood that I was to wait, so I waited.

After waiting ten minutes, I did not understand why we had not left yet. I again attempted to ask if he was going to my destination. He confirmed and pointed to the back seat, so I sat. Soon, a woman appeared and sat beside me, forcing me into the middle of the back seat. Little by little, people appeared with packages, and the back seat filled and then the front seat. The driver packed the car. There were four of us in the back seat and three in the front seat, each with our things. The driver started the car, and we left. I was at once relieved and scared.

We left the narrow streets of the city and entered a lush green countryside. Puerto Rico was an exceptionally beautiful country. I loved staring at it and all its hues of green and blue. We reached a fork in the road and turned left and then another fork, and we turned right. All the time, I wondered if the driver had really understood me and was taking me to the place I wanted to go. I had no idea how much he was going to charge me. Would I have enough money? The driver stopped repeatedly, and people left the car with their packages. It was great having more room in the car. Finally, the car stopped, and the driver pointed to me and motioned that I should leave the car. We were nowhere. We were in the middle of a valley with no houses visible. The driver put his hand out and told me the price. It seemed reasonable; I paid him, and he drove off. I was nowhere, by myself, clueless—and one second from panicking and having a meltdown. I could not just sit down and cry, but I wanted to.

Finally, I picked a direction, grabbed my luggage, and started walking. After a bit, I saw a mile marker. It was not even close to where I should have been. I did not even know if I was on the right highway. I looked at the sky and thought that rain was about to fall. I was desperate. A car approached. I flagged it down. The driver kindly stopped. He had a passenger. I tried to speak Spanish, but they did not understand me. The passenger tried to speak English, but I could not understand him. This made him angry because he saw no reason that I should not understand him. The driver intervened. I showed him my X on the map. He motioned me to get into his car. I did, and within ten minutes, we came into a cluster of houses. He stopped in front of a tienda, which is a small store, often located in a single-car garage—a Latin convenience store. Families used tiendas to supplement the family's income by selling essential products.

The driver motioned for me to get out. I did. I thanked him, paid him, and he was off. He was kind to me when I needed kindness. He did not have to stop to help me.

It was three o'clock, and I had not eaten since breakfast, other than the multiple Cokes I had drunk in Arecibo. I did not know what to do, so I drew a deep breath and entered the tienda. Before speaking, I rehearsed what I thought I needed to say. When the man behind the counter finished waiting on other people, he turned his eyes toward me. They held no expression, and he asked no question. He just stared at me, frowning. I gave him my best Spanish, and a Pepsi appeared over the counter. I smiled internally. He extended his hand. I asked how much. He answered in English. That worried me because I had to speak Spanish, or the staff would deselect me and return me to the US. I paid and stepped outside to sip my soda, biding my time before I had to start begging for a place to stay.

After I finished the Pepsi, it was time for me to find a homeowner who would accept me into his home and feed me for three days. I walked up to the first house. It had to belong to a person with above-average income for the neighborhood because it was much larger than the other houses, and a high wall surrounded the property. I thought this house would offer my best chance. I walked up to the outer fence and rang the bell. After a long pause, an expressionless maid appeared and stared at me. I tried to explain to her what I needed. The maid had no idea what I was saying and made no attempt to understand. She held out her upright palm, indicating I should wait. She closed the door and disappeared. A minute later, I heard someone approaching. A woman opened the door and looked at me. I used my best Spanish to ask her to let me live with her family for three days—a task that took great courage on my part. She said nothing but wagged her index finger back and forth as a definite no. She backed up and closed the door.

She had looked upset that I had brought her into my problem. Really, why would a middle-aged housewife tell a twenty-year-old male American—a stranger—that he could live in her house with her husband and children? If she had, her husband would have been furious. It was not for her to decide such things; only the man could decide, and he was at work.

I went from house to house, asking the same question—a question to which I knew the answer. I knew I was putting these families in an inconvenient situation. Not surprisingly, everyone gave the same answer.

To lick my wounds and build my confidence, I walked down the road in the direction that led out of the village. I wanted to see what was there. On the edge of the village, a couple of blocks beyond the last house, I saw an old, abandoned house. It had no door or windows, and one-third of the roof was missing. I ventured inside and saw that it consisted of one large room, which was mostly dry. It offered protection from weather events, especially if it did not rain. I looked out the window frames in the back of the house and saw a most picturesque view. Puerto Rico was beautiful. It was a dreamland. If I found no place to stay this night, I decided that I would return here for comfort and try again tomorrow. I was like a homeless stray puppy.

Toward the end of the day, I noticed that I had visited all the village's houses except for three. They were located high on the hill above the road. I decided I needed more time before I approached them. I returned to the tienda, overcame my concern for conserving my living allowance, and ordered another Pepsi. This time, fearing that I might not have supper, I added a candy bar to my order. I was famished. I looked at my watch and saw that it was a quarter to six. The sun was fading. I knew that it would be dark by six o'clock. In this region, there was almost no dusk. It was light, and then it was dark.

I finished my snack and headed up the hill to the first house. I told myself that if I were unable to convince one of the three families to take me in, I would have no other choice but to return to the abandoned house and settle in for the night.

My heart sank a little as I visited each house, and each time they denied my request, although in a kind way. The Puerto Rican people were always kind to me. When they told me that they could not accept me, they were respectful and genuinely sad. I knew that what I was asking was difficult for them to grant.

These families were very low-income families who barely had enough to eat. Their houses were small. To allow a stranger into their homes would mean that someone would sleep on the floor, and etiquette would not allow that to be me. They did not have doors on their rooms; therefore, they could not isolate themselves inside their rooms and lock the door. In addition, they would be embarrassed if they did not have enough food to offer their guest and for themselves. In addition, they would be subjecting their families to significant risk by asking a stranger into their homes—a foreign stranger. I understood their hesitancy to accept me. I felt horrible having to ask them.

After the last house denied me, I walked down the steep hill, slowly, pensively. I questioned my decision to leave home. Home was boring, but I always had a roof over my head and food to eat. Right then, those two things became particularly important. I decided I would return to the tienda and find something to serve as food and then return to the abandoned house for the night. As I descended the hill and approached the road, a car appeared.

Upon seeing me in his high beams, the driver screeched to a stop. He reached over, threw open the passenger door, and yelled,

"I hear you are looking for a place to stay. Come on; get in." Yes, he said it in English, but I did not care. I got in and waited for him to explain.

He said that there was talk in the village about the poor stranger looking for a place to stay. They were sorry they could not accept me into their homes. They were embarrassed to have a stranger, especially an American, see how little they had. In addition, during the day, the men were working. In Puerto Rico, a woman cannot allow any man to enter her house without the man of the house being present. This could never happen.

The man said that he lived in the next small city with his wife and two young children. They could offer me a rollaway bed, breakfast, and dinner. I almost kissed him. I told him that the Peace Corps expected us always to speak Spanish, and I needed to arrive early in the village and stay there until late. He agreed to help me with my Spanish, take me to the village early, and pick me as he returned home from work. I could not believe my luck. Puerto Ricans were so kind.

This arrangement worked well. My caretakers had family in the village, and they took turns babysitting me. They showed me a coffee *beneficio* (beh-neh-fee-see-oh), where they processed coffee from freshly picked beans to dried beans. They showed me enterprise operations for cattle and vegetable and fruit production, and how farmers made their livings on ten or fewer acres—some with less than an acre to their names.

By the end of the first field trip, I was building confidence. My Spanish was better, and I had been surviving on my own. I was learning to bridge cultural and speech gaps by incorporating hand signals into my conversations and with heavy use of the bilingual dictionary. I had made great progress, but I had a long way to go. I always had difficulty explaining why I was in Puerto Rico and why I was in their community. They did not let their lack of understanding bother them. They accepted me and did everything they could to help me.

During this first field trip, I had noticed that every house had a photograph of John F. Kennedy. Puerto Ricans adored him. When they learned that JFK was responsible for creating the Peace Corps, they opened their arms and hearts to us, as his representatives. Although people had no idea what the Peace Corps was, they knew and loved JFK. That was enough for them.

When I returned to our camp, I discovered that a dozen of my fellow trainees had come home early, picked up a plane ticket, and returned to the USA. They had experienced demanding situations that they did not know how to manage; they managed it by leaving. Other than the obvious requirement to learn to speak Spanish, a major objective of the Peace Corps was for the trainee to become capable of handling difficult and stressful situations.

Three weeks after our first field trip, we had a second one. For me, it went smoothly. My Spanish was slightly improved, and I was familiar with the place and the people.

September 9, 1967, Puerto Rico—The Fateful

Trip to the Beach

After the tension from the second field trip and the result of our midterm evaluations, our camp director thought that it was time to give us Saturday and Sunday off. The East Coast and West Coast coalition decided they would fulfill their fantasies with a beach party. They arranged for transportation to a beach they had heard about. It was late Friday afternoon.

We did not hear any more from the group until Sunday afternoon, about the time they should have been returning. We spotted excitement around the administration building. We heard that the police had arrested the entire group and were holding them in an Arecibo jail, with deselection from the program the most likely result.

The story, as we heard it, was that they went to the beach that someone had recommended to them for Friday night. They enjoyed the beach but grew tired of it. They sent search parties out on Saturday and found a lovely beach. They decided to move their festivities there early Sunday morning.

They enjoyed their evening partying by drinking, smoking, and doing whatever else healthy young people did in those situations. By

14

morning, they were very drunk or high, many were nude and swimming in the warm waters of the Atlantic Ocean. Meanwhile, not far from the beach, an old man and his wife prepared to have their customary breakfast on their backyard patio, with its unequaled and unobstructed view of the ocean. It was always so peaceful there, and they enjoyed the experience. And that is when things started to go awry.

As Mrs. Old Man carried breakfast out to their patio table on a large tray. She looked up and saw a large group of stumbling, drunk, and nude people doing disgusting things on their private beach. She screamed and dropped her tray. Mr. Old Man ran from inside the house, the best he could with a bad hip, and looked where Mrs. Old Man was pointing a crooked finger with one hand while she grasped her heart with her other hand, almost swooning. He returned inside his house, with his wife in tow. She was attempting to faint but could not because he was pulling her. He sat her down in a comfortable chair, picked up the phone, and started making phone calls. And that was when things went off the rails.

Lickety-split, the police rounded up the misbehaving group and rushed them to jail. As the lack of luck would have it for our stressed-out group of Peace Corps trainees, the old man was on Puerto Rico's Supreme Court; in fact, he was the Chief Justice. When he picked up the phone, he called the head of Puerto Rico's police, the mayor of Arecibo, and the governor of Puerto Rico. These three contacts did the rest for him.

Within minutes, they contacted the State Department and the Peace Corps in Washington, DC, the head administrator of our training camp, and anyone else of any standing in the community or on the island. To say that the proverbial stuff hit the fan would be the understatement of the century.

After a couple of days, they brought our misfits back to camp. The old man wanted them thrown out of the Peace Corps and Puerto Rico. In fact, the Supreme Court Justice would have been happier if the Peace Corps had relocated out of his hemisphere. These unlucky adventurers represented twenty-five percent of remaining trainees. The Peace Corps did not want to lose its investment. Even though they had showed little common sense, these trainees were leaders and could become the most successful Peace Corps volunteers, but it was exactly this type of behavior that could also result in the Peace Corps being embarrassed on the front pages of a country's newspapers and on the evening news on television. It could even result in the Puerto Rican government throwing the Peace Corps from their island. Not everyone would be as understanding and willing to compromise as the old man and his wife in Puerto Rico.

After they repatriated the group with the rest of us in the training camp, the camp director subjected them to a serious scolding before he informed them that they would allow them to finish their training. However, if they even coughed without covering their mouths, they would be on the next flight home. I think after all the attention they received; the group saw the error of their ways.

September 27, 1967, Puerto Rico—Field Trip 3

The party-minded people decided we should have a party before our third and last trip. We all contributed a few bucks to purchase a pig from one of the camp employees. Locals would roast a pig over an open fire. We also hired a steel band, which made tropical music on instruments made from oil barrels, and local people to prepare the food.

We started eating before dark. They made the punch from pineapple. I did not think that pineapple punch could be tasty, but it was delicious. After eating, I played basketball with a couple of trainees.

They had constructed the basketball court on a wide terrace carved from the steep hillside. They carved one side from the hillside, and the other was filled in to make a narrow basketball court. The problem with the court was that every time that the ball bounced to the downhill side, it rolled downhill until a tree or bush stopped it. It discouraged the most enthusiastic player, but on this night, I was persistent.

I played for a bit, and then I laid the ball carefully on the court to keep it from rolling downhill. I walked to the back door (the closest one) of the cafeteria and passed by the food line until I arrived at the punch bowl. I poured myself a big cup of punch. The taste was that of pineapple, but it had a hint of something unknown to me; I liked whatever it was. I walked otut the front side of the cafeteria (now the closest exit for me) and headed back to the basketball court, sipping from my juice cup as I walked.

After a four or five such trips, I noticed that when I shot at the basket, I missed more often. I spent more time chasing the basketball than I did shooting it. As I gained confidence in my basketball skills, however, instead of leaving the ball on the court when I went for more punch, I dribbled the ball past the food line, got my punch, and then dribbled out of the dining hall and back onto the court. Everyone else had long abandoned the court, but I continued to climb down and crawl up the hillside, chasing the ball. During the early morning hours, I finally tired and decided to go to bed. We were starting our trip down the mountain the following morning at seven o'clock for our third and final field trip.

On my way to the cabin, I noticed that no one else was around. The camp seemed abandoned. I started to worry. Had I missed a signal to abandon camp? I entered my bunkhouse; it was empty. Curious, I started walking, although with difficulty, from bunkhouse to bunkhouse. Finally, I found a bunkhouse that had smoke pouring from its screened windows. It was either on fire, or I had found my fellow trainees. They were all sitting on the floor, smoking. I did not smoke, so I returned to my cabin. I looked at my watch; it was five o'clock. The sun would be up in one hour. When I lay down, the cabin started to spin. I could not close my eyes. I had to stand up. I felt uncomfortable. What had been in that pineapple punch?

The next morning, starting at six thirty, the Peace Corps staff went from cabin to cabin, ringing a bell and yelling for us to rise. They reminded us that we were rolling down the mountain at seven o'clock sharp. I felt horrible, but I climbed out of my bed, dressed, threw a few things into my travel bag, and made my way to the loading area. I did not eat. I could not eat; I could not even think about food.

The staff continued to go from cabin to cabin, yelling orders; then the threats started. Any trainee not ready by seven o'clock would have points deducted on their final evaluation score. Slowly, the trainees started to appear. All the trainees looked horrible, including me. Four or five ran to the forest's edge and unceremoniously emptied their stomachs before they could climb into the van. That is when I learned that an evil trainee had emptied several bottles of rum into the pineapple juice. That was the first time I had tasted alcohol. I felt betrayed. How could anything that tasted so good earlier make us feel so bad now? We left closer to seven thirty, but we did leave.

The driver forced us into the back of the vans. In each van, three trainees had the undesirable seats facing backward. Once the doors closed, there was no ventilation. With all trainees loaded, the staff member responsible for driving closed the doors; immediately, the temperature started to rise, and we started to panic. We knew this would not end well.

We began our descent down the mountain. Our convoy consisted of four vans. The road had dozens of ups and downs and curves in the road. Some curves were sharp, tossing us from side to side, and it was becoming hotter in the back of the van. At first, we were surviving, but then someone started gasping and then heaving. We shouted for the driver to stop. We begged him to stop. We did not want the smell of vomit in such a confined place with so many stressed and uncomfortable trainees, but it was too late. Now, more trainees were gasping, and others were already heaving. The situation was critical.

The driver pulled to the side of the road, ran to the back, and threw open the door. He gasped, covered his nostrils, and stepped back in horror. We piled out and sought clean air. More were on the side of the road, grabbing their ankles and heaving, while others were able to recover after a little gagging. Someone had a water jug and tried to wash the damage from the back of the van, but that was only partially successful. We needed more water than that if we were going to erase all the damage.

The other vans drove by, honking, with the trainees laughing and pointing at us. We were too stressed to care.

After the tipsy trainees regained their composure, we reentered the van, and the driver returned to the road. After a mile or two, we passed first one van and then another van, with their trainees lined up at the road's edge, grabbing their ankles. The vans played hopscotch with each other all the way into Arecibo. When one van was on the edge of the road, the others passed, but there was no more laughing or honking. We were in survival mode. That was the longest and most uncomfortable trip I have made in my life.

We arrived in Arecibo at nine o'clock. The drivers delivered us to the American restaurant in the center of town. All but two of the staff left to spend a couple of hours shopping in town before returning to camp. The two staff members were to monitor our progress.

We trainees were supposed to start our trip to the country immediately. We did not. We entered the American restaurant and sat at the counter or claimed a table with our heads hanging. We took turns going into the restroom to wash our faces and rinse our mouths after a new round of heaving.

After a half of hour sitting at the counter with my head leaning heavily on my hands, I ordered a Coke. I drank it slowly. I started to feel better. The Coke settled my stomach. At ten o'clock, staff members returned to check on us. They were not happy when they found us exactly where they had left us. No one—not one trainee—had vacated the restaurant. They reminded us of our duty. I ordered another Coke, which I again drank slowly. At eleven o'clock, staff members returned and insisted that we leave. They went from trainee to trainee and physically walked each of us outside. Once we were all outside, they stood in the doorway until we wandered off. They were a distrustful bunch.

I walked slowly and unsteadily to my little van, parked a mile away, which would take me to my village. They crowded my fellow passengers and I in the back again, with no ventilation. I hoped that I would not feel the need to heave while in the back of the community bus.

When we finally reached a town, I realized that I still was not well, and I did not want anyone in the village I was visiting to see me in that condition. I left the van and found a small hotel to spend the night. I decided I would splurge—only five dollars for a room. I needed my privacy that night.

After dark, I felt hungry. I had not eaten anything during the last twenty-four hours. I found a little restaurant and ordered something light. As soon as I reached my room, I lost it all, but at least I lost it in the privacy of my room. After I recovered, I ordered a couple of Cokes so that I would have them during the night to settle my stomach. I tried to sleep. I found it better to sleep by stacking all the pillows and leaning against them in a near-sitting position. I cursed the rum that someone had put in the pineapple punch. I did not like pineapples anymore. In fact, I did not like anything or anybody.

I finished the last leg of my trip early the next morning. My first assignment was to find the man who had offered me my new place to live. With the help of people that I had met in the village, I found the wealthy, middle-aged farmer who had agreed to allow me to stay in one of his unused farmhouses. He would take me there at night and pick me up in the morning. I had the house to myself. It was a big house and in decent shape. He simply did not need it. Mostly, he stored stuff in it. Its location was perfect. It sat high on a hill with a view of the valley that contained the local town. The view was beautiful. The house had a wide porch on three sides. It was perfect for sitting and thinking. It had running water, a working bathroom, and a cold-water shower. This house also would not meet the Peace Corps' specifications, but I did not know what else to do. I felt lucky that I had a place to stay.

The farmer took me to his house so that I could leave my little suitcase and so I could see where I would be staying. We spent ten minutes looking around. He was short, slightly overweight, and talked constantly. He was mostly bald, with the obligatory mustache. Already, the sun was hot, and there was no breeze. I could feel myself starting to sweat. The day would become uncomfortably warm if the breeze did not appear.

My Spanish was improving, but it was still lacking. Since I started with not knowing any Spanish, it would be a long way to being conversational in Spanish. I hoped my skill would improve this week.

My Spanish improved and they selected me as a Peace Corps volunteer. I was going to El Salvador! I was proud.

Chapter 2

My Journey in El Salvador Begins

October 28, 1967—Off to El Salvador

Everyone was on the plane from San Juan except one volunteer; he was sick and would remain in San Juan until the doctors resolved his health problems.

After a two-hour flight, we landed in Guatemala City, where we were surprised by how chilly it was, given that we were in the tropics. We never realized that Guatemala City was a mile high. We made a quick dash around the airport to warm up. We had thirty minutes before we had to board the plane again for the last leg of our flight.

We took off and landed twenty minutes later in San Salvador. The plane climbed only for ten minutes before it started its descent, demonstrating how small the Central American countries were. As we circled San Salvador for our final approach, I saw the reflection of the moon in Lake Ilopango (e-low-pan-go), a lake formed in the crater of an extinct volcano.

We left the plane and descended to the tarmac and walked toward the airport. There was no band playing, just us volunteers walking into the unknown. Then, from a dark second-story balcony, cheering and clapping broke out. We struggled to see where it was coming from. It was current Peace Corps volunteers who had made the trip to San Salvador to welcome us. I learned later that they were there to view the new volunteers to be the first to stake their claims on someone they fancied. No one staked a claim on me. I could only surmise that I was too young for the much- older female volunteers. I was twenty years old; they were twenty-three to twenty-eight years old.

As soon as we entered the airport, two photographers appeared and took a group photograph. The photograph appeared in the next day's newspaper. We then went to our pensión (pen-see-own), Latin America's equivalent of a motel. By US standards, it was not much, but by Peace Corps standards, it was just dandy. Surprise—a party spontaneously broke out. Someone had found a roaming band of musicians who were happy to serenade us for a small fee.

That finished our eventful day. I retreated to my bed and prepared to sleep, but I could not sleep. I was too excited. I was in El Salvador. I really was in El Salvador, the same country that I studied in the sixth grade. Now I could add to the photographs I had already seen in our encyclopedia, the street noises I heard from my bed, and the scents reaching my nose. I pulled the sheet around my body and smiled to myself. My great adventure had started.

The next morning, a Peace Corps staff member appeared early at our pensión to tell us that we needed to be in the Peace Corps office by nine o'clock. The staff member left the address for us with brief directions. I had no idea where to go. I knew it was too far to walk and too expensive by taxi. We needed to go by bus, but which bus or buses? My strategy was to find the volunteer who spoke the best Spanish and attach myself to him until we arrived at the office.

We spent the next three days filling out more forms and listening to speeches and then more speeches. The U.S. Ambassador invited us to a party   at the U.S. ambassador's house for our first night in-country. I did not feel comfortable because we were supposed to dress up. I was insecure because there were so many high-level dignitaries present. As a Nebraska farm boy, I never saw myself shaking hands with a US ambassador. There were fewer than two hundred American ambassadors in the world, and I was about to meet one of them.

Having arrived at the party, I hung back in a corner and watched while the other volunteers spoke comfortably to the ambassador and his children, whose ages were from teens to twenty. I wondered what their life must be like from day to day. There also were dignitaries present. All my colleagues moved about smoothly from one person to another, with a drink in their hands and a smile on their faces. I had no drink and only a forced smile. I was not happy. I was in the shadows, nervous, and I looked at my watch constantly. I was out of my comfort zone, and I did not like it. I kept an eye open for any other volunteer who showed signs of thinking about leaving. I would volunteer to go with them. Escape was my only thought.

The next day, we received our permanent assignments. This was a huge moment. They were sending me to the city of Sonsonate (sown-so- nah-tay), which was in the northwest corner of El Salvador, close to Guatemala. The city was located eight miles from the ocean, less than two hours by bus from San Salvador. It had about forty thousand inhabitants. At first, I was disappointed. The image I had of being a Peace Corps volunteer was to live far from civilization in a small village, without electricity or other amenities. But no, where I was going, all kinds of fruit, vegetables, meat, dairy products, and coconuts were available. Electricity and running water were available. It even had three movie theaters, although not of the same quality as in the USA. The city even had its own bus system and soccer team.

I would not be roughing it; however, it would be nice to occasionally see a movie or to eat ice cream. The downside to all this luxury was that Sonsonate was located on the flat plains and was hot, hot, hot.

October 29, 1967—My First Trip to

Sonsonate and Nahuizalco

My assignment was to find my way from San Salvador to the Indian village of Nahuizalco (nah-we-zal-co). First, I needed to cross the city from the pensión to the bus station. Second, I had to travel from San Salvador's bus station to Sonsonate's bus station. Third, once in Sonsonate, I needed to find and take the next bus to Nahuizalco, a village five miles northeast of Sonsonate. There, I would meet my Peace Corps volunteer mentors, Bob and Shirley, a married couple who had resided there for one year.

My first task was to take a city bus from my pensión in San Salvador to the intercity bus station, which was located across town. I do not remember how I did it, but I did it. Then, I found a bus that would take me to Sonsonate. I did it, but there was a problem. Unbeknownst to me, there were three types of intercity bus services in El Salvador. First, there were direct buses. These buses left San Salvador and did not stop until they arrived at the destination. It cost more, but the trip was fast and direct. My bus was not this type.

The second type was a bus that went from point A to point B but made several stops in smaller cities and towns located on or close to the highway along the way. These villages were located two or three miles away from the main highway. Once the bus reached each of these stops, it unloaded people and merchandise before loading new passengers and merchandise. This process could take ten to twenty minutes, and they made a half dozen of these stops along the way. A trip on this type of bus cost less than the first type of bus, but it could take twice as long as the direct bus. My bus was not this type of bus either.

The third type of bus not only stopped in the towns along the way but also stopped to pick up and unload passengers along the highway. Whenever anyone wanted off the bus, the driver stopped the bus and unloaded a passenger and his or her merchandise. Whenever a person stepped out from a coffee plantation and waved at the driver, the driver stopped the bus. The passenger boarded and they loaded his or her merchandise. Seldom did the bus travel more than one mile without stopping to drop off passengers and merchandise or to pick up others. This was the type of bus I was riding. Because I had been unaware of the three types of bus service, the fifty-five-mile trip to Sonsonate was unbearably long and confusing.

I only had an idea where Sonsonate was located. Each time we took a turn off the main highway, I thought I had caught the wrong bus. When this happened, I caught the attention of the ticket-taker and asked if this bus was going to Sonsonate. He always answered yes, and then we turned and went somewhere that was not Sonsonate. If I had understood about the different bus services, my trip would have been much less stressful.

Eventually, I saw a highway sign indicating that Sonsonate was fifteen miles ahead. My anxiety decreased, and I relaxed. All I had to do was to stay with the bus until it stopped at the bus station, and I would have successfully reached my second destination.

As soon as the bus stopped at the station, I waited for the bus assistants to drop my suitcase from the top of the bus. When I had my bag, I looked for a ticket window to buy passage to Nahuizalco. I thought I had found it at the front of a lengthy line. I wished I could have been sure. I wanted to go to the front of the line and ask if they sold tickets to Nahuizalco, but that would mean delaying everyone else who was standing in line behind me. This would have been especially annoying to the well-mannered Indians waiting patiently in line. I thought that the better option would be to wait in line like everyone else.

Slowly, the line advanced. Once I was in front of the ticket seller, I tried to ask for a ticket to Nahuizalco. I had been rehearsing what I would say since I entered the line. He told me that I was in the wrong line and that I needed to go to another line, but I was not sure. To avoid delaying the locals, I left the line and started to look around like I knew what I was doing. I walked a few feet and detained a bus driver. I asked him where I could buy a ticket to Nahuizalco. He pointed to another line ten yards around the corner. I went there, waited in another extensive line, and then bought my ticket.

I had to wait two hours for my bus to leave. I tried to be inconspicuous and leaned against a wall at the entrance to the bus station. Yes, right! I was six feet tall, and everyone else was five feet tall and change. I was white, and they were not. I tried to look like I was in my environment. I was not. I kept looking at my watch. No one else had a watch, and they already knew the time, at least close enough to meet their needs. I wondered what Nahuizalco would look like and wished I were already there.

Finally, I saw a bus come in with its sign indicating that it had come from Nahuizalco. I followed it and gave it time to unload. I asked the driver if it was my bus. It was. I climbed aboard. Within a half hour, we crept out of the bus station and started crossing Sonsonate. It was my first look at the city. It was a busy city. People were everywhere. There were so many people in the streets that one person could not move without bumping into another person, and each car, truck, and ox cart risked running over people every time it moved.

As we reached the edge of the far side of the city, the paved road turned into a well-maintained dirt road. We started a slow ascent into the foothills that would take us to Nahuizalco. After thirty minutes, we entered what I assumed was Nahuizalco. I was not sure because there were no road signs. The bus went to the town square and parked. I optimistically grabbed my bag, boldly stepped out of the bus, and looked around, thinking, I am in the middle of an Indian village in rural El Salvador. What am I doing?

I dug out directions to Bob and Shirley's house, written on a small, crumpled paper, from my pants pocket. I had to walk a couple of blocks ahead, turn, and go in another direction. Their house was the third house on the left on that block. I picked what I thought was the third house and knocked. It was their house, and they spoke English. I was happy. After only a half day on my own, I already missed speaking English.

They invited me into their home. They were as curious about me as I was about them. They lived in a large, old, and poorly maintained house. It had one large empty room: a living room located next to the front door. The rest of the house was located around a central open area with dirt in its center. It had enough space to make a nice garden. On one side of the patio were a bedroom and a smaller room used as a study. On the other side were a kitchen and another room that they used for storage. They paid sixteen dollars a month rent. They put me in the storage room. I did not mind; I was simply happy to be someplace. I found a place to live in Sonsonate and started work. After a few months I took my first short vacation for a couple of days.

Chapter 3

My First Trip into Guatemala

February 7, 1968, Guatemala—Day 1

My first vacation was approaching, and I was excited. I was going to visit Guatemala. I remembered studying Guatemala in sixth grade. In my mind, I still could see the photographs of the colorful Indians in mountains from our textbook.

I had a choice of three roads to reach Guatemala City: (1) I could take the paved coastal road, which followed the lowlands into Guatemala before rising sharply into the highlands and Guatemala City.

(2) I could ride a bus for fifty of the fifty-five miles toward San Salvador before turning sharply back toward Santa Ana, El Salvador's second- largest city. From there I would go on to Guatemala—this paved road had the fastest buses, but the distance was much greater; or (3) I could take a slower bus directly from Sonsonate to Santa Ana, before turning toward Guatemala City.

The third option was the most scenic route, because it rose from sea level to more than a mile high before dropping into Santa Ana. The road was dirt but of excellent quality. The bus would make slow progress, mostly because of the steepness of the road. The road crossed the continental divide at over six thousand feet. The scenery was very picturesque. There were coffee plantations, where the coffee workers picked coffee, and the beneficios dried it. I chose this route. It would take four hours.

I caught an early-morning direct bus from Sonsonate to Santa Ana. I was excited but pensive. In less than an hour, I was in territory that I had never seen. My eyes darted from one side of the road to the other, trying to see everything. We were climbing slowly but steadily, higher, and higher. We were in coffee country.

I could see peasant huts on both sides of the road. As we passed each hut, I saw a snapshot of peasant life. I could see women preparing food. They might be at their grindstones, grinding corn that they had soaked overnight in water. They would grab a bit of dough and pat it into a small pancake, which, when heated on a pottery bowl, resulted in corn tortillas. As the women prepared the dough, chickens could be nearby, trying to sneak a beak full of dough.

Girls were helping the women with their chores. Boys often were kicking a homemade ball. The core of the football would be paper held into a ball shape by string ties. At this time of day, the men have already left for the fields.

As we climbed for the sky, a fog appeared and partially engulfed us, and then, as the sun became stronger, it receded again. After a couple of hours, we reached the continental divide and started our descent into Santa Ana. The road straightened, and we picked up speed.

I ate lunch in Santa Ana and started hitchhiking in the early afternoon. I had trouble obtaining a lift, but eventually, I caught a ride with a person who took me to a turn-off. The driver explained that each branch of the road continued to Guatemala City, but since he was following the road less traveled, he suggested I stay on the road more traveled. His logic seemed sound. I thanked him and left his car.

I sat on the side of the road for thirty minutes and noticed that every car followed the road less traveled. I was suspicious that my former driver might have been setting me up for a long wait, but eventually, I caught a ride on a truck. I was moving again but never for long. I managed to make it to the border (about fifteen miles) in four hours. I walked the last two miles. Even if progress was slow, I managed to spend no money in getting there. Speed was a secondary consideration to frugality. I had to make my small travel budget last.

I passed through the border with little effort. I even managed to exchange Salvadoran colónes into Guatemalan quetzals. I returned to hitchhiking. I waited for what seemed forever, and no cars or trucks passed. I was desperate when I learned that a small bus was going to Guatemala City at 5:00 p.m. I waited and decided that spending money was preferable to spending the night on the side of the road.

The bus arrived, and the bus's loading/unloading specialists— two men—spent time loading the bus. They had empty sacks resting on their shoulders for extra protection against the heavy, sharp-edged objects they carried. Finally, we were ready. The driver started the engine, but before the driver could close the door, someone in the bus sent a child out in search of another person. Meanwhile, we had to wait. After five minutes, the child returned, tugging on the arm of a happy drunk. Two police officers helped him into the bus. Finally, we were moving again into Guatemala.

I was happy to see that the driver had a heavy foot. I wanted to arrive in Guatemala City as early as possible because I had no arranged place to stay. I thought we were making excellent time until the driver started pulling into small towns positioned just off the highway. The bus delivered people to their front doors, and frequently, they needed packages brought down from the top of the bus. As luck would have it, these packages were often located at the bottom of a pile of packages. This required the repositioning of packages to retrieve one package; time was passing, and night was approaching.

At one point on the road, there was a minor discussion between two passengers and the driver. The two passengers did not want to pay the full price. They tried to negotiate the price lower. The driver finally had had enough and abruptly stopped and opened the door. Their mouths dropped open, and one of them muttered, "Well, I still think it is too high," as they dug deeper into their pockets for the money.

Again, we were traveling and making time, and then the drunk awoke abruptly. He started making passes at a female sitting next to him. She encouraged him—not too much but sufficient to keep the drunk's mind focused on her. Suddenly, his face became serious, and he muttered something. Everyone around him laughed, and the driver suddenly stopped the bus. The drunk wobbled out and positioned himself next to the truck's back tire. He moaned in happiness as he emptied his bladder. The weight of the world was lifted from his bladder. As he turned to reenter the bus, he broke into another song.

We were gaining elevation, and it was becoming colder. I was wearing only a short-sleeved shirt with no T-shirt under it. I was already uncomfortably cold, and we were going still higher to reach Guatemala City.

We arrived at the bus depot at 8:00 p.m. I went to the police to ask directions. It was logical to ask the police because they were everywhere. They were nice and even found me a taxi. They negotiated the taxi fare as I hid around a corner. If the taxi driver had seen me, he would have charged much more.

The taxi took me to the part of town where cheap hotels were supposed to predominate. It took forever to find a nice, cheap hotel. The one I found was located near the US embassy and the central market. With that problem solved, I took on the next one: hunger. I located and ate at a nice American restaurant. That was how the first day of my vacation ended; I had arrived in Guatemala.

February 8, 1968, Guatemala—Day 2

I froze on my first night. The temperature fell to fifty degrees Fahrenheit, which, for me, was very cold. I went to the bus depot to catch a bus to Chichicastenango (chee-chee-cas-ta-nan-go), a village located to the north, near Mexico. This was a four-hour trip by bus. I was on a tight schedule, so I did not try to hitchhike; that was too unreliable.

I boarded a little, packed bus. They not only squeezed me in, but it seemed that half of Guatemala City entered the bus after I seated myself. When I gazed over the heads of the people already seated, I thought of a Nebraska cornfield in early July. Every time the bus moved from side to side, so did all the heads in the bus, like when a breeze moved across a cornfield—all I could see were the plants moving back and forth, according to the whims of the wind.

There was no visible aisle in the bus because people were sitting in it. I did not know how that was possible until I saw that the bus had custom-made fold-down half seats to make aisle seating more comfortable. I found an "aisle seat." I was thin, but my bottom quickly lost all sensation after fifteen minutes of one side of my bottom supporting my body's full weight. To make life more interesting, everybody had their shopping bags, chickens, and packages that they were carrying with them.

Initially, I longed for a full seat, but then I noticed that the bus had overhead compartments, like the airlines did, except these were open on the sides, and the bottoms were made from steel mesh. There was always something falling from the overhead compartment onto someone's head. Passengers placed their chickens and iguanas (giant lizards) in the overhead compartments, directly over the persons occupying a regular seat, especially the window seat. I know that these animals did not make any effort to hold it in until we arrived at our destination. People sitting below them were at the mercy of the animals' bowel and bladder movements. I did not want to finish the trip with urine or fecal material on my head and shoulders. The aisle seat no longer seemed so bad.

The trip seemed endless. The bus was slow. It was always stopping to pick up people. I did not think anyone left the bus; only more people entered it. It reminded me of putting more water into a balloon that already looked like it should have burst. I expected the balloon to burst, but it did not; it just kept expanding. The only way this bus could hold more people was for it to expand like a balloon.

As we wound around the highland roads, we still gained elevation. Before long, I started to see pine trees and scenery that reminded me of Colorado. I saw large corn and potato fields. The size of fields was relative to those found in my region of El Salvador, not to the US. It looked to me that the Guatemalan farmers were better than those I had seen in El Salvador, but the soil may have been superior.

I arrived in Chichicastenango at 1:00 p.m., ate lunch at the only place in town, and by 2:00 p.m., I was ready to match bargaining skills with the local merchants. These merchants were specialists at spotting foreign tourists and then raising their prices. My goal was to impress on them that although I was a foreigner, I was not a tourist. They were not impressed with my ploy. They could not stop seeing me as an American tourist and kept their prices high.

The merchants were surprised that I could speak Spanish—at least, a little—because most tourists could not. I negotiated as best I could with each merchant on each item. This took time. I bought nothing until I had visited all the market's stands and bargained on all the items that interested me. I then returned for the final negotiation and to make the purchases. I did well. I bargained for an item and then, when they accepted my offer, I bundled it with another item and argued again. I kept adding items until I had what I wanted for a reasonable value. I bought one item for $0.70 and then saw a non-Spanish-speaking tourist pay $2.50 for the same item. I felt proud.

In this region, the people were very colorful. They had been around American tourists enough that they could speak a little English. They knew how to say "Come in" in English, and of course, they knew the numbers.

After I had spent my budget, I caught a 4:00 p.m. bus to the Pan American Highway. This bus was very crowded, as all Guatemalan buses were. It was a sea of heads. I counted seven heads across a row of seats. In a similar bus in the USA, we seated four people. This did not include the chickens, canteens, machetes, hats, and whatever other things the passengers carried. People also read newspapers on the bus.

We reached the highway, and I was uncomfortably cold. I never imagined Guatemala would be cold. I imagined that all Central America was hot. It was the tropics.

I tried to hitchhike to Lake Atitlán (ah-teet-lan), which put me back on the road toward Guatemala City, but I had no luck. One person stopped who was going my way. I asked him to wait while I ran a few feet to grab my bag. As soon as I turned my back, he sped away. At least running helped me to warm up a bit.

I found a bus passing by and waved it to stop. I was surprised to see it was not crowded, but it was night, and it was near its destination. I arrived in the colorful Indian town above Lake Atitlán. I needed to continue another three or four miles to the village, located at the lake's edge. The last bus had left, and traffic was nonexistent. There were no hotels in this town. My only hope was to take a taxi. Unfortunately, the taxi driver also knew that he was my only hope. This fact did not aid my efforts to negotiate a price. It cost me three dollars to travel the four miles. I managed to find a beautiful little room for five dollars a night, which included three meals.

That night I looked over the town. I met two married Guatemalan Peace Corps volunteers. Their assignment had been in a little village near the jungle. The man worked with cooperatives. The people were nice there and wanted the volunteers' help. The only problem was that during the first ten days, the Communists had killed one of his co-op's members each day. The Communists had killed seven co-op members since he had arrived. The Communists disagreed with the cooperative philosophy. I found that surprising because I thought that communists were all about sharing and cooperating. The Peace Corps moved the couple to another site. The bus ride from their new site into Guatemala City was eleven hours.

In Lake Atitlán, flowers were everywhere. They came from bushes that grew up the sides of fences and house walls. They were all bright colors: red, purple, and yellow. Pine trees were everywhere; their fresh scent filled the air.

The next morning, I walked to the lake beach and took a few pictures. I prepared to hitchhike to Antigua (an-tea-gua), another Indian village known well by tourists. I waited a couple of hours in Lake Atitlán but did not find a ride from the village to the town by the main road. I eventually caught a bus that took me to the town— the same town where I had had trouble negotiating with the taxi the previous night.

I walked to the town square and piled into a little bus. I asked when we were going to leave. The response was "Right away." After I sat in cramped quarters for more than thirty minutes, we were still going to leave "right away." I returned to the robber taxis for a ride to the highway. I asked when they were leaving. They did not leave at regular intervals but when their taxi was full. If you chartered the taxi by yourself, the price was high. They were always going to leave "right away." I waited for fifteen minutes before deciding to hitchhike.

I went to the road and waited. Not one car passed me that was not full of people hanging out of the windows. After thirty minutes, I decided to try the buses again. They proclaimed they were leaving right away, but still, no one left. I tried two more buses, but the story was the same. In desperation, I returned to the robber taxi.

The taxi left me on the Pan American Highway. Since it was already afternoon, I had lunch at a restaurant. After I ate, I tried to hitchhike.

Trucks passed, but no one stopped. I waited ninety minutes before a car stopped. The driver owned a flour-milling plant and received his education in the States. He spoke perfect English. He oriented me about the political situation in Guatemala. He told me that cars were not stopping for me because they were afraid. People had been killed after picking up hitchhikers.

The driver explained there were two political factions fighting in Guatemala, the left and the right. One never knew who was responsible for what. Someone would be found dead, and no one would have any idea which faction was responsible. He said that police cars in Guatemala City always circulated in pairs, with at least two police officers per car. The police required all nonpolice cars to drive with their interior lights turned on. Police would automatically open fire on any car moving in violation to this rule. There were officers with small firearms and machine guns on street corners. Officers carried their machine guns in the ready-to-shoot, horizontal position.

My host was interesting and gave me a much better picture of Guatemala politics. In ninety minutes, we covered a distance greater than I could have covered in three to four hours of bus travel. Finally, his road and mine diverged. I thanked him profusely. He had been kind.

I was still twelve miles from Antigua, so I tried to hitchhike. Within five minutes, an American couple picked me up. They had lived in Antigua for five years. They gave me a list of places to visit. They also took me directly to a hotel they recommended. An English-speaking German woman operated it. She gave me a nice room with hot water. That was the first hot water I had felt since I was in the Virgin Islands. She also gave me a discount on prices.

It reminded me of facilities one could enjoy in Colorado or Canada, where hunters might stay. It was beautiful. Each bed had five wool blankets. I would be so comfortable, lying under those blankets at night, especially since there was no way to heat the room. The room temperature would be only degrees above the outside temperature. The best place to be in the room was in bed, under all those blankets.

I took a long, hot shower. I showered with the door closed to save the heat generated by the hot water. I dried quickly because the room was still chilly. From the bathroom, I ran and jumped into bed, pulling the covers quickly over me. I was still cold. I got up and grabbed three more blankets from the backup blanket pile and then jumped back under them. The weight from the blankets comforted me. I was toasty and happy. I immediately fell asleep.

The next day, I walked around the lake and enjoyed German cooking in restaurants. The bright sun helped to neutralize the cold. I went to see ruins, for which Antigua is noted. I hired boys as guides. I tried to hire just one boy but could not hire just one. They each had memorized their monologues in English. Once they started on it, they had to finish it. It was fun to let them complete half their presentation and then ask a question. They always had to return to the start position. The ruins did not impress me, but I enjoyed the people.

It was late afternoon, and I had not eaten. I began looking for a place to eat. While looking, I ran into another volunteer on vacation. Together, we found a small shop and ordered hamburgers. Surprisingly, they came with a green salad, which the Peace Corps discouraged because it frequently made people sick from the strange little things that lived on the leaves.

We ate and enjoyed the restaurant's food while watching the people passing on the street outside the window. That is when we saw our Peace Corps doctor pass. He saw us, stopped, entered the restaurant, and approached our table. He pointed at the salads on our plates and warned us against eating the salads. We were embarrassed but not enough to stop eating the salad. The next morning, I was fine, but my friend was in terrible distress. I had a cast-iron stomach. Those little critters could do me no harm.

I returned to the hotel, changed clothes, and took a hot shower. When I finished dressing, I returned to the park. A musical group was performing from a balcony overlooking the park. They were serenading the people in the park. The music was unusual because it centered on a xylophone, not a guitar.

The night was very chilly. The crowd was growing. I noticed that the people listening to the music had no coats or shoes. What amazed me was that they did not seem to feel the cold. They were not tensing their bodies to combat the cold. They were just standing there, as I would in eighty-degree weather. That was when part of the crowd began milling around the park while the musicians played. At first, it appeared much like cattle in a holding lot when they started to mill. Small groups of people broke rank and milled in the opposite direction. That is when I noticed that the boys were circulating in a counterclockwise direction, and the girls were circulating in a clockwise direction. I learned that this was the way that young boys and girls started courtship, by simply looking at each other in the park. I thought that we did the same thing in the States, only we used cars. Our way required gasoline, and we met fewer people. The children had adult chaperones. They were the ones who appreciated the music as the children walked around the small park's fountain. It was a clever system.

Before supper, I visited souvenir huts to discover the price range of assorted items. I located two sweet little Indian women in   the square who were selling interesting things. I bargained on items, and I agreed to buy those items from them the next day at 9:30 a.m., since I was not carrying money with me. We would meet at the same place to conclude our business.

The next morning, I was sick. I had a sore throat, stiff neck, and a cough. Although my cast-iron stomach had not let me down, my walking around without adequate clothes did me in.

I met another young American doctor. He did medical research in Malaysia. He was traveling to El Salvador and offered me a ride. What a gentleman! He and I had breakfast together, and we agreed to meet at 10:30 a.m. to head toward El Salvador.

After breakfast, I went to the park to make my purchases. I had budgeted three dollars for the purchases and not one cent more. I found the girls. I expected to make my purchases quickly, as I had already negotiated the prices, but I had to start over and renegotiate every price. That disappointed me. I concluded my purchases and started toward where I was to meet the doctor. Suddenly, behind me, I heard loud, shrill screams. I turned to see two more women who looked like the women I had just negotiated with. In fact, these were the women I had negotiated with yesterday. They looked at my purchases in disbelief. They looked at me as if I had betrayed them. I was in a tight spot. I had already spent my allocated budget, but I had no choice. I spent an additional two dollars with them. That was my reserve money. Now, I needed my free ride with the doctor more than ever; without him, I would have to go to the Guatemalan Peace Corps office and beg for enough money to return to my home in El Salvador. I left immediately; I was afraid that more shouting women might appear and that I might miss my free ride home.

Later, I caught my ride back to El Salvador with the American doctor. I arrived home with ten cents in my pocket but very satisfied with my Guatemalan adventure.

Chapter 4

Back to the Grind

El Salvador, Spring 1968

(Exact Days and Months Cannot Be Identified)

Trip to Acajutla

When I introduced myself to the director of the Literacy Education Office and tried to coordinate work with him, he insisted on doing nothing. I had not joined the Peace Corps to do nothing. I tried many ways to meet with him and learn what I was supposed to do, but none worked. Finally, one day, América invited me to join her in her work with the National Agricultural Extension Service. I presented the idea in San Salvador to my Peace Corps director. They presented it to the National Extension Service, and they approved it. I severed all ties with the literacy program and continued going daily to the local Extension Service, only now, my presence was official.

This morning in the Agricultural Extension Office was monotonous and uneventful. As usual, we had no transportation. This was enough to prevent our agronomist from leaving the office. He alleged he had a report he needed to complete.

América and I gathered our things and headed toward the cantón Tres Ceibas. We walked two miles from the office to the edge of town, where the main highway went to the capital, San Salvador. We waited minutes before we waved down a pinga-pinga bus and climbed on. The ticket taker came, and we each paid our own fares. The government did not reimburse us for these transportation costs. The more we worked, the more we traveled, and the more bus fares we paid from our own pockets. That was dedication on our part, and it was worth it to be out of the office.

The vistas were always beautiful in El Salvador. It was a green country, where layered landscapes were marked with different degrees of translucence. The vistas were clear because of the lack of pollution. This was true, except when the sugarcane owners burned the refuse on their recently harvested cane fields. Then air pollution was horrible. But for most of the year, I never tired of looking at the sugarcane fields, the coffee plantations, and the small farmers working in their tiny fields. These gorgeous vistas masked the economic and social injustices that permeated this society.

After a half hour, we came to the cantón. We signaled the bus to stop, and we stepped off. We crossed the road and headed inland. The school was a ten-minute walk. We saw the usual activity, with people coming and going. Dogs ran about on tasks of urgency; oxcarts squeaked down a path with the campesinos walking in front, issuing orders to the oxen via a stick that never broke contact with the wooden harness around the oxen's necks; and women with filled baskets on their heads went to catch buses.

We turned left at Don Miguel's tienda and saw the school. It looked empty. That was not a good sign. We had established a meeting for this time, but no one was there. América and I looked at each other, and we looked around again. The people had abandoned the cantón.

We looked inside the rooms and found no one. We grabbed two student desks and set them outside, where we waited and watched the movement in the community. We should have had five or six men, women, and children waiting for us.

When no one showed up, it was usually a sign that something unexpected had happened in the community. Perhaps someone had died, or they all needed to be in the fields for some reason. After forty-five minutes, we saw a young man who was part of the group. He said that no one was coming because they were busy with something. It did not matter what it was. It happened. It happened very often, in fact. We would go home and return the next week. Our day was spent. There was no way to go to another cantón or to find something productive to do.

América and I returned to the road and reversed the process to go home. After minutes riding, I decided I would not go to work in the afternoon. There was nothing for me to do. I told América. There was no problem. We were supposed to have spent the day in Tres Ceibas; therefore, we had nothing else planned. The truth was no one cared whether I was at the office.

I left América and the bus and walked to my house, where I had lunch. I told my landlady, Doña Maria, that I might be late for supper. I returned to the main highway and waited for a bus to the seaport, Acajutla (ah-ca-hoot-la). It was eight miles down the road. It took only five minutes before I was on the bus. It was a slow bus, but I was   in no hurry. I watched people come and go, and I watched the farms and ranches we passed. There were sugarcane fields and cotton fields. From my city to the coast, the land was flat and fertile. Logically, large, and wealthy landowners owned it. In the middle of a field were small pyramids ten to fifteen feet high. The farmers drove their tractors up and over them, if possible; if not, they drove around them, crowding as closely as possible to them so as not to leave any valuable land untilled. These were remnants of pyramids constructed hundreds of years ago, but today, no one cared.

Upon arriving in Acajutla, I stepped from the bus and looked around. Acajutla was a large village, no more. It was a small and unsophisticated seaport. On the beach, just far enough up from the water that they were in no danger from the ocean, were a half dozen huts with thatched roofs, sand floors, and bamboo sides. In these huts, simple bars operated, each with a half dozen tables and a small counter for a bar, usually located in the far corner. Young ladies, who had nothing to do, hung back in another corner.

I went into the first hut, put my book about fertilizers on the counter, and ordered an aguardiente (firewater) and Coke. I drank slowly and read about fertilizers. When I glanced up from my book, I saw the young ladies watching me, amused and curious. When they saw that I was looking at them, they all giggled, as if on cue.

I ordered a second drink, but I closed the book and started to think. I thought about home. I missed it very much. It was so far away in distance and in time that I did not know what to do. I was less than one year into my service, not yet at the midpoint, and that fact made the loneliness I felt for home even worse.

These moments were difficult. I had to change the direction of my thoughts. I decided to go for a swim. I did not have a swimsuit, but I learned from the ladies that I could rent one. They offered to bring it out. They were helpful. The rent was reasonable, so I rented it. I went into the back where they had a room enclosed with bamboo, and even with the cracks between the bamboo poles, I changed my clothes. I took all my possessions with me to the beach for safety reasons. I carefully laid my things on the sand and entered the water.

I was a young man and not accustomed to the drink. My head was floating merrily in its own world as I headed for the water. I ran fast into the first wave, which was larger than I had envisioned. It flipped me upside down, rotated me head over tail, and deposited me near my clothes. I was happy to lie there. If that were where I was needed, I could lie there for a moment. I looked up. The sky was blue. The sun was warm. The sound of the ocean made relaxing sounds. The afternoon was still young. I was at peace with the world.

That was enough swimming for the moment. I returned to my bar. I was the only client. A bored bartender sat in one corner. In another corner, four young ladies were milling about. At this point, I noticed the young ladies did not seem to be drinking or doing anything. I ordered another aguardiente and Coke and sat at a table without opening my book. I looked at the ladies and smiled. They smiled back, and two even approached my table and sat down. We talked. They were nice. I did not understand what nice young girls were doing there. I asked them. They said they were working. I found that strange because the bartender only had to fix one or two drinks per hour. When I mentioned this, they looked at each other and laughed but offered no explanation. We talked about their families and my family. They asked what I was doing in El Salvador, and we talked while I drank. They helped me to feel less lonely.

Later, I decided to take another dip in the ocean. I was far less steady on my feet as I ran into the water, but I was more confident. Again, the wave was larger and much more powerful than I had expected, and it flipped me end over end and deposited me on the beach. This time, though, I swallowed water. I decided I had swum enough and changed into my clothes.

By now it was growing dark. It was between 5:45 and 6:00 p.m. At 5:40 p.m., it was afternoon. By 5:45 p.m., the birds were fluttering around like something crazy was about to happen. They chattered and flew from tree branch to line pole and back again. There were desperate to find a safe place to spend the night, and then, at 6:00 p.m., there was no light and the birds had disappeared completely.

I asked the ladies at what time the last bus returned to my Sonsonate. They said 8:30 p.m. I had more than two hours to continue my meditation before I would have to return to the ugly real world.

More people entered the bar and occupied the other tables. The two young ladies stayed at my table. I did not understand. Women had never found me so interesting before. I was pleased with myself. The men in the bar were ordering "cylinders" of aguardiente. These were glass bottles in the shape of a thin cylinder and contained about ten ounces of pure aguardiente. I contemplated doing this also. I thought and I thought, and then I ordered it. The cylinder came quickly. The women in the corner watched with interest. I opened the bottle. The women stopped breathing in anticipation; their eyes were frozen on me. I did not understand why anyone would pay so much attention to me, especially now, as I opened a small bottle. I sniffed the bottle and bravely sipped it. It was not a big sip. In fact, it was a small sip. It was, however, enough to wake every cell in my mouth, esophagus, and stomach. I had burned these cells severely, and they were not happy. I tried to keep an all-is-good facial expression for the ladies, but they knew better. It was difficult for me to conceal my gasping for air. In fact, every time I inhaled, it provided more oxygen for the fire inside me to burn brighter. When I started to cough, the ladies broke into laughter.

Not to be a wimp, I practiced my drinking of straight aguardiente. The excitement being over, the girls found other people to talk with, but they always kept one eye on me. Finally, one nudged me and said that it was 8:35 and that I might have missed the last bus out of town. I went into panic mode. I started grabbing my stuff. I found that I did not have hands enough to grab everything. I stuffed the empty cylinder into my back pocket and ran to where the bus should have been. It was not there, but I could see it up the street. I ran after it as best I could. I did not run as much as stagger. I fell forward, and my feet tried to keep pace to prevent my face from smashing into the pavement. The bus stopped to pick up people on its way out of town. I caught it—just barely. I found an empty seat in the back and sat down. Life was good.

The trip back to Sonsonate was enjoyable, except that I was now starving. It was dark, and I could see campesino campfires here and there in the distance. There were no lights in the countryside because there was no rural electrification. The only light in the night was either gas lanterns or campfires, which is what the campesinos used for cooking and light.

The bus pulled into the bus station. I staggered off and pointed myself in the direction of my house. It was almost two miles away. I tried to walk naturally, but it was not possible. I knew that people were watching me, even more than they usually did. I tried to keep them from knowing that I was drunk, but I was certain everyone knew.

As I walked, I hoped the alcohol would loosen its grip on me, but it did not. I was hungry, and it was not possible to walk in a straight line. As I drew nearer to my house, I saw all my neighbors sitting on their front steps. All my little friends were still up, and their mothers and their distrusting fathers were all there. When they saw me approaching, they stopped talking and watched me. I did not want them to know I was drunk. I focused all my energy on walking a straight line. I knew that I could not say anything, or they would know that I had been drinking. I walked straight past each of my friends who were sitting less than one yard from me. I looked straight ahead and said nothing to them. I was proud because I reached my door and turned and walked through it without falling. When I sat down to eat, I felt the tall, cylindrical bottle in my back pocket. A bottle that size and shape had only one use: aguardiente. The next day, I realized that everyone on the street had seen that bottle in my back pocket as I struggled to walk past them without falling. I had fooled only myself.

A Peasant's Saint's Day

Each peasant had a special saint's day. It was customary for peasants to give birthday parties on their saints' birthdays to honor them. The custom was for the peasant to give the best party possible. If he hosted the best party, within his financial means, he would have good luck during the next year. Although each peasant farmer tried to give the best party, they only invited close friends.

It is important to understand what a chicken meant to a peasant family. Chickens were not just a source of meat for special occasions or for the eggs they provided most days. They represented a peasant's savings account. Chickens represented money in the bank; peasants could only dream of having bank accounts, so they had chickens. If a member of the family became ill, they could grab a couple of chickens and head to town. They could easily sell the chickens and then see the doctor. Chickens were a very liquid asset.

Shirley snagged an invitation to a saint's party. Of course, she would take Bob, but this time they also invited me. They considered us special guests. I got up early so that I could arrive early at Bob and Shirley's house. We started walking immediately. I learned that the walk would take a couple of hours. We crossed the hammock bridge and climbed the steep hill on the other side. We went down roads, up roads, and across roads. We entered coffee plantations and then exited them again. We were so far out of any territory I had seen to date that I was lost. Only Shirley knew where we were and where we were going.

Finally, we came to a fork in the road, whereupon Shirley announced that we had arrived. The dirt-floored, grass-roofed, stick-walled house was located between the forks in the road. As soon as they introduced us, we shook hands all around with all the farmers and their wives, as was the custom among peasants. Mrs. Peasant escorted us into the house and gave us each a tiny bench, about six inches from the ground, and invited us to sit down. All the other guests were outside around the cooking pot, which hung from three sticks tied together at their top over the fire pit. The women conversed in a group, while the men talked in a separate group. I did not see any drinking. This festival was too serious for drinking.

As we waited, they brought us a full glass of pineapple drink. They had removed the pineapple's outer layer and then chopped it into small pieces, poured water on it, and then poured the resulting mixture into a glass. In lieu of a blender, they cut the pineapple into small pieces—as small as they could—but the end effect was to have small pieces of pineapple floating in water; it was refreshing. We were grateful for it after our long walk, although we were all worried about the quality of the water. Still, it would be the supreme insult to refuse their drink.

Later, they brought each of us a metal soup dish with chicken soup and a metal spoon. The spoons had rusted, thus giving the soup a rusty taste. It was imperative that we consumed the soup with a smile. We all knew this. None of us would betray the soup's rusty taste. They gave us these special utensils because of our status as special guests. The other guests had bowls made from pottery and spoons made from wood.

We each had a piece of chicken in our soup. By piece of chicken, I mean half a leg or half a thigh. It was not a full piece by our standards in America. There were too many people and too few chickens. I am not sure if they used one or two chickens for the party, but they used all they felt they could safely spare. A responsible parent never would spend so much on a party that it would put the family at risk. A peasant's chickens were also like a health insurance policy. In the peasant's world, children could quickly become sick, and when they did, they needed their chickens to pay for medical services.

When we finished, we returned our soup dishes, and we complimented the peasant's wife on her cooking. She blushed, smiled, and lowered her head in humility. We saw our host remove anything left in our bowls onto small plates and give it to their children to eat. They chewed on our bones. After the children cleaned the bones, what remained went to the dogs. The dogs were very skinny. At this time, they served us coffee. It was horrible coffee, but we all drank it with smiles on our faces. I doubt they drank coffee normally and did not have experience preparing it. We knew that we were being honored, and we could never permit any of our actions to appear to disrespect our hosts.

Our hosts had thrown a magnificent party. I cannot imagine how they could have done more to honor us, or their saint. We felt truly honored.

We had spent months developing a relationship with community leaders in one Indian village. The village was fortunate to have a new school that offered classes through the sixth grade. The director of that school, Don Napoleón, was very helpful in our work. He was the key to our work in that village because everyone respected him.

June 20, 1968—The Malnourished Child

Don Napoleón was walking to his home in Izalco when a thief assaulted him on the sidewalk. When he resisted, the thief shot him. He went to the hospital where the doctors expected him to recover, but his wounds will take time to heal. El Salvador had the highest homicide rate in the world.

I was positive that a very dark cloud was following me. I was feeling mentally sick. My work was at a standstill due to Teachers' Day and a fiesta in Nahuizalco. They celebrated Teachers' Day by letting school out on Friday and all the following week. After they returned, they had a week of exams, and then the term ended. Most of my work was in Nahuizalco, so when they were on vacation, my work ceased.

The Teachers' Day celebration provided the campesinos with a reason to drink until they collapsed in the streets, sidewalks, doorways, bushes, or on park benches. Drivers needed to be vigilant to avoid running them over. Sometimes, I saw two or three drunks sharing a spot on the ground, even next to sleeping pigs or chickens scratching for food. It was common to see a man's wife and children sitting in the shade near the father, waiting for him to awake and become sober enough to walk home together.

I was in San Salvador and was hitchhiking back to Sonsonate when a married Peace Corps volunteer couple gave me a ride. They were taking barrels to their village for a public health demonstration. They offered to take me to see their village. It was close to the highway and would not delay me more than one or two hours. I found their offer agreeable.

We were eating lunch in a small sidewalk café when a nurse approached us. She asked if we were returning to San Salvador any time soon. The couple replied that they would be leaving within twenty minutes. The nurse asked if they could take a child to a hospital there because she had two broken ribs. The nurse motioned for an Indian lady, who was expecting a child, to approach with her thirteen-month-old baby. The side of her head was black-and-blue. We could not see the baby's ribs because her parents had wrapped her in a blanket. Her feet, however, were exposed, and we could see they were black-and-blue, with pieces of flesh hanging down.

The female volunteer said that she had seen cases like this. Malnutrition and parent brutality typically caused them. I did not see much of this in my work, but Shirley confirmed that she had seen this often in her work in the countryside. This was typical of El Salvador's peasant poverty. The worst months for this were from December to May—the dry months. When the rains came, fruits and vegetables became more abundant, peasants' diets improved, and cases of malnutrition abated.

Yesterday was a boring day from the beginning. I went to work to discover that the head of the office—the director for the livestock part—had decided we needed to move to another office. This was a surprise to me. When I arrived, one desk was already missing—mine—so I found an empty desk and sat down. Within five minutes, they came and carried away that desk. I had no place in the office to sit. I saw one of the veterinarians' jeeps and settled into the back seat to read. Within minutes, the vet, who was responsible for that jeep, had to leave on a job. I did not have any place to sit. It was then that my amigo Bob, the volunteer from Nahuizalco, came by and suggested we go to Acajutla to play Frisbee on the beach. Finally, there was something for me to do. We left.

The next morning, everyone—and I mean everyone—asked me where I had been the day before. Usually, they did not notice if I was gone.

July 4, 1968—The Little Girl

Last Wednesday evening, I came home, showered, and retired to the outer tienda to wait for supper. I always leaned a chair against the wall and pulled out a Spanish book, opened it to a random place, and studied. As customers entered the store, I might look up to see who it was, but mostly, I studied my book. Then, I noticed a little girl enter the store. She looked like she could be eight years old, maybe ten. She asked for frijoles, but there were none. My landlady informed her that she was expecting a shipment any minute, but it had not yet arrived. I noticed that the little girl was neat and clean. It looked like her long, straight black hair had just been washed, and she had a contagious smile, one that caused anyone who saw it to instinctively smile too.

She said something to my landlady and pushed herself from the counter that she had been leaning against. She exited the same door she had used to enter the tienda. As she reached the sidewalk, she ran into the street by crossing upstream. She should have seen it, but she did not. There was a huge thump, followed by the release of air brakes. Microseconds later, I saw a blur pass outside the second door in the tienda, followed by screams from the women in the street.

I did not need to see what had happened. I already knew. I could not tear myself from my chair. Within seconds I heard a woman running toward us from where the girl was headed. She was desperately yelling, "Lupita, Lupita!" I could not bring myself to watch more. I retired to my room to try to think of something else. I played records to drown the cries.

July 5, 1968—A Peace Corps Colleague Dies

About ten days ago I went to Nahuizalco to visit the campesinos in Pushtan. After we concluded our business, Bob and I went to

Acajutla to swim and take part in local refreshments. I was now twenty-one years old. It was good to laugh and speak English. Bob would be leaving soon, and I would leave in fifteen months. He asked me what I would do when I returned to the States. I had not thought about it. Until now, the act of leaving had never crossed my mind. I had just arrived, but now I started to give it consideration.

The next morning, I went to the office. As I approached my desk, I saw a telegram. I picked it up and panicked when I saw the word URGENT on the envelope. I opened it, and its message was "Come quick! Alex is very grave!" I showed it to América and ran to pack a few things and hitchhike to San Salvador. I had a tough time hitchhiking. It took forever to catch a ride, but I caught one with a couple of married missionaries. They had already served four years and were excited about returning home in thirty days. We talked mostly about their excitement of returning after living so long in El Salvador.

As I traveled to San Salvador, I thought that Alex could not be sick. Sickness does not work fast. He must have been in an accident. Alex was an intelligent young man who had graduated from a top university on the East Coast. He was a lawyer. His assignment was in the poorest barrio in San Salvador. I had heard rumors that his living conditions were the worst of any volunteer in El Salvador.

Walking toward the Peace Corps office, I walked faster and faster. I found volunteers already there. I asked what had happened to Alex. They told me that Alex had died. He had committed suicide the previous morning and had never regained consciousness.

July 7, 1968—Dealing with Death

All volunteers and staff were upset. They notified the family. The embassy managed to keep the news out of the newspapers until all volunteers arrived from their rural sites. We lived with him for fifty-one weeks; we shared the most important experiences of our lives together, and hence, we had many of the same experiences. We thought we knew each other as only people can after going through basic training together. No one ever suspected that Alex could do such a thing. Mostly, we were sad that he had suffered alone.

The Peace Corps had a simple service for him that night at a Protestant church in San Salvador. After the service, we went to the funeral home for a short viewing and for us to say our goodbyes to him. Since there was a bus strike in San Salvador, Peace Corps jeeps brought his Salvadorian colleagues from his site to the funeral and the viewing. The Peace Corps insisted that we stay another day in San Salvador.

They hired a psychiatrist to lead a discussion about what had happened. Their concern was that there might be one or two other volunteers among us who might have considered suicide. They were worried that with one volunteer following through with the idea, it might make it more acceptable to others and create a chain of events that no one wanted. The discussion was productive, soothing, and necessary. It helped everyone. There was much red tape with repatriating the body to the USA because the embassy was already using all its resources in preparing for President Johnson's forthcoming visit to El Salvador. The Secret Service and CIA arrived by the plane loads. There were many men to house. They took over the two best hotels in San Salvador. They even moved guests with long-standing reservations to alternative—and inferior locations.

These men had short haircuts, wore sunglasses, dressed the same, and talked constantly into walkie-talkies. They were not difficult to spot around the city.

One of our apartment mates found a castaway American walking the streets with no place to stay. He alleged that his Harley-Davidson motorcycle had broken and was in a shop being repaired. I say alleged because when we later spoke about our interactions with him, his story was slightly different to each of us, and sometimes, it was completely inconsistent. He was a little too "hippie," and he could not sell the image. He dressed like a hippie and talked like he thought they talked, but when we looked at him, we did not see a hippie. We saw a CIA agent trying to infiltrate a group of Peace Corps volunteers.

I should provide a backstory. The embassy's security detail for the president called our Peace Corps director and told her to send over a list of the volunteers who would protest the president's trip. She flatly refused. I liked her. Although most of us were not fond of LBJ, El Salvador was not the place to protest. We all loved the Peace Corps and would never embarrass it or do anything to jeopardize our work there. It was the next day that the hippie appeared and magically crossed paths with one of us. The Peace Corps had already asked us to welcome stranded people into our apartments as part of the relocation program after the embassy occupied the hotels. The protesting students shut down the university.

We went to the airport to see Air Force One land. It was a 737. I must admit that I felt immense pride when it landed, even though I disagreed with the policies pursued by LBJ. There was much pushing to gain a better position to see LBJ. Short people had no chance.

I learned that all US government employees would have a chance to see Johnson at the embassy when he gave a speech. We were excited, but I had not brought my suit from Sonsonate. I had to rush back to Sonsonate to retrieve my suit and hurry back to San Salvador. That was my third round-trip in one week between Sonsonate and San Salvador.

All the male volunteers from the apartment traveled together to the embassy. We found an advantageous position. What I noticed was the feeling of power in the room. I cannot describe it, but its presence was as real as that of the Secret Service. I do not remember what the president spoke about, but it was a good speech. We also saw his wife, Lady Bird, and their younger daughter, Lucy.

When we returned to the apartment, we noticed that the hippie had gone. It was a Sunday. I doubt that he could have picked up his motorcycle at a repair shop on a Sunday evening. He most definitely was a CIA plant in our apartment.

August 10, 1968—A Message from Jerry in Guatemala

I received a letter from my Peace Corps friend Jerry, in Guatemala. When I left him, he was still selling his potatoes in the San Salvador markets. The potato buyers boycotted him from the market and threatened to run him out of San Salvador. I did not understand exactly, but he had to return to Guatemala City with half a truckload of potatoes.

I offered to move around San Salvador and take orders from restaurants and markets. He could then load their truck with the required potatoes to meet those specific orders, but he had had enough of San Salvador and declined my offer.

Jerry had spoken with the Peace Corps office in Guatemala. They were still open to my visiting Jerry, but they wanted to delay the trip.

In the Peace Corps, we could terminate our service one month early if it were to attend college. If I did this, it would mean that I was halfway through my assignment. I could not believe it. I had felt that the end of my assignment was so far away that I could not even think about it. Now, I could think about it. I was starting to slide down the backside of my assignment.

Last Saturday I went to Izalco to visit the teachers from the school. We visited a farm, where we drank coconut water all morning. It was so delicious and healthy. It was a wonderful day away from home.

The Joneses and I made plans to go to a beach near the Guatemala border. They only have another two weeks before their assignment is complete. I will miss them. They will return to school in San Francisco. It will be good for them to be in such a stimulating environment. It made me homesick, just listening to them make their plans because I wanted to go home too. They already had their airline tickets. I envied them their excitement, but before I could feel that excitement, I needed to complete my assignment.

August 13, 1968—The Joneses and I Go to a Beach Near Guatemala

When the Jones and I went to the beach, it was really an island sandbar, with a swamp between it and land. We arrived midmorning after walking in the hot sun for two miles after we left the bus. We had to hire a dugout canoe, which, with the help of a push-pole, took us to the sandbar. The trip was absent of sound, as the canoe owner pushed off the swamp bottom. We marveled at the silence. The canoe owner agreed to pick us up late in the afternoon. We had to pay forty cents for transport each way.

August 24, 1968—I Get Sick

I started to feel bad after my meeting with Sonsonate's mayor last night. I walked all the way home without buying an ice cream cone from any street vendors. I often bought more than one, but today, I bought none.

When an ice cream street vendor saw me coming, he opened his little top door on his pushcart, and he started pushing cones this way and that way, as he looked for the kind I liked. When he found it, he replaced the door and shifted his feet this way and that as he waited for me to reach him. When I approached him, he opened the cart's top door and pulled out the ice cream cone that I had recently been buying. The ice cream man would be crushed if I did not buy it. I had to buy it. It was my act of kindness for the day.

As I continued to walk home, I felt weaker and weaker. I was so relieved when I turned into Doña Maria's tienda and dragged myself through the front room into my room. I removed my shoes and lay down hard on my cot. Doña Maria saw me come in. She recognized that something was wrong and followed me into my room. She felt my forehead. She ordered me to stay put while she brought me pills to take. She returned with a glass of orange juice and mysterious pills. I took them and finished the orange juice. Sleep came quickly.

August 30, 1968—Casa Clark in San Salvador

I was feeling much better, but the last few days had not been easy. The doctor believed my discomfort had been something I had eaten or drunk on Saturday. After I reached my room last Saturday, I lay for a while, resting, and then the diarrhea and vomiting started. A severe headache accompanied these symptoms. I was unable to eat and could not keep liquids down.

By evening, Doña Maria called a local doctor, who made a house call. He brought liquids that I took intravenously.

By Monday morning, I was able to take the bus to San Salvador to see the Peace Corps doctor. I was nervous about the possibility of having to exit the bus in a hurry and scurry into the coffee plants, but I survived.

Monday noon was the first time I had eaten in two and a half days. The doctor sent me to rest and recuperate at Casa Clark. I was not able to weigh myself, but I know I lost weight. My pants fit loosely, but Casa Clark's excellent food would remedy that.

There was another Peace Corps volunteer there for a similar reason. We went to three movies in two days. It was wonderful seeing the big screen and experiencing the wonderful sound system. We saw *The Planet of the Apes, The Fox,* and *The Party.*

We will both return to our respective sites tomorrow. I was sad because Bob and Shirley's group was leaving tomorrow for their homes. I will miss them.

At this point, I had been gone from the USA for only fourteen months. It had not been long, but I already felt disconnected from the USA.

This summer had many interruptions, my trip to Guatemala, my illness, the president's visit, and my colleague's suicide. That made it difficult to stay engaged in my work. Now, my friends, the Joneses, had left, and I had no one to talk to. I had the Mormons, but they had no idea about my work or interest in it, just as I had no interest in their work. I needed to dig in and make myself think about El Salvador more than I thought about home.

In November or December, I will travel to Honduras, Nicaragua, Costa Rica, and Panama. The Panama Canal Zone is a tax-free zone. I want to see if I can save enough money to buy a Pentax camera. All the Peace Corps volunteers are doing it. It makes sense to me. I am having the adventure of a lifetime, and I want good photos to remember it; so far, half of my attempts to take photos have failed. I hope to buy a good wide-angle and telephoto lens. I cannot wait. This dream of traveling through these countries with my new camera helps me to stay focused on El Salvador. It is difficult to wait twelve months to go home, but I can wait two or three months to take an exciting trip, and then I will have only nine months before I can go home. That is how I am surviving twenty-seven months away from home. I break it into bits and survive each bit.

September 7, 1968—No News from Jerry

I heard no more from Jerry, the Guatemalan Peace Corps volunteer, about my helping him with his producers' potato problem. I did not think I could do anything to help. My knowledge of potatoes was practical, not technical, and the Guatemalan potato producers' problem was technical in nature.

September 24, 1968—El Salvador Has the

Highest Homicide Rate in the World

The Peace Corps had received six new agricultural trainees. They were undergoing further training at the National Agricultural Extension Service's facilities in Santa Tecla. The Peace Corps had chosen me as their guide and translator. We slept on army cots in a dorm room. We had afternoons free.

One afternoon, I received a phone call from our Peace Corps office. The secretary had no idea what it was about, but I was to go immediately to the office. I learned that the Peace Corps Guatemala's official had requested that I spend two weeks with Jerry, the Peace Corps volunteer. I would fly out of San Salvador on Monday, September 30, and spend two weeks on site with Jerry in the Indian village of San Juan Ostuncalco.

Last month, I had been in the American restaurant in San Salvador when the painter I had been trying to meet happened to be talking with

the restaurant's owner. The owner saw me and introduced me to Oscar Manuel Garcia, the painter. I arranged to buy one painting a month for ten dollars each. I had the right to reject any painting that I did not like. I paid him in advance for the first painting. He was pleased.

Because of my buying one painting a month, I had little free cash. My upcoming trip to Guatemala would be painful for me because they had the most beautiful clothes, blankets, wood carvings, and other things that I had ever seen. And I had no money.

One Monday morning, I learned that over the weekend, one of our 4-H members had been murdered. An unknown assailant wielding a machete had decapitated him and robbed him of less than one dollar.

One weekend in Sonsonate, there were eight murders. Four of them occurred due to a dishonored husband. The husband thought that his wife had cheated on him, so he killed his wife and the man involved. Unfortunately, the man involved was a bus driver, and two innocent passengers were also killed. The other four were killed at the soccer stadium, where there had been a spirited game between Sonsonate and their number-one rival. These games often became a little testy.

El Salvador had far-right political groups and far-left political groups. They called the far-left group the White Hand. A person considered rich could wake up and find a white hand painted on his front door. The implied message was that he had seventy- two hours to liquidate his assets and divide them among the poor, or dreadful things would happen to him and his family.

One far-right group simply killed people they did not like. There was a pharmacy located three blocks from where I stayed. The pharmacist received many free samples, which he happily passed on to poor peasant Indian farmers who could not afford medication. For that, the far-right group entered his pharmacy with machine guns and destroyed everything, including the pharmacist. They claimed that the pharmacist had been Communist because he had been giving away free medicine samples to the Indians.

Chapter 5

I Try to Help Jerry in Guatemala

October 5, 1968—I Will Fly to Guatemala to Help Jerry

I left San Salvador by plane for Guatemala City on Monday at 7:30 a.m. Within the hour, I was in the Peace Corps office in Guatemala City. They gave me thirty-two dollars to cover my living expenses in Guatemala and sent me off for two weeks. Since the first bus for San Juan Ostuncalco was at 2:30 p.m., I went to the central market and bought a leather carrying bag and two beautiful all-wool blankets. I envisioned that my children's beds would use these blankets if I ever had any. I assumed the nights would be cold where I was going and that the blankets would be useful.

At two thirty, a new Greyhound-like bus pulled out of the station. It had huge windows, giving every passenger a view of the panorama as it slid by. To me, the region seemed like Colorado, but there were differences. There was no snow on the mountain peaks. The needy farmers cleared the mountain forests to their tops to plant more potatoes. There were few rocks in the soil; in fact, the soil was sandy.

The peasants in these areas wore a special kind of shoe, on which the toe and heel were open. At first, I could not figure out why they would open the toe and heel for a shoe. Then I walked in the sand and saw the peasants walk. As they did, sand slid out their toes and heels, keeping their shoes sand-free.

Beautiful, fragrant pine trees covered the mountaintops. El Salvador had no pine trees, with minor exceptions. I arrived in Quetzaltenango at dusk, elevation eight thousand feet. It was too late to go on, so I found a cheap place to stay and eat. I was hungry because I had not eaten much that day. I had weighed myself the day before. I weighed 155 pounds. When I started training, I weighed 177 pounds. When we started our work in El Salvador, I weighed 166 pounds, and I had one year left, during which I would lose more weight.

I began to explore the city. As I walked through the streets, I saw two gringos approaching, and I recognized one of them. He was the Mormon who had left Sonsonate three weeks ago. He was waiting for a bus to his next destination. We had a soda together and caught up on the news.

October 6, 1968, Tuesday—I Arrived in

San Juan Ostuncalco

I caught the bus to San Juan Ostuncalco the next morning at six thirty. I found Jerry in an Indian language class. Most Guatemalan Indians spoke only a little Spanish and mostly spoke their Indian languages. In fact, if a Peace Corps volunteer arrived speaking only a little Spanish and even if he committed glaring errors in pronunciation or grammar, the Indians mimicked that manner of speech. The Indians always figured that the white guy knew more Spanish than they did. That made it difficult for new volunteers to improve their Spanish. Plus, new volunteers had to learn the local Indian language.

Indian languages varied. There was another Indian village about every five miles. Each village often had different words in their vocabulary for the same thing. If you traveled three or four villages away, they might speak the same language, but much of the vocabulary was different. This made Peace Corps work challenging in Guatemala.

When Jerry's language class ended, we sat to drink a coffee and plan my two-week visit. Then we walked around his village, and he introduced me to people.

He walked toward a steep mountain slope. I followed him. As we started climbing the steep hill, he told me that this hill belonged to the area's voodoo priests. Soon, we saw a man kneeling and praying. We kept our distance but continued to watch him. He was burning something as he prayed.

He saw us and motioned for us to approach him. We did. He was very pleasant and talkative. He spoke of freedom of religion and mentioned that he was praying for improved health. He said he visited the slope daily and always prayed at that spot—that spot belonged to him; no one else prayed there. All the dozens of other spots that we could see around us belonged to other voodoo priests.

He said that each May they had a convention and met on the slope of a nearby volcano. Last May, he claimed that one thousand priests attended. Suddenly, he told us that our conversation was over, and he returned to his praying.

In the afternoon, we visited a nearby cooperative. There were eighteen members present. We discussed production and marketing problems. After the meeting, we established meeting times on Saturday to visit their individual farms. We returned to Jerry's house, ate, and left for another cooperative meeting at 7:30 p.m. in a town six miles away. This area was mountainous; therefore, these six miles had many ups and downs between the two villages, and we were riding bicycles.

Jerry had his own bicycle. He borrowed one for me. As we started our first descent from a mountain peak, Jerry mentioned that my bicycle did not have any brakes or lights. I quickly overtook him on the descent, but luckily, we had a full moon so I could make out where the road ended, and the steep mountain slope began. At the bottom of the hill, the road turned sharply to the left and then sharply to the right before going up another steep hill. I almost tinkled my pants from trying to keep my bicycle on the road, but after forty minutes, we arrived for the meeting. Sixteen enthusiastic cooperative members were present. Our meeting did not end until nine o'clock.

Jerry wanted to show me more of the beautiful scenery that the full moon offered. I accepted his invitation to deviate from our normal path. He turned and started uphill again. The road was so steep that we had to get off and push our bicycles uphill. Once we crested the mountain, the view of the fields in the moonlight was unequaled. We remained silent for a few minutes and admired the view.

We started down the mountain at nine forty-five and reached home at eleven o'clock. We ate and then slept. We were exhausted. It was very cold inside the house, but my newly purchased blankets saved me.

October 7, 1968, Wednesday—Making Field Visits

We were up early and had a modest breakfast of French bread and coffee. Jerry had his Indian language class at six thirty. After class, two retired married missionaries drove by and offered to take us for a ride. We went to a nearby town, where they produced the most beautiful woolen blankets. They were gorgeous, with flawless workmanship, and so inexpensive, but I had no money. As a Peace Corps volunteer, I had become accustomed to that feeling of having to walk away from something that I wanted. That was an important part of the Peace Corps experience. I did it many times that afternoon.

In the afternoon, we went to our third cooperative meeting. We had to travel several miles to this meeting. The first half of the trip involved climbing a steep slope; mostly, I pushed my bicycle. The last half the trip was downhill. I had to be careful to keep the bicycle under my control, which I did, except for the moment when I almost hit a horse. When we arrived, sixteen members appeared. I was impressed with Jerry's organization. He was flawless—the perfect volunteer.

While the cooperative members were finishing business, Jerry and I climbed a mountain to its summit. From there, we had hoped to see the sun setting over the beach, which often one could see from this point, even though the beach was tens of miles away. Unfortunately, we saw dark clouds roll in one thousand feet below our elevation. It was unsettling to watch them from above.

We returned to the cooperative meeting that finished at 6:30 p.m. It was already dark. We grabbed our bicycles and started pushing them up the mountain to the summit. It took an hour and a quarter to reach the summit. We mounted our vehicles and pushed off into the darkness. There were rocks in the road. This made our lives more exciting. If we hit them, they could bend our tires' rims and throw us from the bicycles. We also had to keep from hitting each other and going off the road. It took fifteen minutes to reach our village at the base of the mountain.

We ate and were almost ready for bed by eight o'clock, but first, I wanted to visit the local agronomist. Jerry took me to his house and introduced me. I wanted him to explain the local agricultural practices.

October 8, 1968, Thursday—We Were Almost Caught in a Rainstorm

After Jerry's language class and breakfast, he went to another village to see people about a new classroom addition. I accompanied him just to see.

The students attending this school were mostly poor Indian children. Since this area had Protestant missionaries, children wore clothes that this region normally did not see. The missionaries collected these clothes from the United States. I saw one student dressed in overalls. People in Latin America never wore overalls, but there he was. Patches covered his overalls.

On our return to our village, a rainstorm nearly caught us. Traveling in wet clothes would have been horrible. A wet coat did not offer warmth from the season's coldness. The houses did not have heat. I would have no way to dry clothes other than the natural process, which took a long time at the low temperatures that we were experiencing.

I wore a T-shirt, a long-sleeved shirt, and a coat. I wore these everywhere, even in the house. When I wrote letters, I was fully clothed. Shaving was no fun, although that task was not a difficult one, because my beard was barely visible. We bathed by heating a bucket of water on the stove and using a sponge in a dark corner.

October 9, 1968, Friday—We Feasted with

the Missionaries

We traveled to the community called The Hope. We ate lunch in the house of a cooperative member. On the way back, a heavy downpour caught us. We stopped cycling and waited under a tree for a bus to come. We flagged it down, had our vehicles loaded on top of the bus, and climbed in for a safe, dry trip back to our village. We returned to Jerry's house at five in the evening. We had half an hour to change into dry clothes and prepare for dinner with the married missionaries.

The missionaries hosted an excellent dinner party. We drank milk and ate mashed potatoes with two kinds of gravy, peas, creamed corn, carrot sticks, coleslaw, white bread, and whole bread with butter, and all the meat we could eat. They also served two distinct kinds of jellies and ice cream. Wow! To heck with the Peace Corps, I wanted to be a missionary!

Later, because they were going home in two weeks, they gave Jerry and me each a pair of warm socks. I felt like we had been honored. The meal we had just eaten must have taken a couple of people all day to prepare. I was thankful for that meal—and still am.

On our return trip, we took the main highway. As we started, we noticed a car parked on the side of the road. The driver smoked a cigarette. Jerry and I found that to be unusual. That night, I began to feel pains in my stomach.

October 10, 1968, Saturday—I Get Sick

We noticed the police had stopped a truckload of peasant farmers along the highway. Jerry said they were on their way to the coast to pick coffee. The police stopped them because they wanted a bribe before they would release them. The truckers picked this route because its roads were in the worst condition. They thought it was more likely to be free from police patrols.

That morning, my stomach cramps continued, but we had to leave to visit more peasant farmers.

We met four farmers in the community of The Conception. These farmers were ready for change. One farmer discovered that chemical fertilizer obtained better results if spread on the ground with organic matter. This was a great observation because it was based on scientific fact.

In the afternoon, we went to Quetzaltenango for a piece of pineapple pie. By nightfall, my stomach had neither worsened nor improved.

By three in the morning, I had severe stomach cramps. I had to stand and walk around to gain a small degree of relief from the pain. Then the vomiting started, and I was sick all of Sunday. I was unable to drink or eat anything. There were three things available to drink: soda, coffee, or a local tea. I was unable to keep anything down. Even worse, I could not lie down or sit down. I could walk, but I had to walk bent over. During this time, the house was very cold, and I was uncomfortable. It rained constantly.

I became very depressed, and I wanted to go home. I wanted to leave Guatemala and El Salvador. I wanted to be warm again, and not have any pain, and eat and drink whatever I wanted. Finally, at seven thirty in the evening, I was able to lie down and sleep.

October 12, 1968, Monday—More Farm Visits

We left early to visit eight farms which were located at a high elevation and far from our village. We pushed our bicycles uphill for forty-five minutes. Jerry said we were at 9,500 feet elevation. It was misty and cold. We completed our visits and did what needed to be done. We started our return trip at 12:25 p.m. It started to rain when we reached the summit. By the time we reached home, the rain had soaked us.

I concluded my time with Jerry and returned to my site in El Salvador.

I had seen a beautiful painting in an American restaurant and asked who had painted it. The restaurant owner told me that it belonged to a local painter. As luck would have it, on a later visit to the restaurant the painter was there, and the restaurant owner introduced us. I made an agreement with him that I would buy one painting a month for ten dollars, but I had the right to reject any painting I did not like. He gave me his address and I told him that I would visit him within the month. Ten dollars represented ten percent of my salary. It was not an insignificant amount, but I liked his painting style.

October 18, 1968—I Visit the Painter and His Family

I went to San Salvador and ordered another painting. The painter, Oscar Manuel Garcia, and I were becoming good friends. He promised me that I would love the next painting. I knew he would do his best, so I paid his asking price, but now I wanted his best quality. Usually when he needed money, he made a quick-and-dirty painting in one day and gave it to his wife. She walked about the streets in the market, trying to sell it for the best price she could, allowing them to eat that day.

The painter, his wife, and their two young children lived in a poor community. Their children were malnourished—at least that was my opinion each time I saw them. They were under weight and looked sickly. I felt horrible, but there was nothing more I could do. Buying one painting each month left me without financial reserves. It was the maximum sacrifice I could make.

Each time I visited them, he would invite me into their front room and asked me to sit in a soft chair. He then excused himself and disappeared. Moments later, his wife entered from the backroom and greeted me before she rushed into the street. Minutes later, she returned with a sweet roll from the bakery. She went to the kitchen and prepared coffee. Finally, she reappeared with a silver-like tray that held a small cup of coffee and the sweet roll. They gave me the royal treatment. I had never felt more important.

After the formalities were complete, I looked at his new paintings. Typically, I accepted one of them because it was good. I gave him the money for it and authorized the painting for the following month.

One day when I visited, I learned that one of his children had died. The cause of death was from complications from malnutrition. I wished I could have helped more, but I was now struggling myself. I had allocated ten percent of my living allowance to purchasing his paintings. That was all that I could do.

Chapter 6

My Trip to Panama

December 19, 1968—San Salvador, El Salvador

I had been planning a trip to Panama for months. Now the time had arrived, and I was off. After spending the night in San Salvador, I took an early direct bus to Managua, Nicaragua. After three hours, we entered Honduras. Honduras was semi-arid, poor, and desolate. Two hours later we entered Nicaragua where the vegetation was greener. We arrived in Managua in early evening. I rented a cheap room and ate a cheap meal. My standby meal was always chicken and rice. It was what the workers ate. There was always a huge volume of rice with peas, corn, and chicken. It was the meal with the most food for the dollar.

December 20, 1968—Managua, Nicaragua

I boarded another direct bus to San Jose, Costa Rica. As soon as we entered Costa Rica, we gained altitude. We were traveling in the clouds. The mist and beautiful flowers were everywhere. Droplets of water accumulated on the plant leaves and dropped onto the mossy rocks, where water again collected before it fell to the roadside and ran downhill. This was where a river was born.

The houses were like the small houses in El Salvador, except they painted these houses in bright colors. They planted flowers in the ground surrounding the houses and hung them on the outside walls by rope and planted in dried coconut husks. They were neat and beautiful. They painted their oxcarts in bright colors and in carefully created geometric designs. As soon as we reached San Jose, I rented a cheap room and ate chicken and rice.

The next morning, I took a direct bus to Panama City, Panama. The road from San Jose into Panama was dirt and full of ruts. Once we entered Panama, the road was paved, and we sailed on into Panama City. Again, I found a cheap room and ate chicken and rice.

I was up early and took a taxi into the Canal Zone to buy my new Pentax camera, tax-free. I already knew the name of the store with the best prices. Peace Corps volunteers who came before me had already done the market research. All I had to do was to go to this store and buy the product, which I quickly did and then headed to see the canal.

I was impressed when I first saw the canal. When I looked across the city, I saw a huge ship that looked like it was sailing down a street. It was in the canal. The lock gates were enormous, but the water pumps still filled them quickly.

I took a slow-moving train to the other side of the Isthmus of Panama, to Colón. The train tracks paralleled the canal. There were many ships crossing the isthmus in the canal. Some were gigantic, and others were tiny. The train crossed swamps that must have required much work before they could support a train. Finally, I reached Colón, at the opposite end of the canal. I looked around, took photographs, and returned to Panama City.

I bought my bus tickets back to San Jose, Costa Rica.

December 30, 1968—Traveling to Costa Rica's East Coast

Once we were in Costa Rica, we started gaining elevation until we reached an altitude over eleven thousand feet. I have no words to express how beautiful it was. Costa Rica was a gorgeous country. At last, we reached San Jose. I rented a cheap room and ate chicken and rice.

The next day I wandered the streets, meeting people. So many people were traveling. All North American land travel to South America goes through Central America. There is only one main highway—the Pan American Highway. If you sit in a bar on that highway, you can see the entire world parade by, eventually.

I met a Canadian with an engineering degree who planned to travel for a couple of years. I ran into an American trying to sell his car so he could keep traveling. A married German couple was headed to South America. I met another Canadian with a master's degree in electrical engineering, and we decided to travel together for a few days.

The next morning, we boarded a slow-moving train to the Caribbean coast of Costa Rica and the village of Limón. The train took seven hours to travel 103 miles. It was a *pinga-pinga* train; it stopped for everyone who came out of the cocoa plantations. It stopped for every woman with a container of milk or a basket of fruit. It never went more than thirty miles per hour. But that was what we were looking for—a way to observe out-of-the-way people fulfilling their normal duties. These people were just that; I could not believe how many people could appear at the tracks through miles and miles of cocoa plantations.

Eventually, we arrived at Limón. There people spoke English because of the former slave trade, but most people were of African heritage. They did not speak English as I knew it; I could not understand them. They spoke what had been English more than 150 years ago, but to me, it was unrecognizable. Unfortunately, not many people spoke Spanish. We spent a couple of hours looking around and took the next train back to San José.

The next day, we went to the Costa Rican bullfights. These were different from Spanish bullfights because they never harmed the bull. He became tired and bored, but they did not harm the bull. It usually was people who were harmed.

To watch the bullfight, we had to pay an entrance fee and sit in the bleachers. If we wanted to be *in* the bullfight, we paid nothing and they allowed us into the bullring, where one hundred or more confederate bullfighters accompanied us.

In the center of the ring was a pole. Around the pole was a small pool of water that was about eighteen inches deep. It had a radius of about ten feet. Its purpose was to offer protection to fleeing bullfighters from an angry bull. The hope was that the bulls would not jump a twenty- four-inch wall and jump into eighteen-inch-deep water. My experience was that the bull was not aware of this arrangement. Fighters who were fearful of being hit by the bull could run into the pool in the center to escape, but the bull sometimes followed the fighter into the pool.

To start the fight, the cowboys coaxed the bull into the arena. When he saw the dozens of annoying humans, he quickly became agitated and charged through the bullfighters. On a good day, the bull wounded about one hundred fighters, they took some to the emergency room. On any given day, the bull could seriously hurt from two to four bullfighters, but the bullfighters kept coming back to annoy the bulls. While this was very entertaining, I did not think the amateur bullfighters were very bright. And then I spotted one of my Peace Corps colleagues in the ring. The Peace Corps had given clear instructions to all volunteers vacationing in Costa Rica that were not to enter the ring. Yet there he was, in the ring.

When the bull showed signs of tiring, two cowboys came out on horseback and approached the bull from each side. They roped the bull and walked it out of the arena to the applause of the spectators. This process of walking the bull out of the stadium did not always go smoothly. Sometimes the bull was not as tired as the cowboys thought he was. In one instance, the cowboys were on each side of the bull and were casting their ropes about the bull's head. One cowboy succeeded at lassoing the bull, but the other failed. The bull took off running. Since the cowboy, who had roped the bull's head, and his horse were anchoring the bull, when the bull bolted, he ran only in an arc, effectively clotheslining dozens of bullfighters who did not see that coming.

My Canadian friend had met a Costa Rican family with four daughters, aged twenty, nineteen, seventeen, and fourteen. The Costa Rican family invited him to their home to celebrate the holidays. They lived in a nice middle-class house that they had built themselves. In addition, the girls knew how to cook, sew, knit, clean, and paint beautifully. The family was ultra-talented.

As guests, all we did was sit and watch. It was interesting. The mother stayed in the kitchen, preparing things, along with the older sisters. The younger sisters brought things from the kitchen to the dining room. Lively Latin music was playing, and the girls moved to the beat of the music. They did not walk; they glided but always to the rhythmic beat of the music. I could have watched them all night. They were art in motion. I loved Latin America.

January 1, 1969—My Canadian Friend

Continues His Journey

I awoke midmorning and found my Canadian friend packing. He had decided to continue his journey. He had been in Costa Rica for one month. He felt he needed to continue toward South America, or his money would run out before he had traveled to all the points he wanted to see. I saw him off at the bus depot.

I also packed my things and bought a ticket to Managua, Nicaragua. I would go straight back to Sonsonate without any delays.

Chapter 7

My Work in El Salvador Continues

January 5, 1969—A Peace Corps Volunteer Goes Native

I arrived in San Salvador on Friday evening and went to our apartment to rest. I found a couple of colleagues there. We went to a good movie, *The Graduate*.

The next day, as I approached the *tienda* in Sonsonate, I was surprised when someone asked me, "Did they leave you without clothes also?" I had no idea what the person was talking about. I continued to the *tienda*. When I entered the patio in the back, I saw Doña Maria. She seemed nervous about seeing me. Here is what happened:

The previous night, thieves jumped over the patio wall and gained entrance to Doña Maria's patio. They opened the door on the two vets' room and stole all their clothes, money, jewelry, and everything that was not tied down. The vets were asleep and did not awake. They broke into the second room, but it was not occupied and contained nothing. They tried to break into my room, but my lock was too strong for them, and they chose to run. Maybe one of the vets made a sound, but they spared my room from being invaded. This was good because I had my record player, records, and my clothes. I also had my month's one-hundred-dollar living allowance, my trunk, and its contents. Doña Maria said that when she pulled on my room's lock to determine if it was safe, it popped open. That was how close the thieves had been to gaining access to my room. I felt grateful.

The funny part of the story was that the vets awoke to no clothes. They only had the clothes they had worn to bed. They begged the maid for the loan of a bath towel. I was sorry for the Spanish vet, but the disgusting Salvadorian vet deserved it.

Next week, the painter was to have three or four paintings ready for me to view.

One set of parents who lived on the East Coast were worried about their son. He was stationed in northern El Salvador, near Honduras. He had long ago stopped answering letters from his parents. Finally, his parents contacted Peace Corps Washington, DC. They forwarded the parents' concerns to our director's office. She tried calling the Salvadorian agency director for the office in which he worked, but they had not seen him either. Now, our Peace Corps country director was concerned. She sent our doctor to visit him. He located where the boy had previously been living, but no one had seen him for months. By asking around the village, the doctor heard that people had seen the volunteer in and around another village that was far away. There were no roads that led directly there. The doctor hired one of the men to serve as his guide. They drove as far as they could, and then they walked. As they walked, he asked the peasants if they had seen the volunteer.

When the doctor finally found him, the volunteer was dressed like a peasant farmer, with the hat, the white shirt, pants, and the tire sandals. The doctor learned that he had built a house, married an Indian woman, and received credit on a one-acre plot of land that he had bought. The scene startled the doctor. After talking with the Peace Corps volunteer, the doctor retrieved a syringe from his medical bag and filled it with something. Without the volunteer's knowledge, he poked the volunteer. The volunteer immediately slumped down.

The doctor said that he needed a local ambulance to take him back to his car. A "local ambulance" consisted of a thick tree branch with a hammock tied to each end, carried by two men. When the ambulance arrived, they placed the Peace Corps volunteer inside the hammock, and then they wrapped its sides over him to prevent anyone from knowing who they were transporting. When the volunteer woke up, he was on an airplane on his way back to the States. His parents met the *former* Peace Corps volunteer and the doctor at the Washington, DC, airport. What had happened to the volunteer was that he "went native." This happened occasionally.

Chapter 8

My Last Vacation

My Last Vacation in Honduras, Belize, and Guatemala

The first leg of my vacation was to travel to southern El Salvador, near the Nicaraguan border, and then turn northeast to visit a Peace Corps colleague, Tom, with whom I had trained. He would be waiting for me in the central market in San Miguel, the third largest city in El Salvador.

The bus that operated from San Salvador to San Miguel was a newer school bus from the US. When they traded used school buses in the US, they were often taken to countries in Latin America and sold to transportation companies. The bus had to be in decent shape because this was a nonstop route between two major cities. If this bus company wanted to be competitive on this route, it had to have a comfortable bus.

The trip took four hours on a paved highway. Everyone had their windows open because it was hot, and the bus offered no air conditioning. The countryside was beautiful. For me, that was all I needed to pass the time. I never tired of staring out the window at the ever-changing landscapes.

When we arrived at the bus station, I took a taxi to the central market. I was worried that I would not connect with Tom. He had told me that he would be buying potatoes because that was his main food in his village. All I had to do was look for a six-foot white guy in the potato section of the outdoor market.

Tom ate only potatoes. He had no refrigerator; in fact, his village had no electricity, except for a couple of hours during the early evening. A small *tienda* had a generator that operated a half dozen lights and a beer cooler every night between six and eight o'clock. By that time, most people were already in bed.

We greeted each other. He said we should seek a taxi to the bus depot. He had completed his shopping. He had eaten a good hot meal with a steak-like meat and vegetables. He had ordered a big banana split, and now, he had purchased fifty pounds of potatoes. We were ready to head to his village, located in the highlands near the border with Honduras. After a brief wait, a long bus with high guardrails on its roof parked in front of us in the stall assigned to the bus going to his village. A host of people were already waiting for the bus, and they crowded forward, carrying their purchases from the market. One man climbed onto the roof while the other man passed bags and sacks of merchandise to him. The man on the roof grabbed the merchandise, carried each load to the back of the roof, positioned it, and then returned for more. After Tom gave up his potato sack, he entered the bus and motioned for me to follow. We sat in the front.

When every person had their merchandise situated on the roof and had found a seat in the bus, the driver started the engine and closed the door. We were off. We drove across the city and found a road headed northeast. The road started as a two-lane paved road.

We made suitable time, until we turned onto a dirt road. At this point, the driver stopped, looked at Tom, and opened the door. Tom tapped my leg and waved for me to follow him. We climbed onto the roof of the bus and sat at the front, where we could hang on to the guardrails, should the need arise. When we were seated, Tom banged the bus's ceiling twice, and the driver continued our trip.

It was great having the breeze in my face. There was dust behind us but not in our faces. Soon, the road turned sharply upward. It became rougher, and we made slower progress. The bus rocked from side to side as it maneuvered over bumps and holes in the road. We also had to be careful because there were trees growing on each side of the road, with branches growing over the road. We had to take care so that a branch did not knock us in the face, in extreme cases, dislodge us from the bus's roof. It made the time go by faster.

Finally, we turned a corner, and I saw a bell above the treetops, then the church, and finally the village. It was small, even for a village.

The church was small and was a faded white color; it had not seen a paintbrush in decades. At the base of the walls was a brown stain, from rain hitting the brown soil and bouncing back onto the church walls and bringing with it brown soil particles.

The town square was more like an extra-wide street. Opposite the church on the town square was the small *tienda*. Tom led me to his house, which was located near the *tienda*. He had a large old key to open a large, flimsy old lock. When Tom opened his house door, it scraped the entire distance on the floor. Its hinges were loose and barely hanging onto the door. Any drunk falling against the door would have knocked the door down. Safety did not appear to be any concern in this village.

I looked at his house. It had an open and weedy patio surrounded by unused rooms. He had strung two hammocks on posts that were used to hold up the covered part of the patio. He had an old dresser where he stored his few clothes. When I had thought of how a Peace Corps volunteer lived, before I joined the Peace Corps, I was thinking of Tom's house.

It was early afternoon and hot. He proposed we take a nap. We both settled into the hammocks, he in his and me in the guest hammock. A couple of hours later, when the afternoon had become less hot, Tom volunteered to show me the village. He carefully locked his front door, and we headed around the *tienda* and down the street, away from the church. He showed me where the market was once a week. A small area was allocated for it, so it must have been small. He said that he occasionally could buy eggs there. He did not like rice or black beans, so he was destined to eat potatoes—boiled potatoes—every day, without even the benefit of butter.

At the lower edge of the village, we turned and followed a path around the edge of the mountain. After a mile or so, he paused at a spot that overlooked the village and the surrounding area. He sat on a rock and motioned for me to do the same. Then, he pulled out a cigarette and lit it. That was when I noticed it was not a normal cigarette. He inhaled and motioned for me to do the same. I turned him down. I could not even smoke normal cigarettes without getting a horrible migraine headache. No smoking for me. I positioned myself so as not to be downwind from where he was sitting.

The sun was quickly setting. The landscape was green, with layers of blue separating us from the green. The blue became darker and darker until we saw no more. Tom put away his stash, and we retraced our steps to the village. Because Tom had no trouble finding the path in the dark, I assumed this was a path he had taken many times.

When we approached the *tienda*, I heard the motor of the generator running, and then I saw the light emanating from inside and shedding light in a small arc outside the establishment. The *tienda* owner had already placed a small table with a white tablecloth and two chairs just outside the door. I imagine that he had seen Tom and I pass his place earlier in the afternoon. He had a phonograph with an old needle playing Latin music on scratched records. Tom walked in and sat down in one of the chairs and motioned for me to do the same. He held up two fingers, and instantly, two cold bottles of beer appeared. Tom was the only person in the village who could afford to buy a beer.

Tom quickly drained the bottle and ordered more. I was a slow beer drinker, but Tom did not wait for me. He lunged ahead, marching to his own music. The empty bottles accumulated under our table. Tom was now singing to the songs as they played on the record player.

I watched what was occurring around us. The light extended only ten feet beyond our table. A dog appeared from the darkness and approached our table, sniffed our feet, and then continued its path. A peasant silently stepped out of the darkness, carrying his machete and a small net containing his lunch container and the gourd he used to carry water. His lunch often consisted of a stack of corn tortillas; if he were lucky, the tortillas would have cheese or refried black beans in their centers.

Then, I heard a horse's hooves clomping on the cobblestones, slow but steady as he came closer under the cover of darkness. Suddenly, the horse stepped from of the darkness carrying a rider. They crossed our field of vision, continued down the street to the lower village, and quickly were swallowed again by the darkness. The steady clomping slowly faded into silence.

At eight o'clock, the *tienda* owner tried to close, but Tom begged for just one more beer. The owner gave in. Tom drank and sang while the *tienda* owner started to put things back inside. He turned off the record player in mid-song as Tom finished his last beer. Finally, we started across the street to Tom's house. The light disappeared, silencing the generator. There was nothing left to do but sleep. Tom did not even have a candle in his house. He knew where everything was and could easily find his way around his house in the dark. I needed a candle, but I had none. I found my hammock, climbed in, wrapped myself into a ball, and slept.

There was nothing left to do in Tom's village. I took the next bus back to San Miguel and caught the first bus to Tegucigalpa, Honduras. I spent the night in Tegucigalpa and caught a bus the next morning to Puerto Cortes via San Pedro Sula. Puerto Cortes laid on the Caribbean Sea.

I arrived in Puerto Cortes at noon. I found a restaurant frequented by local workers and ate chicken and rice. I enjoyed a small, strong, but sweet coffee after my meal. Drinking this coffee gave the meal more time to settle before I continued the day. After minutes of rest, I got up and walked around the port. I saw large ships at dock; at least, for me they were large.

My next task was to find transportation from Puerto Cortes to Belize. I asked around and found a small boat, forty feet long and about twelve feet wide. It was taking shipments of bottled beer and sacks of cement to Belize. The boat had two crew members—a captain and a worker/cook. Both crew members were shoeless and shirtless. They only wore dirty and ragged shorts. They agreed to take me for two days and three nights for ten dollars. That included the transportation, food, and a bunk to sleep. I signed up immediately.

We left by late afternoon. The sky was clear, and the ocean was calm. I loved sitting on top, watching the waves and listening to the clunk of the old engine. It seemed old and tired, yet I never doubted that the next clunk was coming. An hour before dark, the crew stopped the boat and turned off the engine. One man jumped into the water and disappeared. Moments later, he reappeared with a fish. He repeated this procedure two more times until he had a fish for each of us; then he joined us onboard, and the engine started its clunking again.

The cook started to make rice and cleaned the fish. As soon as he had one cleaned, he threw it into another skillet. Within minutes, the cook called me to the small table to eat. The table was inside the galleon, but I had to sit on a small stool outside the galleon to eat. The spaces on the boat were small. After I ate, the captain ate, and finally, the cook ate. The cook immediately washed the dishes, dried them, and put them away. It was now dark. I sat on deck, but there was nothing to see. There were no lights anywhere, save a pipe that emitted a glow every time the smoker drew from it. The sounds included the waves hitting the boat's hull and the clunking of the motor.

I went below deck to my bunk and tried to sleep, but I found myself slowly becoming seasick. I had to return on deck to avoid becoming sick. Eventually, I became so tired that I went to sleep as soon as my head hit the pillow.

We arrived in Belize on Sunday morning, but the customs office would not open until Monday morning. We had to dock in the bay and stay on board. That was boring. Spending twenty-four hours on a stopped vessel in sight of land was more than I could tolerate. I wanted to continue my adventure.

When I arrived on shore, I found a nice, cheap hotel, where I took a long shower and ate a breakfast of bacon, eggs, and toast. I noticed that Belize had good-quality food, and I enjoyed it. I slept for the rest of the day, got up, ate chicken and rice, and slept all night. My only problem was getting the bed to stop moving back and forth. I had left the sea, but the sea had not left me.

Early the next morning, I bought a ticket to the border between Belize and Guatemala. Even as we left the capital for the rural area, the road was a well-maintained one-lane road with a layer of crushed rock and the bus had empty seats. We had the windows open, and since it had rained the previous night, it was almost cool. We could hold our hands out and touch the jungle as we sped by.

After two or three hours, the bus stopped, and everyone disembarked. The border guards ordered the people to grab their bags and walk across the border. Another bus was waiting for us there. I had never seen the case where the guards did not allow the buses to cross borders, but because the Belizean and Guatemalan governments were not on good terms, this was not possible.

There was an encampment on the inside of the Guatemala border. I found a cheap place to sleep and stashed my suitcases. I grabbed my camera equipment and started walking about. I met a Frenchman who also had a camera. He was traveling around the world. He paid for his trip by taking photographs, developing them, and selling them. He camped out under an abandoned boat near a small nearby lake. I viewed his photos. They were excellent, much better than anything that I had taken. I found it interesting that I spoke no French, and he spoke no English, but we communicated perfectly in Spanish. I loved being able to speak Spanish. There were so many benefits.

The next day I caught a bus to Las Flores (which translates to "the flowers"), a village located on an island in a lake in the middle of the Petén jungle. I arrived at dusk and took a dugout canoe, powered by a motor, to the island. Once there, I looked for a place to sleep and eat.

I learned that I was not supposed to take any photographs of banks, soldiers, or military installations. The problem was with the Communist guerrillas who were hiding in the jungle. They would take photographs of the banks and military installations and then use them to attack the military installations or rob the banks. They needed to rob banks to pay for their activities. They were active all over Guatemala, but they mostly hid in the Petén jungle area. The government was following their activities and interested in anyone who might support their activities.

The next morning, I walked around the island and took photographs. Two soldiers were patrolling outside a bank. When they saw me, they asked me to take their photographs. Why not? I thought. They posed with their weapons in front of a bank, and I took a couple of photographs. In fact, I used up the last film that I had with me. They wanted me to take more photographs, so I kept taking them, even though I had no film. I guess these soldiers had not received the order about not taking photographs in front of a bank.

Once I had seen everything that Las Flores had to offer, I took a bus to Tikal, the famous site where Mayan Indians had built pyramids hundreds of years ago. It took a couple of hours to arrive. I saw a tiny village and the pyramids. Of the people from the bus, I was the only one who headed toward the pyramid area. The rest disappeared into the houses located around the village. I was the only tourist.

I walked around the area and was surprised there were no restaurants, restrooms, gift shops, or anything. There was nothing except the pyramids. I walked to the tallest of them and started to climb the stairs to the top. I was surprised how steep they were. I felt dizzy and leaned forward until my hands reached the steps. I started to climb with my hands outstretched, like a child. I saw a chain secured to the steps on one side. I grabbed hold of it and slowly climbed to the top.

At the top, the surface area was small. I went to its center and stood up. I felt dizzy and had to widen my foot stance to prevent myself from falling. It was high. I looked out over the jungle. I saw other pyramids that the jungle still claimed. They had reclaimed only a couple, with a couple more partially reclaimed. It was a tourist attraction in development.

After a couple of minutes and a couple of photographs, I started to go back down the steps by holding on to the secured chain. Once on the ground, I walked around a bit and did a quick disappearing act into the jungle for a tinkle break, since that was the only choice I had. My thoughts then turned to my egress from Tikal. Since I was the only tourist, I started to worry about how I might get back to somewhere— anywhere.

I found a man walking on a street and asked him when the next bus left. He thought it would be on Wednesday. Today was Monday. I did not see any hotels, motels, *pensiónes*, or empty houses. I was becoming nervous. I took three deep breaths and asked if there was any other way of leaving.

He pointed at a lone truck in town. "The driver usually leaves the village in the early afternoon."

"Where does he live?"

"He most likely lives in one of those houses behind the truck," he said and then turned and continued his journey.

I went to the truck and noticed that it was loaded with roughly cut mahogany planks. I picked a house and knocked. After a few attempts, I located the driver. He was leaving about two o'clock. I negotiated a price and he agreed to it. I was so happy that I never thought to ask where he was going. I assumed he was going down the same road that had brought me into the village. I was wrong.

I was starving. I had managed to only drink coffee with French bread early that morning. It was noon. All I could do was sit on the shady side of the street in full sight of the truck and wait. I dare not miss my only way out of town, but I could not get my mind off my empty stomach.

At two o'clock, the truck driver approached his truck and motioned for me to climb into the back. We were off. He found what looked to me like the same road on which I had come into the village. It was narrow and covered in crushed rock, and both sides were thick with grassy vegetation. Every few minutes, a man popped out of the growth along the side of the road and stopped the truck. He and the driver negotiated, and then he climbed on back with me. At first, there were only two of us, then three, and eventually there were six or seven of us. The men seemed to enjoy staring at me.

A boy of ten or eleven came out of the bushes, pulling a heavy sack, and stopped the truck. He negotiated with the driver, but it was not for a ride. His sack was full of pineapples, which he wished to sell. I motioned for him to send one up for me to examine. It was gorgeous, huge, and it seemed perfectly ripe. I asked him how much it was. He gave me a price that was equivalent to a dime each. I bought all ten of his pineapples. He passed them up to me, one at a time. I paid for them, and he disappeared into the jungle.

All the men's eyes were on me and my pineapples. They were curious what I was going to do with them, especially since I had no way to carry them, and I had no machete. I asked if any of them would like to share my pineapples. They all did. I asked if one of them could slice one up—they all had machetes on their belts. One volunteered. Those were the tastiest pineapples I had ever eaten. In no more than twenty minutes, we had finished all the pineapples. I was not as hungry as I had been, but the pineapples were acidic, and that much acid in an empty stomach was not an ideal situation.

After two or three hours, the driver pulled into a village and stopped. I asked when he was leaving again.

"I'm not," he said. "The road ends here, and my trip ends here."

I asked myself, *where is "here"?* My gut feeling was not good. There were fewer houses in this village than in the previous village. They constructed their houses from bamboo sides, dirt floors, and grass roofs. The last village had adobe-brick walls covered by plaster and tile roofs. My gut told me that I was farther inside the jungle than I had been and farther from where I needed to go than I was in the previous village. I needed to take three deep breaths.

I learned that they had loaded a small barge on the river with sacks of corn and was leaving within the hour. Again, I did not ask where it was going, but it was pointed downstream, and that had to lead out of the jungle. I found that reassuring. I negotiated a price and paid my fare, but before I climbed on, I needed to try to secure food to neutralize the acid in my stomach. I asked about places to eat. They told me that the village had restaurants, but they had no food.

The eating establishments in this village had food ready at eleven in the morning, and they served food as long as it lasted. When the food was gone, they closed. It was not possible to special order food. They had no menus. I went to a few places; they were all out of food and closed. I was able to find one place with two pieces of two-day- old bread and a bottle of Guatemalan wine. I bought them and headed toward the barge. I would learn that the bread was too hard to eat, and the wine was too bad to drink.

At least a dozen other people already were sitting on the barge. I made my way to the front of the barge and moved three or four corn sacks here and there to create a soft easy chair. I sat down. I was ready for whatever came.

The boat that was to pull us seemed tiny and underpowered, but as it pulled forward and tightened the tow rope, I felt the barge move— slowly at first, but it gave way and followed the little boat down the river that separated Belize and Guatemala. I estimated the number of fellow passengers at eighteen. Most were small-business people. I met a man who carried soda from civilization into the jungle to sell and then took the empty bottles back to where he bought the soft drinks.

He and I talked for hours. We talked about our families and about the Communist revolutionaries. He said they never came into this part of the jungle; we were safe. He also mentioned that he had heard there were ladies of the night in the boat. They were relocating. The pilot did not think they would be safe on the barge, so he shared his boat with them. He must have been a kind person.

Darkness fell upon us. There was no rural electrification, so there were no lights. As we silently drifted downstream, we occasionally passed a peasant farmer's bamboo hut. On one occasion, the peasant had a fire going. I saw a peasant, who appeared to be squatting over an emery board sharpening his machete. The woman in the hut was preparing either corn tortillas, or *pupusas*. *Pupusas* were tortillas that they split down the middle, like two slices of bread. They had inserted something tasty between the two slices and cooked. I loved the *pupusas* with smashed black beans or cheese. The corn tortillas by themselves were uneatable, but adding smashed beans or cheese made them not only eatable but delicious. They stuck to your ribs. I was hungry and wished I had a couple of them to eat.

The sky revealed all its stars. Every star was visible to the naked eye because on this night, there was no moon. I did not understand how the tow-boat pilot was able to see to guide his boat and our barge down the river, but he did.

At 3:00 a.m., the pilot swung the barge into the river's edge, where crew members secured it. They informed us that this was a barge stop. We would leave at exactly 6:00 a.m. They told us that we could order chicken soup if we liked, and we could rent a hammock, if we wished. I ordered chicken soup, as did other people including the ladies of the night.

The barge stop included a grass hut with an outside fire. They had three crude tables with chairs around them. Nearby there were posts placed in ten-foot squares. Each post had from one to four eyelets used to secure a hammock. People who wanted to sleep had rented a hammock and were fastening them to the posts and climbing in. They wrapped the hammock edges around themselves to protect themselves from the mosquitos and the chill of the night.

Two women had grabbed machetes and headed to a small bamboo building toward the jungle's edge. Seconds later, we heard chickens protesting, and then it was quiet. Minutes later, the ladies reappeared carrying two plucked and dressed chickens. They dropped them into the pot that already had water boiling.

I was sitting at a table watching people when the ladies of the night joined me. They did not see many tourists in this area and were curious who I was. I enjoyed talking with them. We talked of our families and of our travels and our dreams. It was refreshing. Later, I did not remember the details, but I did remember that they all seemed so innocent to me, perhaps because we forgot what they did for a living and only talked as normal people talked.

The soup came and I ate with so much gusto that I was embarrassed. I wanted more, but I dared not ask because they had a limited supply, and everyone wanted more. I laid my head on the table to rest. I did not want to pay to rent a hammock for one or two hours. Then, the sun popped up, and it was six o'clock. The pilot called everyone on board—without any breakfast.

Within an hour, I was surprised to see we were leaving the river and entering the ocean. Now, this concerned me again. I knew I should have asked where we were going. I asked my friend, and he told me that we were going to Puerto Cortes, Guatemala, which was near the Honduran border. He said that we would be traveling three hours on the ocean, which was not as steady as the river. I was not fond of traveling in small vessels in the ocean.

We arrived in port at 11:00 a.m. I was happy to be out of the jungle and out of the ocean, and I could shower, eat, and sleep, which I did in that order. I slept the rest of the day. At night I walked around to see the port town; then I ate again, and I slept some more.

In the morning, I caught a bus to Guatemala City and then to Sonsonate. I was home again. That made me happy. I had had enough adventure.

Chapter 9

Almost Home

The Soccer War between El Salvador and Honduras

Shortly after I returned from my last vacation, El Salvador and Honduras had a soccer game. I no longer remember who won, but the rivalry was great, and a fight in a hotel bar resulted in broken glass in a door. For some reason, the world's correspondents thought that this scuffle resulted in the hot war that followed soon after. They were poorly informed.

The real reason for the war was that Honduras wanted to secure its borders. El Salvador was a densely populated country, with land for farming being impossible to obtain. Honduras, on the other hand, had much land and sparse population. El Salvadorians noticed this, crossed the invisible border into Honduras, and rented land. Being hardworking and good farmers, they prospered and moved from renting land to buying land. These farmers had to be good to survive in the difficult conditions that existed in El Salvador. All the lazy peasants had already perished in the struggle to survive. Eventually, there were so many El Salvadorians inside the Honduran border that the Hondurans started to react and complain. At some point, the Honduran government became aware of the problem.

There was a second condition that created the hot war. It dealt with unfair trade policies. I cannot remember which country was complaining; it does not matter. Those two reasons were what started the war, not the soccer game.

I awoke one morning and walked into the street to head for work, and I saw a huge cloud in the distance. I asked Doña Maria what had happened. She told me that Honduras had attacked El Salvador by blowing up an oil depot in Acajutla. I wondered if my favorite bar was safe. She also said that they had dropped bombs in other places.

The first bomb dropped by Honduras in El Salvador landed in the patio of a house owned by a Honduran. It failed to explode. Most bombs dropped in this short war failed to explode. They had purchased them from the US after the end of World War II as surplus. The bombs were twenty to twenty-five years old. Storing the bombs so long in a humid environment could easily render them useless. The army constantly sent bomb squads to remove a bomb from a parking lot or a highway. The only bomb that I know exploded was the one that caused the oil storage tank to explode in Acajutla.

Once the war broke out, it made the nightly news in the States. Reporters commented that crazy soccer fans had caused a shooting war. The war they were reporting was so far from what I saw that I thought they were describing another war. I thought they were all holed up in a Miami bar and making up their reports as they drank Cuba Libres from the comfort of their hotel bars.

The El Salvadorian public and I were always looking for more news about the war. All national papers produced extra copies and publishing editions twice a day to keep an interested population informed.

They surrounded the airport terminals with sandbags at least five feet high. They placed sandbags at each corner on the roof, with a fifty-caliber machine gun in place. A crew was always on duty.

I heard a story about a Honduran bomber pilot who executed several bombing runs at the airport each week. The plane's engine was not firing on all pistons. It always sounded like each piston's firing would be the plane's last gasp, but somehow, it kept flying. On each trip, he flew over the airport and dropped a single bomb. Time after time, the bombs hit the tarmac without exploding. After each mission, the bomb squad had to dig it out and try to explode it safely. No one seemed to mind. The El Salvadorian air force was not going to expend the energy to shoot him down because he posed no threat. Each flight made by the Honduran bomber created excitement for an otherwise bored military regiment guarding the airport.

My friend Tom lived in a village near the Honduran border. His village's water supply originated in Honduras. The village elders had a meeting and decided they needed to lead an incursion into Honduras to protect its water supply from the Honduran militia. They formed a group of peasant farmers, armed themselves with machetes, and started their mission at midnight. Tom, bored, accompanied them. They went to the pond and saw no evidence of any military activity, so they returned to their village and slept.

El Salvador's National Guard was moving quickly, even unopposed, toward Tegucigalpa. With less than a week into the shooting war, Honduras proposed peace. Their alternative was to wait and have El Salvadorian troops march into Tegucigalpa. The war was over. Both countries returned to their starting positions.

Chapter 10

My Return Home

Preparing for My Trip Home

During my last week in-country, Peace Corps called me into San Salvador for my exit language test. The possible scores were from zero to five. When I had left training, I had scored a 1+, the minimum allowable to remain in the program. They reserved a score of five for college-educated native speakers. A 4+ was as high a score as a nonnative speaker could achieve. I scored a 4+ on my exit exam. I was fluent. I thought in Spanish. I dreamed in Spanish. I was proud of myself.

The last few weeks had been difficult. My leaving created tension between me and my friends. I knew that when I left, I would never see them again, and they knew it too. They were good friends, and I could not imagine a life without them.

I had daily routines that I enjoyed. These routines would change completely when I left El Salvador, and that would cause me consternation. When Americans leave the US to go to another country, and we suffer an adjustment when we arrive, they call this culture shock. Later, when we return home and suffer an adjustment when we arrive, they call this *reverse culture shock*. I had heard that *reverse culture shock* was worse than culture shock. This worried me because I had been living deep inside the El Salvadorian culture.

América and Doña Maria would feel my absence more than my other friends. They were both like my adopted mothers and I their adopted son, especially Doña Maria, who had no children of her own.

By my last night, I had already given away everything I could not take with me, and I had packed my trunk and suitcase. I was concerned how I was going to carry my trunk and suitcase the half mile to the main highway to wait for the bus on the highway's edge. I had my passport and airline ticket ready on top of my trunk. I had hung the clothes I would wear the next day from the chair.

I visited Celia and said my goodbyes. She cried softly. We hugged. I went next door and spoke with Juana and her mother. They were both sad to see me leave. I had spent so many hours conversing with Juana's mother that I knew she would miss me. I spoke briefly with Juana's father, alone. He asked me directly if I was a CIA spy and wanted to know why I was leaving now. I was speechless. He told me that all the men on the street knew that I was a CIA spy, and there was no need for me to deny it; they knew.

Doña Maria closed her tienda. I had never seen her do that. She had promised me a wonderful meal, and she fulfilled her promise. Just the two of us ate a small steak, rice and black beans, and fried ripe plantain with extra-thick cream on top—all my favorite foods. We had orange juice with the meal and coffee after the meal. Doña Maria had purchased an eight-ounce cylinder of aguardiente, which she mixed with orange juice and gulped a shot. I followed suit, and she finished it off. Doña Maria did not typically drink alcohol.

When we hugged and said our final goodbye, she was tipsy and had tears in her eyes, but she was trying not to cry. As soon as she locked herself into her room, I could hear her crying. In the morning, I would leave early, before the *tienda* opened, via the side door to avoid having to say goodbye to her again. I would see none of my friends again. I went to bed sad.

I could not sleep. I tossed, turned, and thought about how my life was about to change dramatically. I wondered if I could manage it.

Before my alarm sounded, I was up and dressed. I grabbed my trunk and suitcase and carried them outside the house. I carried them a hundred feet before setting them down to rest. It was a good thing I started early. Finally, I reached my spot on the highway from where I knew I could catch the Greyhound bus for my last trip to San Salvador. I never enjoyed the view more than I did that day, knowing it was my last.

In San Salvador, I took a taxi to the Peace Corps office and left my luggage. I had to make one last trip to say goodbye to my painter friend, Oscar Manual Garcia. When I approached his house, he saw me, and his wife immediately appeared from the kitchen, smiled, shook my hand, and ran to buy me my last sweet roll. Oscar asked me to sit down. He said he had a present for me. He gave me a small painting as a gift. In fact, it was still wet. He told me to carry it carefully or the paint would smudge. His wife returned, and I drank my coffee, ate my sweet roll, and treasured every minute with my friends.

I returned to the Peace Corps office, but before I grabbed my things,

I said goodbye to the Peace Corps director and subdirector. I

appreciated their support and help over the last two years. I grabbed my things, found a taxi, and headed to the airport.

I checked my bags and waited for the airline to call my flight. After they called it, I walked across the tarmac to the stairs leading into the airplane. I remembered what I felt as I descended from the plane two years ago. I was a different person now. I entered the plane and found my seat, and I only wished to be alone. I was excited yet anxious.

My Return to the US after Twenty-Six Months Away from Home

On the first day, I flew from San Salvador to Mexico City to Houston, where my flight ended, and I had to spend the night. As the plane descended and positioned itself to land in Houston, I saw countless mansions and large patches of green lawns. I thought how nice it would have been if my peasant farmers could have had access to the area dedicated to lawns for them to plant and grow food for their families. I knew already that I had just entered a rich country. Any time people dedicated so much land to growing grass that fed no human or animal, and yet the grass received copious amounts of fertilizer, herbicides, and water, the country had to be wealthy. How wasteful and useless! How unfortunate that there could not be a more equitable way to divide land resources among people.

I was fortunate that my family had a friend who lived in Houston, Christine. She met me at the airport and took me to her and her husband's house. She was very conversant and asked questions. I was slow to answer and then only gave brief answers. I was in shock. I did not want to be a rude guest, but I was. I was not accustomed to any of it. The houses were different; the roads were different; there were no people in the streets; the language was different—and I was different. I wanted to speak Spanish because that was the language I normally spoke. I was not used to speaking English.

I had a tough time sleeping. I was in a nice fluffy bed with a fluffy pillow. In El Salvador, I slept for two years on a canvas stretched tightly across two support beams. I had a pillow, of sorts, but it was not fluffy.

In the morning, Christine fed me a wonderful breakfast and took me to the airport. I was grateful for her help and understanding. She likely knew that it was difficult for me and was not offended by my quiet rudeness.

I caught my plane to Dallas, Lincoln, and then Grand Island. I was not looking forward to what was coming. It would be overwhelming. The plane landed and taxied to its position on the tarmac. People exited the plane and walked across the tarmac to the gate. People waiting at the gate greeted those arriving by given them hugs and kisses, and then, together, they moved on. My family searched for a sign from me, but I was still waiting in my seat. I stood only when everyone else had left the plane, and I inched my way forward. I did not want to leave the plane because that would mean that my Peace Corps experience had ended. I was not ready for that. Once I reached the inside of the airport, I saw my family. There were hugs and kisses all around.

We waited nervously for my baggage and then started home. Everyone was talking, except for me. I was silent. All the English being spoken seemed strange to my ears. On the way home, I looked out the window, and I missed the hues of blue and green from El Salvador. I missed the people walking and waiting by the side of the highway. I missed the old school buses that should have been cruising the highway, dropping off and picking up peasants.

Once home, I moved my baggage into my old room downstairs. Because it was Saturday night, Mom had called for a family dinner in my honor. Grandma, Grandpa, and all my aunts and uncles and cousins came. I did not want to be honored. I wanted everyone to leave me alone, but I had to tolerate this because the family needed the celebration. It was good to see everyone, but the talking was unnecessary. My sensory systems were overloaded. There was too much noise, too much talking, and too much commotion. I yearned for my little quiet room in Sonsonate.

At one point I escaped outside and walked around the farmstead. There was a tall pole located in the middle of the farmstead with a bright light that allowed me to walk around the entire farmstead without a flashlight. I walked into the machine sheds and around the steel bins. I drew a deep breath to smell the smells of the old iron junk pile outside the machine shop, where we always went to scavenge for a piece of metal to weld something. All the buildings were just like I had left them; nothing had changed. It was strange to reach out and touch them.

I returned inside the house, grabbed a plate of food, and sat by Grandpa. He was silent, and I was silent, but we understood each other. When people started leaving, I mentioned that I might go into town for a soda. Mom quickly lectured me that I had to be home early so I could go to church the next morning. I was shocked. I had not had anyone tell me what to do in my personal life in over two years. That alerted me for what was coming. I understood now. No one thought I had changed. Everyone assumed that I would pick up exactly where I had left off two years ago, like going to church on Sunday, working on the farm (when I had no land to farm); free labor for anyone who needed help. I would be donating my labor to other people's land and crops. I would need to win my freedom all over again. I was ready for the fights that were coming.

The next Sunday, I had to move into the dormitory at the University of Nebraska in Lincoln. I had to prepare for that. I had not bought any new clothes since I had left home more than two years ago.

I had stored my 1962 Chevrolet Impala that I dearly loved in the back of the machine shed, with strict instructions for my family that I wanted to find it with the same mileage and in the same condition when I returned. On Monday morning, I went to the machine shed, brushed off the dust, and backed my car out of the shed. It seemed different. I drove it to the farm gas pumps and found that it drove like a lumber wagon. I could not believe it. I abandoned it at the pumps and went inside the house. I learned that a "few times" during irrigation, the farm was short a vehicle, and Dad had to use it for irrigation. It had held shovels, even irrigation tubes and plastic dams. They had used it as if it were an old pickup. It drove like an old pickup. I was furious. It was impossible to have any personal things at the farm. Everyone assumed that what one person owned could be used by anyone for anything.

Dad had always been conservative when it came to spending money on cars. He told me that a car for me was not an investment. It was an expenditure. It was something that, once bought, only decreased in value, even if it were not used and did not generate revenue. That was when I became intrigued when Dad insisted on going with me to buy my next used car for school because I refused to accept the 1962 Chevy anymore. He also insisted that we go to the Pontiac dealership in Central City.

When we arrived at the dealership, I told the salesperson that I wanted a good second-hand car for school. Dad winked and asked the salesperson to first show me what they had in new cars. Dad had obviously been at the dealership before and had everything arranged for them to show me a 1969 red two-door hardtop Pontiac Lemans.

I sat in it and found it comfortable and desirable, and the fact that Dad strongly approved added to its appeal. I had saved the money to buy it, but I was accustomed to used cars; in fact, I was used to walking. I had not driven a vehicle during the last two years, except for a few times after our extension office received the old Dodge panel truck. Looking at a new Pontiac was too much for me. I did not feel comfortable with it, but Dad was so happy. I could not take this moment from him, so I bought it. Dad was ecstatic. I now understand that Dad was proud of what I had done, and he wanted to reward me.

I moved into the university dormitory on Sunday afternoon, eight days after leaving my life in El Salvador. The dormitory had thirteen floors with fifty rooms per floor and two people per room, which amounts to 1,300 immature male students living in one building. Next door was an all-female dormitory, with rooms for 650 females. The two dormitories shared a cafeteria that was located between the two buildings.

The buildings were new and were in excellent condition. The rooms were small but adequate; in fact, I had more space in my dormitory room than I had in my room in El Salvador. They designed the bed, desk, and bookcase to be efficiently adequate. The food was excellent. For breakfast, we had our choice of bacon, sausage, eggs, toast, and a host of other goodies. The cafeteria offered us meat, mashed potatoes with gravy, and our choice of salads, and I could eat cake and ice cream every day. In El Salvador, I had never eaten cake. I was ready to start my junior year.

I soon learned that I had a good roommate, and my courses were challenging. I was happy, although I kept to myself. I found most people uninteresting, even antagonistic. In class, I once overheard a conversation between a couple of guys. The gist of it was that one boy had blown the engine in his car while showing off in the street. He was telling his friend that his father had better replace it with an improved one soon. My only thought was that this was a young person who had not been spanked enough. I overheard other conversations that were in the same vein, spoken by spoiled and entitled children.

I also overheard conversations in the cafeteria line. Guys complained about the horrible food, which they referred to as pure garbage. They said they could not wait to visit home so they could eat a respectable meal again. I boiled inside. I quickly resented these arrogant, entitled children who had something missing in their home education. My reverse culture shock nearly overwhelmed me.

Girls in the cafeteria line had other complaints. They needed a larger allowance so they could buy more dresses, perfume, cosmetics, and other important material items. Inside, I was fuming, but on the outside, no one could detect what I was feeling. One of my female friends in El Salvador had no more than three dresses total in her closet. Both her parents were teachers, a profession that paid little; they had to be very economical. Her parents' top priorities were to keep food on the table and to keep everyone healthy. Their children were all thankful when the parents accomplished this and did not complain about how many clothes they had in their closet.

Little by little, resentment accumulated, and I became hostile to the student population. I did not want to make friends. I did not want to converse with them because they, in general, were immature and spoiled. We had nothing in common. Outside of my dormitory roommate, I lived in isolation.

I had classes and professors that I enjoyed, but a few disappointed me. My adviser was one of them. He taught a class on fertilizers. The exams were fill-in-the-blanks. For example, the question asked might be what percentage of organic matter was in sandy soils; if the answer was 3 percent, and I put 3.1 or 2.9 percent, he counted it wrong because the book had shown 3 percent. He was not practical or flexible. I constantly visited him during his office hours and asked him questions. I am sure he understood that I had become frustrated with his pickiness.

I also shared with him my thoughts from my two years' experience in Central America, including my thoughts on the United Fruit Company. The United Fruit Company was widely known for their people-exploiting practices and their negative impact on the peasants in Central America. I frequently let my adviser know my beliefs on Central American politics and the unfavorable impact that resulted from the United States backing these countries' military and political structures. It always benefited the rich at the expense of the people.

Weeks later, another professor, who was my good friend, warned me to be careful of my adviser. This good friend had been a Peace Corps subdirector in Venezuela. He understood the nature of my reverse culture shock and what I was going through. He said that he had been looking at my folder in Human Resources and saw that my adviser had tagged me as a Communist. I learned that his main investment in his retirement portfolio was the United Fruit Company. I no longer confided in any professors, other than my Peace Corps subdirector friend.

By spring, I was missing all my friends in El Salvador. I missed speaking Spanish. I often found myself thinking in Spanish and still occasionally would start to answer a question in Spanish before catching myself. I was not happy with what I was learning at the university. I was learning facts but not how to solve problems. I did not feel I had acquired any skills that I could take home and use. In El Salvador, I learned to speak a language fluently and how to produce tropical crops.

I learned a new culture, a new way of thinking. I felt cheated by the university, and I did not know what to do.

The semester ended, and I returned home to help on the farm. This time, I started out being happy to do the work, since I had not done   it for three years. I loved cutting stalks, disking, harrowing, operating a scraper, and all the other tasks. Performing these tasks provided immediate reward. As the machine and I crept across the field, the field became transformed. Every day that I operated the scraper, at the end of the day, I had cut off a high spot and filled in a low spot. I saw the benefits from my work. During the two years I spent in El Salvador, any reward from our work was rarely, if ever, visible.

Eventually, hilling corn—the process of opening little ditches between the rows of corn so that water released at the high end of the field could flow by gravity to the low end of the field—started. One day, I was hilling in a quarter section of corn that was at least four feet high. A quarter section consists of a field that is one-half mile by one- half mile. I had to finish it quickly because, with the elevated temperature and bright sun, the corn was growing rapidly. Under such conditions, corn could grow more than an inch a day. If this corn grew a couple of more inches before I finished hilling, the extra growth could cause stalk breakage by the tractor passing over the stalks, and that would damage the ultimate yield.

The corn had a deep, dark, almost black color. On that afternoon, there was a breeze that blew the corn's leaves in all directions. It made the corn rows disappear, which made it difficult to keep the tractor centered inside the rows. The rows were one-half mile long. All I had to do was point the tractor down the correct rows and then keep one hand on the steering wheel. It was so boring. I dreamed. I thought of El Salvador and how I missed it. I was tired of attending the university and not learning what I thought I should be learning. I was unhappy. I knew that to stop being unhappy, I needed to change something.

At lunchtime, Dad picked me up and took me home. While eating dinner, I was quiet, but no one noticed because there was always so much conversion that it was difficult to get a word in. Suddenly, as everyone was finishing their dessert, I told Dad that I was not returning to the field that afternoon. I startled everyone. All conversation ceased.

He did not believe that he had heard me correctly. I repeated my statement. He asked me why. I told him that I was going to hitchhike to El Salvador. The hired men decided they were done eating and asked to be excused from the table. And the conversation between Mom, Dad and I grew serious.

Mom reminded me that other people were depending on me to help them. What would they do now? I replied that a good manager faced problems daily and should be able to overcome them. Dad was concerned with my not working anymore and with my hitchhiking. It was not safe, he argued. I compromised and agreed to take a bus. Mom wanted to know when I would come back. I had no idea. She asked about the university. Would I return for my last year? I told her that I was not happy with the university and did not know if I would be back by then. Now, my parents were not happy, but I felt better.

Chapter 11

My Return to El Salvador

I Travel by Bus

In the end, I did not return to work that day. I went to the bank and withdrew a safe amount of money for my living-on-the-cheap trip. I bought a bus ticket that same day, leaving town at 6:00 p.m., that would take me to Laredo, Texas. After the hornet's nest I had just kicked at home, I was not going to stay around and be stung. I packed and had my sister take me to catch my bus. My family may have thought that I was crazy and unreliable, but they could not call me indecisive.

My Trip to Mexico City

It was daytime when I arrived at the Mexican border. Our bus stopped and unloaded all passengers. Passengers went through customs and walked across the border, where I bought a bus ticket to Mexico City.

I enjoyed looking out the window while watching the geography change as we proceeded toward Mexico City. I snoozed a little and watched out the window a little. I was excited. I could not wait to see what would happen when I saw my friends in El Salvador again.

In Mexico City, I had to visit the Guatemalan embassy to obtain an entry visa into Guatemala. As soon as the bus stopped, and I claimed my backpack, I hailed a taxi to take me to the Guatemalan embassy. Once there, I found the waiting room for visas. It was packed. I was disheartened at the thought of how many hours it might take to obtain a little ink stamp.

As I waited, I noticed two tall white guys. I thought they were Americans, but I could not be sure. I tried to listen to their conversation, but there was noise in the room. I approached them and asked where they were headed. The shorter one replied that he was an American soldier, headed to join his unit in the Panama Canal Zone. His friend was accompanying him to keep him company and to help him drive. The soldier was taking his car with him because that was often what soldiers stationed in the Canal Zone did.

I asked if they spoke Spanish. They did not. I volunteered to accompany them and translate for them, even help drive—all the way to the Canal Zone, if they needed. They accepted. We were now the three musketeers.

We received our entry visas for Guatemala and took off for the border. We experienced no problems traveling down to the border. Even so, I felt better once we crossed into Guatemala. I was familiar with Guatemala. I thought of Mexico as mysteriously dangerous. Once we entered Guatemala, it was like we were almost home. It did not take long for us to enter El Salvador and to reach Sonsonate. I needed to contact my sister and ask her to send me money because if I went to Panama, I would be short of funds when I returned to El Salvador.

I introduced my travel mates to América and Doña Maria and Celia and Don Chepe. Somewhere along the way, the soldier contracted a bad case of food poisoning, and we had to extend our time in Sonsonate by a few days.

After the soldier improved, we continued our trip to Panama. We passed through San Salvador and were heading toward Honduras when two men stepped out of a coffee plantation and onto the road. One held up a weapon above his head. I thought it best to stop. It was a National Guardsman and a National Policeman. They had been at a wedding and needed a ride to their next assignment, located about an hour's drive from where we were and where, just one year ago, the war with Honduras had started.

I quickly noticed that these two men were hopelessly drunk. In fact, they kept asking me to stop the car so they could buy firewater. They would even buy us a drink, they said. I translated everything to the soldier and his friend. Finally, the National Guardsman begged for a drink. In desperation, he volunteered to let us shoot his weapon, should we decide to help him. When I translated this, my friends thought that was a reasonable trade. As soon as I saw the next *tienda* on our side of the road, I pulled over. The National Guardsman ran to the *tienda* and disappeared inside. After a moment, he walked out again with his head down; he looked as if the world had just cast him a lethal blow. When he reached us, he explained that they could only sell him firewater if he had his own container.

The American soldier said they had a nearly empty whiskey bottle in the trunk. He offered the bottle to the National Guardsman. In turn, the National Guardsman offered to empty the bottle first. As the American soldier handed the National Guardsman the bottle, the National Guardsman smiled again as if he has just been saved by Jesus. As soon as he finished the bottle, the National Guardsman headed back to the *tienda* in a determined manner. When he came out again, he was smiling, and the again the world was right.

We drove farther down the road and found a quiet spot along the road, and we stopped. We were on a road that was climbing a hill. This spot was forty feet above the coffee plantation that lay below. As we crossed the highway, the National Guardsman carried his weapon loosely with one hand. He gave the weapon to the soldier first. The American soldier examined the weapon and looked down the sights. He loaded a bullet into the chamber and fired three or four rounds. He smiled and handed it to me. The American soldier had to show me how to fire it. I pointed at the sky and pulled the trigger in fully automatic position. The barrel kicked up, and I stopped firing. I then pulled and released the trigger a few times to fire one bullet at a time. When we finished, we returned to the vehicle, and within minutes, we dropped our friends at their destination. The National Policeman had to steady the National Guardsman because he was top heavy but humming happily to himself.

After that, there were no more adventures all the way to Panama. Upon reaching Panama, I said goodbye to my friends because the soldier had to report for duty. They entered the American military compound, and I grabbed a taxi to a cheap hotel.

I went to a little restaurant to order my chicken and rice. I picked a long empty table and sat. After ten minutes, I had not even received a menu. The restaurant was not busy; in fact, most of the tables were empty. Finally, I started snapping my fingers to call for a waiter. One looked at me with dagger eyes. He grabbed a menu, walked within about ten feet of the table, and threw the menu at me. I had to catch it to keep it from hitting me.

I tried to get his attention again when I was ready to order, but he seemed determined not to see me. I got up and walked toward him. I asked him for draft beer and chicken and rice. He grabbed the menu that I was handing him, and he walked away without saying anything. He returned with my beer, and he flung it at me from the opposite end of the table. If I had not reached out to stop it, it would have slid off the table. It looked like the service in this restaurant was not going to be great that night. I decided that I would not leave a tip.

I ate my chicken and rice and paid for the food. I would not eat there again. The problem was that Panamanians were going through a political movement. They thought the US should leave Panama and give the Canal Zone back to them. As part of this movement, Panamanians hated Americans. That was all.

When I reached Sonsonate, I had less than one dollar in my pocket. My sister Shelli had wired me money. When I went to the bank and found the money, I was elated; otherwise, my future would have been bleak. I rented a room and ate chicken and rice in a little restaurant, where they appreciated my presence.

During the next week, I visited all the villages in which I had worked and saw my friends. After another week of visiting my friends, I had seen that everyone was fine. I felt reassured and was ready to return to the US. I went to San Salvador and bought my ticket home.

Mom and Dad were happy to see me. I had arrived in time to attend my last year at the University of Nebraska–Lincoln. I worked on the farm doing whatever they asked me to do for the rest of the summer. I was at peace, and my parents were happy.

I attended my classes, passed my exams, and received my diploma— in the mail. I did not go to my graduation. I had gone to my high school graduation for twenty-five students and thought it would never end. I did not care to see how long it would take to walk a few thousand students. No, I went to Colorado and climbed a mountain instead of attending my graduation. On Sunday morning, I hiked down to the nearest village and bought an *Omaha World Herald*. They carried the complete list of students who graduated that May 1971. I also bought a six-pack and hiked back up the mountain. After two beers, I checked the paper. I had graduated. Surprise!

Life was good, except I had a problem. When a person graduates from the university, he should know what he wants to do in life. Not me; I was confused from the two years I had spent in the Peace Corps.

The process of reverse culture shock had not yet run its course. I no longer felt at home in the US. In addition, I had no confidence in my technical ability as a college graduate. I had had misgivings about what I was learning before I joined the Peace Corps and how applicable it was. When I returned from the Peace Corps, my hope was that the last two years at the university would pull my learning together and make me feel competent. It did not happen. I always went to class. I studied, and I asked questions, but in the end, I had a feeling of disappointment in myself and in the curriculum that I studied. I had always imagined that a university degree provided one with knowledge that could open the secrets of the universe. I was wrong again. Later, I would learn that the university had provided the foundation that was necessary. What I lacked was experience. No amount of technical knowledge can compensate for a lack of experience.

I did not look for a job in agriculture. Instead, I looked for work at the Lincoln Regional Center because I had a friend who had worked there. They hired me to work with boys with emotional problems, aged twelve to seventeen. The boys had serious emotional problems, although they often seemed normal. There was no chance of advancement in that job, but it would give me time to find myself and choose a direction in life that would be more compatible with my personality. I did not feel competent enough to seek employment in the agricultural sector.

At work, we always had to be on guard. When one child became nervous, for whatever reason, he could cause the others to feed on that nervousness. The result could be a sudden shift in the collective mood from one of peacefulness to one of danger.

One evening, there were only two of us on duty. They hired my colleague in the same batch as   I was. We both had the same experience, and neither of us had verbal control over the patients. We took our group to recreation in the basement. Some patients played basketball, while others played pool, and still others stood around. It was our job to keep everyone engaged. We encouraged the idle ones to find something to do. Suddenly, they tired of our insistence that they engage, and they became angry. Their mood changed quickly, and they raised their voices and became aggressive. From one minute to the next, we were in a serious bind. We had thirteen angry male teenagers ganging up on two inexperienced employees. One boy picked up a couple of pool balls, one in each hand, and started swinging them around, while another couple of boys picked up pool cues and started to bang one end in their other hand. The boy with the pool balls challenged me to make them do what they did not want to do. The others only stared at me to see how I would react.

My colleague slipped into the office and called the second-floor section that managed another group of male patients. As luck would have it, they also had only two employees. It was against state law for either of us to work with fewer than two employees; therefore, he could not legally leave his post to help us. My colleague gave me the unwelcome news as we tried to figure out how to deal with our problem. Before we knew what was happening, our friend from the second floor burst open the entrance doors, which I knew was for show, stopped, placed his hands on his hips, and looked from one boy to another without saying a word. He was a longtime employee and had instant respect from our patients. They surrendered, and we took them all to quiet rooms on the first and second floors and locked them up for the remainder of the shift. I still give thanks for the second-floor employee's help.

I did not like working at the center, but each morning I had a destination and at the end of every two weeks I had a paycheck. It was one way of treading water while I was in my completely confused stage of life.

After six months, I realized that I needed to look for a better job. I began to summarize the strengths and weaknesses of what I had done in the Peace Corps when I worked as an Agricultural Extension agent. I liked doing that. If I was successful at teaching a peasant farmer a new agricultural technique, he and his family were less hungry the following year. That was positive reinforcement. Any work that I did in the US would be to make money for someone. For me, increasing profits for someone was far less gratifying than decreasing a family's level of hunger. I was not interested in increasing anyone's profits. I wanted to decrease hunger. I wanted to work in Latin America.

I started to prepare a work proposal for an agricultural school for peasants to learn the basics of better agricultural practices. I sent this proposal around to various agencies. One day, I received a phone call, but that will be a story for another day

Living in Nicaragua

Chapter 12

How It Started

I graduated with a degree in agriculture from the University of Nebraska at Lincoln in May 1971; yet I was unhappy, and without goals. I always thought college graduates should know what they wanted to do in life. Not me, I was confused from the two years I had spent in the Peace Corps in El Salvador from 1967 to 1969. That experience had changed me profoundly and I was having difficulty dealing with those changes.

I still suffered from reverse culture shock--the inability to adjust to one's native culture after returning from an extended stay in a foreign culture. I no longer felt at home in the US. I always felt on edge and irritated. There were reasons for this.

I spent the last two years living with students at the University of Nebraska. To me, these students felt entitled, ungrateful, and unaware of the world's dark side. For example, they wasted food at the cafeteria and were fussy about what they ate, always complaining about the quality of the food. For me, the food was excellent and available in unimaginable quantities. They had never been hungry for more than a couple of hours. Food always tasted good to a hungry person and there was never enough of it. I had seen too many hungry and desperate people to not appreciate it.

These students were in college, which was only a dream to most young people in third-world countries where most children did not study beyond the sixth grade. Yet, at the university, students skipped class and did not pay attention when they went to class. To me, these were unforgivable sins for someone who had a chance of a lifetime. I met so many young people in El Salvador that would have fought for an opportunity to go to the university. Anyone could enter a US university, yet students seemed not to value the opportunity that our society gave them.

From what I saw, students had closets full of shirts, blouses, shoes, shorts, and coats. In El Salvador, I knew people who had two or three changes of clothes, at most. Many had only the clothes on their bodies. That was a fact. There was no complaining because complaining did not produce more food or clothes.

In addition, to reverse culture shock, I had no confidence in my technical ability as a college graduate. Before I joined the Peace Corps, I had misgivings about how applicable what I had learned at the university was. When I returned from the Peace Corps, my hope was that the last two years at the university would pull my learning together and make me feel competent. It did not happen. I always went to class. I studied and I asked questions, but in the end, this left me with a feeling of disappointment in myself and in the curriculum that I studied.

I always imagined that a university degree would provide one with the knowledge that could open the secrets of the universe. I was wrong again. Later, I learned that the university provided the necessary foundation. What I lacked was practical experience. No amount of technical knowledge can compensate for a lack of experience.

I did not look for a job in agriculture. Instead, I looked for work at the Lincoln Regional Center--a state-run institution for troubled minds. They hired me to work with boys with emotional problems aged twelve to seventeen; although, they often seemed normal. There was no chance of advancement in this job, but, it gave me time to find myself and choose a direction in life that would be more compatible with my personality.

At work, we always had to be on guard. When one child became nervous, for whatever reason, he could cause the others to feed on that nervousness. The result could be a sudden shift in the collective mood from one of peacefulness to danger.

One evening there were only two of us on duty. They hired my colleague and I in the same batch. We both had the same experience, and neither had verbal control over the patients. We took our group to recreation in the basement. Some patients were playing basketball, others played pool, and still others were standing around. It was our job to keep everyone engaged. We encouraged the idle clients to find something to do. Suddenly, they tired of our insistence that they engage and became angry. Their mood changed quickly, and they raised their voices and started to become aggressive. From one minute to the next, we were in a serious bind. We had thirteen angry male teenagers ganging up on two inexperienced employees. One boy picked up a couple of pool balls, one in each hand, and started swinging them threateningly, while another couple of boys picked up pool cues and started to bang one end in their other hand. The boy with the pool balls challenged me to make them do what they did not want to do. The others came closer and stared at me to see how I was going to react.

My colleague slipped into the office and called the second-floor section that managed another group of male patients. As luck would have it, they also only had two employees. It was against state law for either of us to work with fewer than two employees; therefore, he could not legally leave his post to help us. My colleague gave me the unwelcome news as we tried to figure out how to deal with our problem.

Before we knew what was happening, our friend from the second floor burst open the entrance doors, which I knew was for show. He stopped, placed his hands on his hips, and looked from one boy to another without saying a word. This employee was a long-time employee and had instant respect from our patients. They surrendered, and we took them all to Quiet Rooms on the first and second floors and locked them up for the remainder of the shift. These Quiet Rooms were about eight by nine feet and had no light bulbs. The clients could break the light bulbs, and the clients could use them to harm themselves. The windows were covered by bars and screens to protect the clients. I still give thanks to the second floor's employee's help.

I did not like working at the Center, but each morning I had a destination and at the end of every two weeks, I had a paycheck. It was one way of treading water while I was in my completely confusing stage of life.

After six months, I realized that I needed to look for a better job. I began to summarize the strengths and weaknesses of what I did in the Peace Corps when I worked as an Agricultural Extension Agent. I liked doing that. If I were successful at teaching a peasant farmer a new agricultural technique, he and his family were less hungry the following year. That was positive reinforcement. I wanted to decrease hunger. I wanted to work in Latin America.

I started thinking about the ways that I could work to decrease hunger. I thought about the shortcomings of the agricultural extension system. Traveling to all the different villages took time, and without a vehicle, we could only visit one village per day. Running around the villages trying to find people to work with also took time. It took time to find people willing to allow us to establish an experiment on their property. These farmers had such small plots of land with which to produce the following year's food that they were usually hesitant to cede any of it for an experiment. I was hesitant to encourage them to change their production method because it could fail and cause the peasant family harm. Experiments failed. This could significantly reduce their total food production and allow hunger into the household.

I began thinking of another way of dispensing useful knowledge to the peasant farmers. I thought about an agricultural school. It would have a fixed location with fixed and well-developed experiments. It could have small enterprises: a couple of cows, three or four pigs, a hundred chickens, both to lay eggs and for meat production, some corn, black beans, bananas, and other crops. If an experiment failed, our farm suffered, but no peasant would feel hunger because of it. It would be cheaper to bring a dozen peasant farmers, and/or their children, the future peasant farmers, to the farm than to develop these projects in each of dozens of communities. We could use a bus or van to bring them to the school for a day's show and tell, or we could bring young people, future farmers, to the school for them to do an internship for weeks or months. We might even create a certificate that they could obtain if they completed a prescribed course at the farm.

That was it! I would create an Agricultural School Project and then try to find a place to apply it. I developed the project on paper and sent it around to organizations that I thought could benefit from such a project. For months there was no response, then, one day, I received a letter from the First Baptist Church in Cleveland, Ohio. They were associated with a church group that owned approximately eighty acres of land on the edge of Managua, Nicaragua. They asked if I would be interested in knowing more. Oh, yes, I would.

The Baptist churches in Managua were active. They had a Baptist School and a Baptist Hospital that people considered the best in Nicaragua. The school, the hospital, and the church were all started through the leadership of Dr. Arturo Parajón. His son, Dr. Gustavo Parajón continued his father's work as a physician in the hospital and as an elder in the church. If I were to work in Managua, Dr. Parajón would provide any medical care that I might need for free. The farm had a nice house that the church occasionally used for meetings, but graciously would allow me to live there for free. The church had a fund that could pay me forty-five dollars a month. As a comparison, Peace Corps Volunteers in Managua earned one hundred dollars a month. My lifestyle would have to be modest, much more so than the one I had led as a Peace Corps volunteer in El Salvador.

The Baptist church in Nicaragua encouraged all young members to provide one year of service to a rural community after they graduated from high school. The church also received groups from its associated church in Cleveland, Ohio during the summer. They went to a rural community and worked for its betterment.

For me, the decision was easy: new adventures in Nicaragua, or continue to work with twelve to seventeen-year-old problematic children. I was not good at working with these children. I was not bad at my job, but I had colleagues who had developed a rapport with the children and could maintain control over them. That was our job: to control them. I notified the Cleveland First Baptist Church that I accepted their offer.

I prepared for my trip. I already had a passport. I obtained a visa and packed my bags and a trunk. I had just bought a high-quality stereo set with wonderful speakers. I decided that if I were going to

110

rough it, I could do so while listening to my music. I took my trunk and the boxes with my stereo to the Post Office and mailed them to Nicaragua via ship. It would take six or eight weeks to reach me. I could not afford to have them shipped by air.

The day arrived for my departure, and again, I was going to the airport, but this time my sister took me. This was different from when I left for my first Peace Corps tour when my entire family accompanied me. She waited with me at the airport until they called my flight. We hugged and she left. I boarded the plane and found a seat in the back. I was again left to my thoughts. This time, I had no idea when I would return unlike my Peace Corps tour to El Salvador which was twenty-seven months. The job had no ending date. I did not care. I wanted to speak Spanish again, and I wanted to confront the challenges of living and working in Latin America. I was ready for whatever might come.

I Arrived in Managua

Juan, a young man with a wide smile and a bounce in his step, picked me up at the airport. He kept the conversation flowing as he drove to the farm using the one-hand-on-the-wheel-and-the-other-on-the-horn method of driving. It seemed to be the most popular method used in Managua. It had been the same in El Salvador, but to a lesser degree than it was in Managua. Drivers in Managua had mastered that driving style.

After driving seven miles south from the airport, Juan turned left without warning from the highway onto a narrow dirt road. The road was not easily visible from the highway, at least, not to my untrained eyes. There was a vine with purple flowers growing from one side of the road entrance. It grew up and over the entrance, making the dirt road even less evident from the highway. The narrow dirt road continued after the flowery entrance. Located on both sides of the street were small houses. Most were hidden behind either an adobe brick wall or a wire fence covered in flowers and bushes.

We drove a half-mile and turned right onto an even narrower path. This path was only wide enough for our Land Rover to pass between the overgrown brush and small trees growing in the fences located on both sides of the path. After a quarter mile on this path, we turned left again. I had to get out of the vehicle to open a barbed wire gate. The path led us to the farm property with a white farmhouse located on a hilltop overlooking the city of Managua. A smaller storage shed was located on this side of the house. There were twenty or thirty beehives located on the far side of the house with a couple of large shade trees providing shade for the bees.

The house had a wonderfully large front porch that allowed people to sit and view the farm below it. The house had a bathroom and two bedrooms. I claimed the bedroom closer to the bathroom. The house also had a combination kitchen and dining area. Windows in the house provided a panoramic view of Managua. The floor consisted of tiles that were cool to the touch of my bare feet. Juan placed a scissors cot for me in my chosen bedroom. We unloaded my suitcase and placed it in my bedroom. Juan then took me into the city to buy sheets, pillows, and other accessories that I needed.

Within the first week, I learned that I needed to make my bed every day. I stretched the sheets tight because I had luckily unmasked a large scorpion when I shook the upper sheet. That created a habit that I would never lose while I lived in Nicaragua--the daily shaking of the sheets. To that, I added the daily habit of holding each shoe upside down while shaking because, once, as I was about to put on my shoes, I heard a noise in my shoe. Curious, I looked inside but I did not see anything. I turned the shoe upside down and shook it and a large black scorpion dropped out.

Juan introduced me to the current peasant farm manager--Don Luis (Don is a title of respect). He had been responsible for supervising the three workers who kept the farm running. Now, he would report to me. I would use him to oversee the workers in the field.

The field workers consisted of two adults and a seventeen-year-old. All field workers struggled with their reading, writing, and arithmetic. They could sign their names and read a little. The boy, Julio, could also perform calculations. Because I wanted to collect data to determine the cost of production for everything we produced, I would require one of the workers to keep track of the hours each worker spent performing each task during the week. Don Luis could not do this because numbers confused him. The record keeper, in addition to his regular work, would need to weigh every item harvested and know from which field it came. I needed at least one worker to be good with numbers in addition to reading and writing. I thought that it would be Julio. He showed the most enthusiasm when I discussed what we needed from the workers.

The First Baptist Church worked to fight illiteracy. The church created learning centers around the country. In these centers, local community leaders helped teach the illiterate to read and write by using teaching methods that the church had developed or adapted from other people's work. I wanted to apply these teaching methods and use their materials on the farm for the workers who were interested in improving their reading, writing, and mathematics skills.

When I presented this option to the workers, they all opted into the program. We agreed that we would do this after work each day at the farmhouse. On the first day, the workers were all present and excited. We found four school desks inside the house's dining area. I brought them out onto the porch. I explained the program to the workers and gave each worker his personal book and a pencil to use. They worked at their own pace. I drifted among them to give them encouragement. They were timid and would not ask questions at first, but later, they became less intimidated. No one showed more excitement than Julio.

While the workers were studying alone, I developed worksheets on which we would collect data. One documented the crops produced and the areas of each. Another documented how we used the workforce's time: the hours devoted to executing each task for each crop. After becoming satisfied with each form, I redrew it and showed it to Julio. The next day he would start to collect data. He was so enthusiastic that he gave me a smile that was so wide that it engulfed his ears.

For work, we started producing vegetables. Since the rains had not yet come, we only planted a small area. Without rain, we needed to irrigate the seedlings every couple of days. We only had water from our house pump and a garden hose. This limited the scale of our operations.

We had to think about how we should market the products. Nearby was a modern hotel in which Howard Hughes occupied the seventh floor. I thought that we could obtain the highest price there for our quality vegetables. We established the hotel as our primary market. Because we had no vehicle to carry our production, any excess not sold at that hotel would go to the community market, which we could reach on foot; even though, their prices were lower.

Meals Taken on Site

The workers slept in our storage shed. They either did not have a home, or they lived too far away to commute, so they slept onsite. On weekends, they mostly disappeared. I did not ask questions.

The workers paid a cook to prepare their meals. Their meals were simple: mostly pasty spaghetti, eggs, rice, and black beans. Since I made about the same money as they did, I joined their group. We pooled our money and paid a cook to buy and prepare food for us.

At mealtime, the cook called us. She always placed the food on a small wooden table under a large shade tree located between the house and the shed. She prepared the food in the shed where the workers slept. She covered the food with a tablecloth to protect it from the swarms of flies that occupied the area. When we removed the tablecloth, we had to defend our food and fruit juice. We ate with our right hands and swatted flies with our left hands. It was an impossible job. If I swatted my food, a swarm of flies landed on my juice glass. If I swatted around the glass, a swarm of flies landed on my food. My workers were having no better luck.

The flies became such a problem that we agreed to take the tablecloth that had covered our food and fully unfold it. We placed it over our heads creating an extra barrier between the flies and our food. That allowed us to eat while defending our plates and food, but that was not good enough. The flies still found our food and ate as much as we ate. That was when I had the idea. I would take my knife and tap my juice glass. The ringing noise would scare the flies away. It worked for a few days, but then, even more flies appeared. My only explanation was that the flies must have associated the glass ringing as a call to eat and came with that single purpose. In the end, our only defense was to swat fast and eat even faster. It must have appeared strange to anyone watching us eat: four men under a tablecloth with both arms moving rapidly in all directions.

The Lapa

The house and large tree came with a Lapa, a large colorful parrot. Mostly, he stayed in the tree and screeched. He had a very loud and shrill screech. It was very annoying. His favorite time to sing the song of his ancestors was at six in the morning. I could never sleep beyond that time. I could set my watch to the beast's morning screech. I hated that beast.

Sometimes he climbed down the tree, waddled to the shed next to the house, climbed up the water gutters, and screeched there for a while. If I was standing in the shade of the tree, he often climbed down the tree trunk, waddled to my leg, and climbed up using his beak. He grasped my pants with his beak and pulled himself up. He slowly and deliberately climbed my pants and then my shirt. If his beak found flesh under my pants, I screamed in pain, but my screams did not influence where he clasped his feet or his beak. He climbed until he was on my shoulder.

Sometimes he seemed so cute and cuddly. He stood on my shoulder and rubbed my ear with his beak. Then the evil devil would bite my ear with enough force to crack a walnut. I could not defend myself by knocking him down because he would have taken a piece of my ear with him. I had to apply pressure on his body by slowly increasing it until he released my ear. All the while, I had to be careful not to harm him. When freed, I threw him back into his tree. I had no idea why he was so mean.

I Retrieve My Stereo

Finally, I received a message from customs that my packages had arrived. I was elated. I wanted to listen to music on my stereo. Juan drove me to customs. I expected to sign three or four papers and claim my things, but that was not the way they did it in Somoza's (the dictator) Nicaragua. I can no longer remember what the difficulty was, but something was wrong. I could not take my things until I did something. I really did not understand what the problem was. I was very unhappy. I had to turn and walk out of customs without my things. Juan said that he thought they were fishing for bribes to release my property.

When Dr. Parajón heard of this, he was able to clear part of his day's business schedule within a couple of days and accompanied me to customs. He straightened it out, and I walked out with my property without paying a bribe. Dr. Parajón was a well-known and highly respected man in Nicaragua. What I remember most about Dr. Parajón was that he was very soft-spoken. His voice was so soft that everyone had to pay attention to hear him, yet they always heard him. Dr. Parajón was my hero. He was super-human. He was a force. He faced so many impossible problems each day, and somehow, he resolved them without raising his voice or saying a bad word about anyone. He was a true Christian.

Meanwhile, I was teaching Julio how to use the newly developed data collection forms to collect data. He had bought an inexpensive watch so that he could time the activities. He periodically took notes during the day to allow him to accurately fill in the forms at the end of the day. The idea was simple, but it was not easy to achieve with accuracy. It took us a couple of weeks before I was receiving usable data. I had never seen anyone respond to words of praise as much as Julio did. He was a delight to work with.

Each day, after work, we continued our literacy training. I was surprised by how excited the men were to learn after a hard day's work. They wanted to be able to read and write. Julio's training included mathematical problems so that he could calculate hours worked, each day's crop production, and overall totals.

Every night I prepared more data collection sheets because these were each hand prepared. I collected Julio's sheets, prepared summary sheets, and shared my results with Julio, who was ecstatic to be included in the process. He loved to be learning new things and for me to take him into my confidence when I shared the results with him. He loved the attention given to him.

Going to Panama to Buy a Motorcycle

I needed transportation. I was unable to leave the farmhouse. For a twenty-five-year-old man, that was too confining. I looked at motorcycles in Managua, but they were expensive due to Nicaragua's high import taxes. That was when I remembered that the Panama Canal Zone was tax-free. I could buy a motorcycle in Panama tax-free. When I told Dr. Parajón of my plans, he informed me that when I brought the motorcycle into Nicaragua; I would still have to pay Nicaragua's import tax. He told me that, if I wanted to buy a cycle in the Canal Zone, he could produce a document declaring that I would use the motorcycle for the church's purposes, and then I would no longer need to pay import taxes. The only restriction he placed on me was that, should I leave the country, I would sell my cycle to someone doing the church's work.

I flew to Panama City and bought a Honda 350 cubic centimeter dirt bike and a helmet. It was wonderful. With my new cycle, I drove to a hardware store and bought six feet of heavy chain with a heavy-duty padlock to secure my cycle whenever I parked it. With this in hand, I started up the Pan American Highway. I could not believe that I could go anywhere I wanted, anytime I wanted. I fell in love with the rumble of my cycle's engine as I headed north toward Costa Rica.

Panama was a green country. Everywhere I looked, it was green. The Pan American highway ran through flatlands, but it was never far from the hills. I judged their distance by their blue hue: the closer vegetation was dark green while the farther from the highway; the deeper the blue hue.

It was relaxing to feel the cycle's vibration, hear the hum of the motor, and see the highway disappear under its wheels. I was not in a hurry. It was a moment I wanted to extend as much as possible. It was very cloudy, and rain was imminent, especially since the rainy season was already overdue. That was one disadvantage of being on a cycle-- the exposure to the weather. I accelerated. The next city was David, a city located in north Panama and named after President Eisenhower. I hoped to reach it before the rain came.

117

The highway passed along the eastern edge of David. I noticed a rooming house sign next to an area surrounded by a high white wall. The rooming house was located inside the walls. I thought this would be a secure area for my motorcycle. I entered the compound and parked my cycle. I rented a room for the night and convinced the owner to allow me to park my cycle inside the house. She was a very understanding woman. Even so, I applied my chain and padlock. My cycle was a beautiful machine. I would not risk losing it.

The next morning, I ate breakfast and was off. I was only an hour from the Costa Rican border, which I reached without incident. The road from the border into San José was dirt with deep ruts left from last year's rainy season. These ruts could be catastrophic to a car, truck, or bus; but to a motorcycle, they could be deadly. If either of my wheels were to fall into a deep rut, it could flip my cycle sideways or stop it in its tracks--throwing me from the cycle. I had to avoid the deep ruts, or if they were unavoidable, I had to transverse them at an angle so that my wheels could cross the ruts without falling into them. This required me to drive very slowly or to think and react very quickly.

I entered Costa Rica and raised my bottom from the cycle's seat a little and supported my weight on my legs. This allowed me to increase my speed to a moderate level. I had to keep my eyes glued to the road to avoid my tire dropping into any ruts. After less than an hour, my cycle stopped suddenly. It did not sputter or make any conking sounds; it just stopped. All efforts to restart the cycle failed. I was devastated.

I was well inside a rain forest area of Costa Rica with a dead motorcycle. I pushed the cycle to the edge of the oversized road and thought. I had not seen any villages behind me. I had no idea what lay ahead of me. I started pushing my cycle, hoping the rainy season would hold off another couple of days. After a couple of hours, a small truck stopped and asked if I needed help. I asked the driver where I could find a mechanic. He said that a few miles back there was a village a couple of miles off the road. He agreed to haul me and my cycle there--for a modest fee. I agreed.

The village had a mechanic, a market, a bank, and other businesses. It was modest, but it was what I needed. They located the mechanic. He was twenty-something years old, had long greasy hair, a thin scraggly beard, and two teeth. He was wearing flip-flops, a greasy, torn shirt, and an old pair of pants. He had grease smudges on his arms, hands, and face. When he understood, he was going to work on a new motorcycle, he took a step back, examined the cycle from stem to stern, and opened a broad smile that fully exposed both his teeth. At that moment, I was in deep trouble. I did not think he had a clue how to repair a cycle. He explained that he would not be able to complete any work until early the next day. Luckily for me, there was a small hotel in town, in fact, located almost next to the mechanic's shop. I rented a room from the hotel, found a simple restaurant, ordered chicken fried rice, and settled in for the night. I was grateful that I would spend the night in a cheap hotel rather than on the side of the road in a rain forest.

The next morning, I ate breakfast and walked to the mechanic's shop. I wanted to stand and watch him work on my cycle, but that was unnecessary. I found that he had already made the repair. It was a sweet moment when I gave the cycle a slight crank and the motor responded. I was so happy that the motor started immediately that I did not ask him what the problem with it had been. I only asked him how much it was. I do not remember how much it was, but it was a reasonable amount. I tried to pay him in US dollars, but he only accepted Costa Rican money. I had to wait for the bank to open at 10:00 am, which did not make me happy. Once it opened, I exchanged the money, paid him, and pointed my cycle back toward the road from which I had come.

When I reached the Pan American highway again, I turned right and accelerated as I picked my path among the deep ruts. After an hour's journey, the cycle again stopped, and my heart accelerated. What was going on? I had a new cycle. Again, in the middle of nowhere, I was pushing my cycle. After four hours, a truck appeared and stopped. They gave me and my cycle a ride up the road to a lone gas station that happened to have a mechanic. I accepted their kind offer.

After twenty minutes, the truck driver pulled to the side of the road by a gas station. There was no village, just a gas station located on the side of the road. The owner was in the process of closing. I quickly paid the driver, unloaded my cycle, and pushed it toward the gas station attendant as fast as I could. I begged him not to close until he had looked at my cycle. My pleas did not move him. He was done for the day, and he closed despite my pleading for him to stay open and check my cycle. He said I could keep my cycle inside his building, and that he would look at it first thing in the morning, and he left me standing.

Darkness was but thirty minutes away; I was hungry; I had no place to stay, and there was no village for many miles in any direction. I looked around and found an old, abandoned bus pushed off to the side of the road. The jungle concealed it. It consisted of only an old body. It had no wheels or motor, but the seats inside were still mostly intact, although mischievous people broke most of the windows. I noticed that in the back, the windows and seats were still intact. That would be the safest place for me because no one could position themselves behind me. I walked to the back of the bus and situated my things under my seat and sat down. I evaluated the seat and was satisfied that I would be safe there. I tried to sleep and finally did, despite the hungry mosquitos.

I awoke the next morning to find that travelers and their merchandise occupied most of the seating. I grabbed my things and camped out in front of the gas station. After ten minutes, the owner arrived and opened the station. He started to work on my cycle. Within minutes he had found the problem. This motorcycle had a "kill" switch located next to my left-hand handle. Its purpose, I think, was for the driver to hit it with his thumb if any dangerous situation arose, and that would kill the engine. My thumb had hit it twice as I and my cycle bounced around the rough road. I felt like an idiot. He charged me an appropriate fee and I was back on the road--this time without any more unscheduled interruptions.

The dirt road ended just south of San José. With the aid of pavement, I made suitable time; although, my bottom was raw from the hours of riding on a cycle and bouncing all around. Even so, I was going to try to arrive in Nicaragua yet that day. With straight pavement, I could travel at high velocity with my 350 cubic centimeter cycle. I had no problem maintaining high speeds while climbing steep grades.

Midafternoon, I arrived at the Nicaraguan border only to find that, even as a permanent resident, I could not reenter Nicaragua without an entry visa. Luckily, I could obtain this at a consulate located one hour back in a regional city. I turned my cycle around and opened it up, quickly arriving at the consulate. I obtained my visa and was back at the Nicaraguan border lickity-split. The entire process only took a couple of hours. Now, I had to hurry to make it home before dark, which I did.

Making Payroll

It felt good to be safely home with my beautiful new cycle. Now that I had my stereo, I could listen to music and, with my cycle, I had mobility. Life was good, even though it still had not rained. I was worried because everyone said that the rainy season in Nicaragua was already late.

Every Friday afternoon, I had to travel into Managua to cash the church's check for that week's payroll. In the bank, there was a beautiful, young, and charming teller. She had jet black hair and always had a smile that reached all the way down to her soul. I always stood in her line, even if other tellers were available. She had to notice my strange behavior, but she did not say anything. She smiled when it was my turn for her to wait on me. She was very professional and efficient. I tried to delay the transaction, if possible, to learn more about her, but that was not easy. She was friendly, but volunteered no personal information, even if there were no more clients in her line. As for pay day, I put the cash in a small backpack and took it to my house. For safety, I put it under my cot and pulled my sheet down to cover it.

Once a month, I went to a small hotel called *La Florida* to eat three blueberry pancakes with maple syrup. I always ate them slowly to extract every bit of flavor from them and to enjoy the air-conditioned environment. They were so good.

On an alternative weekend, also, once a month, I bought a banana split at an air-conditioned restaurant. I ate it as slowly as possible to maximize its savory taste, but I could not eat too slowly, or it would melt. That was all the luxury that I could afford each month, especially since I now had to set aside money for gas for my beloved motorcycle.

One day, we received an encouraging rain that more than settled the dust. We were in the second year of drought; consequently, we were in a celebratory mood. I was driving my cycle to a bar to have a couple celebratory beers when I saw a Dutch friend in his yard. He was the master brewer at the largest brewery in Nicaragua. I stopped and we talked about the prospects of more rain. He was not optimistic. I was. Farmers must be optimistic. He invited me into his house to try a few beers. I carefully guided my cycle through his front yard gate and hid it behind shrubbery while he locked the gate. In his house, he handed me an all-copper mug and the coldest beer I had tasted in months. We drank several beers as he told me his story of traveling from Holland to Nicaragua. After a couple of hours, I carefully drove back to my house. Fortunately, my drive only required me to drive on narrow paths with no traffic.

Despite the short shower, most farmers were afraid to plant because the rains were late. When rains were late, they were often unreliable, but after today's rain, I was sure that the more optimistic farmers would start to plant more crops. For the remaining farmers, more rains were required before they committed their cash to planting. They could not afford a false start. If they planted seed, applied fertilizer, and the rains stopped; they would lose their investment.

I obtained permission to hire more workers to clear the weeds and brush in expectation of planting vegetables. I hired fifteen to twenty workers because, if the rains started for certain, we would be able to plant the seeds before the sun could dry the ground surface. I had to make sure that Don Luis kept a close eye on the number of workers that came each day. This was necessary because workers often disappeared for a day or two and then reappeared. In addition, I wanted to know what each worker did and how much work he accomplished. Don Luis and Julio needed to be on their toes. When it came time to lay off workers, we could lay off our less productive ones.

Friday at noon, Don Luis and I prepared the payroll sheet. For our calculations, we assumed that all workers would work Saturday morning. On Friday afternoon I went into Managua to the bank. The next day at noon, the men stopped work and gathered under the shade of the big tree. I pulled a small table and stool out onto the porch from inside the house and sat my backpack on the table. I arranged the bills in stacks by each denomination. I called the first man on the list. I confirmed with each man how many days he had worked and how much he had earned. If the man agreed, I counted the money and gave it to him to count, if he could count. If he was satisfied, he made an X on the line indicating that he had received his money and the line moved on.

As each man received his money, he disappeared quickly because he wanted to make it to Saturday market before all the good fruit and vegetables were sold. After I completed the payroll, I climbed on my cycle and headed to visit a friend or to buy my banana split or blue berry pancakes. Sometimes, I just rode around to hear my motorcycle's engine when I accelerated and to feel the engine's vibration.

Traffic in Managua was dangerous, especially for someone riding a motorcycle. Drivers failed to respect signs and signals. They did not even consider them as a strong suggestion. You could never assume that a green light meant that you could safely cross an intersection. Narrow intersections made this even more dangerous. The street was twenty feet wide plus three feet on each side for sidewalks. If this were the case, drivers only could see twenty-six feet and beyond that they were blind. When a driver entered an intersection with a green light, he did not know if there was a driver from the other street about to run a red light. Traffic needed to creep up to the intersection, look up and down the other street, and then cross the intersection. Of course, no one did that. They took their chances. Some people slowed down for intersections, but many did not. There were numerous accidents.

Security on the Farm

At night, I locked all outside doors in the house, and then I locked myself inside my bedroom. In addition, I had a paid armed night guard who walked around the outside of the house. During the day, Don Luis was always armed.

Managua was a dangerous city, and we had the worst neighborhood in the city positioned on the east side of the farm. In this *barrio*, most people were unemployed, and crime was high.

Our farm had at least five acres of excellent bottomland nestled between the steep slope east of the house and the *barrio*. Before I arrived, the church had tried to plant crops on the bottomland, but they only had losses because *barrio* people stole (we believe) most of the production before it was fully ripened. The church then placed a night security guard to guard the area, but I heard that mischievous people had killed him. After that, the church decided it would not use violence to protect its assets. Instead, they abandoned those acres and allowed the *barrio's* people to work out a way to share the land and to plant their own vegetables. That was the way the church had to turn an unpleasant situation into a good situation. I never visited the area.

The farm had sixty acres of good grass, although, at that moment, it was mature and not palatable to cows. For the next year, even if the drought continued, we should have enough grass to support cows. I convinced the powers-to-be that we should buy a cow. Don Luis knew the perfect one. He found her somewhere and convinced her owner to part with her, and thus, we bought our first cow. She gave eight quarts of milk daily.

If we were going to have cows, we should have a way to make silage to keep them producing milk during the dry season. I convinced my supervisor to allow me to build a small horizontal silo near the building site. I needed a bricklayer, and again, Don Luis found me a bricklayer. We ordered the huge stone bricks, which were the most economic building material. I hired three brothers to help dig the opening needed on the hillside, and construction began.

I discovered quickly that the self-proclaimed bricklayer, even with the Don Luis's stamp of approval, was no guarantee of ability. I noticed that the bricks laid by our bricklayer were not straight. Our bricklayer did not know how to lay bricks. I learned that he was simply an unemployed man who would do anything to work, even misrepresent himself.

I had to find another bricklayer. I went to Don Luis and explained that we needed a real bricklayer. He could not afford to be wrong on this selection because it reflected badly on him and on me. He disappeared for a couple of hours and reappeared with another man carrying a toolbox with his tools. He swore he knew how to lay bricks. I asked him to show me. He dismantled what the previous bricklayer did and started over. I verified that he knew what he was doing and approved him to start work.

In anticipation of completing the silo, we had planted six acres of sorghum to fill the silo. It was growing nicely, but we had problems that I had never seen on our farm in Nebraska. The sorghum produced heads, which opened and started to produce seed that was easily accessible to birds. Then the parrots came. They came in mass. Great flocks of little green hungry parrots feasted on the milo heads. It was obvious that if we allowed them to continue, nothing would remain to chop for silage. We had to act.

We discussed our alternatives. We discarded having a person periodically discharge a gun because it would be too expensive. We discarded the idea of having a person periodically set off firecrackers because it would also be too expensive. The problem was that whatever we did had to be done for the twelve hours of daylight for each day until we could cut it for silage. That would consume a large volume of firecrackers or bullets. We agreed to hire a young boy who would carry a large biscuit can, the equivalent of a five-gallon can, and a stick. He would walk about the field and bang on the can with the stick.

This also failed because the parrots just avoided him and ate the seed-heads in another part of the field. If we hired a second boy to bang on another can, it would be too expensive. Our choice for a crop was simply not feasible in Nicaragua. We had no way to protect the seed. Even though milo was better suited to the area's climate, the bird problem made it inviable. Any future crop would have to be corn. That was the price of inexperience in the region. We were building a silo and, we had little to chop to fill the silo. I thought that I had taken on more than I could manage.

One day, Dr. Parajón learned how I went into town to collect the cash payroll and left it overnight under my bed. He became nervous and told me never to do that again. It was too dangerous. Neighborhood thieves had committed murder for far less cash than I stored overnight under my bed. First, he said that a different person would do the payroll every week. Second, we would make payment at a different place every week. We would reveal the place on Saturday at noon under the shade tree at the house. It would never be far away, but still, these methods would make it more difficult for anyone to rob our payroll.

One day, while we were eating our lunch under the tablecloth, I heard three shots fired in rapid succession. The workers and I pulled our heads from under the tablecloth, dropped the tablecloth onto our plates, and looked toward the house where the sound originated. I saw Don Luis standing with his arm extended aiming for another shot. I looked toward where he was pointing his pistol and saw a man running fast down the path away from the house. He was far enough away that Don Luis had no chance of hitting him. When I asked Don Luis what had happened, he told me that he had come around the corner of the house and found this man standing on the porch and looking inside the house. He thought the man was about to enter the house. That was when Don Luis shouted a warning, drew his pistol, and started firing. The man quickly perceived the spot he was in and decided to vacate the premises. He may have only been looking for work.

One night we had a celebratory dinner in town and the group was taking me home after it was over. We passed onto the farm through the wire gate and arrived at the first turn where we had to turn left to reach the farmhouse. As the Land Rover made the left turn; its headlights swept across a field. In full view, we saw three men hunched over and fast walking toward the farmhouse. They carried machetes, but then all workers carried machetes. It could have been that they were workers from somewhere who worked late and were trying to arrive home as fast as possible, or they could have been moving toward the farmhouse with bad intentions. At that time of night, we thought the second option to be the more likely.

We quickened our pace to the farmhouse and awoke our three workers who resided in the tool shed. They dressed, grabbed their machetes, walked around the house, and then walked toward the place where we had spotted the intruders. They found no one. I was sure that the invaders took a different direction as soon as we spotted them. The workers returned to their slumber. We alerted my night guard to be on the lookout for any suspicious activity during the night and went to bed.

The three brothers finished digging the silo hole. They knew that without rain we would not need their services. They asked to speak with me, and I accommodated them. They told me that, if I were to release all the workers cutting weeds, they could take over and accomplish as much as all the others. I consulted with Don Luis, and he concurred.

We were far enough into what should have been the wet season, and still without enough rain to plant; we decided to abandon our idea of planting a large area to vegetables. Without the rain, it was unlikely that we could produce a crop without incurring economic losses. To minimize our losses, I would release fifteen men who had been clearing the land of stumps and weeds. I would tell the workers on payday. I decided to retain the three brothers because they never complained, always arrived on time, and gave me a good day's work each day.

On payday, it was my turn to hand out the money. I decided to make the payment on the house porch on the farm. The workers that I laid off were not surprised. They had been expecting it. Their look of despair still overwhelmed me, but I could not show it. The workers being unemployed meant, that once they spent this money, their families would experience hunger. I had already understood that I, or the church, could only help a few people for a short while--and we had already kept hunger from their doors for several weeks. We had done what we could. We were out of resources and could help them no more. Nicaragua had no relief system, no unemployment insurance, or food stamps. Every man had to provide for himself. Men had extended families that could help them, but these agricultural workers were in the second year of a drought. Most extended families were also drained of resources.

There was one man who, when I informed him that this was his last paycheck, had an expression that was different from the others. I noticed that he carried a fish knife in his belt. In fact, most peasant workers carried fish knives, but I never noticed them. His fish knife caught my attention because it was in plain view. I had not noticed him before, but today I noticed he had a huge scar that started at the corner of his mouth and formed an arc down his jawbone, back toward his ear, and up and around to his eye. I could only imagine that it was a fish-knife fight, and it did not look like he had won. His expression was emotionless. It caused me concern.

I paid my scar-faced worker and he disappeared. Only he reappeared an hour later, lurking about at a distance, and approached the house little by little. Don Luis saw him first. After a few minutes, Don Luis approached the worker and asked what the worker wanted; Don Luis smelled firewater on the worker's breath. The agitated worker demanded to speak with me. Don Luis searched for me, and when he found me, he warned me that the former worker might be confrontational. He suggested that I get on my cycle and disappear until night, to give the worker a chance to sober up. I locked the house and told Don Luis not to close the wire gate on the edge of the farm's property until I returned. He agreed. I cranked my cycle and left.

I went into town and entered an air-conditioned restaurant. I ordered, and slowly drank, two very cold Coca Colas, one after another. I then visited friends until dark. At dark, I started back to the farm. Once I left the highway and turned onto the dirt road, I slowly rode the cycle while standing on the pegs and flashed my lights from low to high beams. My objective was to catch a reflection if cretons had strung thin wire across the road at neck height. This was a recent method that the thieves had developed to steel motorcycles. I drove slowly, but deliberately. If I failed to see the stretched wire, it would hit my chest and do minimal damage at my low speed.

When I reached the property, the gate was supposed to be open, but it was not. This could have been a trap. Even though there were no trees on our property, there were trees, brush, and tall weeds on the other side of the fence. Any number of people could have been hiding, and I would have no clue. I had no choice but to stop, open the gate, pass through, and close it behind me. Then, I had a clear drive to the farmhouse.

On Monday morning, one of the three brothers did not appear. His name was Antonio. I asked the two remaining brothers where Antonio was. They said that he would be back on Wednesday. I asked if he was sick. No, he was not sick. I pressed for an answer. One brother finally said that he was in a little misunderstanding in a bar over the weekend and had killed someone. Now he was hiding. I asked how he was going to return to work on Wednesday with the police looking for him. They told me that, in Nicaragua, the police only look for murderers for three days. If they did not find them, the case goes cold. The police have so many new murderers to find that they cannot dwell on old cases, which are all cases four or more days old. On Wednesday, Antonio was back and gave me a full day's work.

As I walked around the south side of Managua, there was a large prison. It had high, thick walls. On three sides there were no windows or doors, only small openings which were fewer than six by eight inches and were located high on the walls. These were for air circulation; however, the prisoners had another use of them. The prisoners managed to fabricate small containers, tie them to string and throw them up and through the openings near to high prison ceilings and lower them until they hung at street level. They just hung there until someone walked by. At this moment, the prisoners started yanking on the string and the containers came alive by moving up and down rapidly as they tried to gain the passerby's attention. The prisoners were begging for money so they could buy food to eat.

In this prison, the prisoners were not fed. It was the prisoners' responsibility to have a family either bring them food each day or pay for prison food by any means possible. If a prisoner did not have a family that would take money, or food, to the prison, they had to find a way. Usually, this involved the prisoner finding a small paper bag and roll down the top thus forming a lip. He then tore his t-shirt or other article of clothing into strips and formed a rope. He attached the clothing rope to the paper bag with a safety pin. The next hurdle was to toss the paper receptacle up and through the ventilation hole and coax the bag to drop to street level.

The sight was sad to me of all these paper cups jiggling as people walked by.

The Arrival of the Church Volunteers

One day the church bus arrived on the farm filled with singing passengers. When it stopped, it offloaded a bunch of young people with a smattering of middle-aged people. These were the volunteers from the church in Cleveland, Ohio. Church volunteers had already placed cots around the house to receive them. One room had cots for the female volunteers while they housed the male volunteers in my room and the kitchen area. We had fifteen young volunteers and three supervisors--and we shared one bathroom.

There were a couple of high school graduates, college students, and college graduates. This was a happy time for me. First, I could eat with them, and their food was much better than the food that I had been eating. Second, they laughed and joked at mealtime. I admired how intelligent and quick-witted they were. Finally, there was a young female volunteer that caught my eye. I wanted to become better acquainted with her. Her name was Nancy.

The volunteers helped water plants, harvest, and package lettuce while others grabbed a hoe to help weed the growing vegetables. We sold the lettuce to the fancy hotel where people said Howard Hughes staid. People were everywhere. It was hard to keep track of who was doing what, but it was nice having so many people around. It made keeping records difficult, especially for labor because the volunteers were shifting jobs at will and Julio could not keep pace with them. Also, they were not as proficient at performing tasks as the regular day laborers were.

At night, after we finished our work, and we ate and washed the dishes, Nancy and I would go for a walk. It was nice to have female companionship. She was a good listener and had a wonderful smile and laugh. That was the best part of my day. I had to be careful because the group's elders were always watching us. We made a point of always staying in view to avoid any suspicions or confrontations.

After five days they transferred the group from the farm to the north-coastal region of Nicaragua. It was even hotter there than in Managua. They would stay in the area's school and work with the school children.

I decided to follow their bus later the same day. The farm, without the volunteers, seemed excruciatingly quiet and intolerably boring. I could not bear it. I hit the road just after lunch and was making suitable time because the paved road was mostly straight, although it did not always have a shoulder. If any driver needed to pull off the road for whatever reason, it would be dangerous without a wider shoulder.

I was traveling about sixty miles per hour going uphill and approaching a curve to the right. The car in front of me and the curve severely restricted my forward vision. I noticed a truck in my side vision trying to pass me. He was entirely in the passing lane. An oncoming car appeared ahead of me from around the curve. The truck was only three-quarters passed me when he saw the fast-approaching car. The truck driver simply moved his truck into my lane to avoid the oncoming car. Unfortunately, I was occupying that space. I had a second to figure out what was going to happen. I tried to slow down and move to the edge of the road, even though there was no safe shoulder area. I survived and continued my journey. I had come close to a serious and, possible fatal accident. All I could do was shake it off and continue down the road.

A couple of hours later I turned off the highway onto a dirt road and started to kick up dust. Without too much trouble, I found the school, and my *amigos,* who were busy setting up their cots and familiarizing themselves with the outdoor toilet situation. The supervisors appointed people to give each toilet a good scrubbing because they needed it. That was when the girls discovered spiders inside the toilet confines and inside the toilet. The cleaning girls came back to the group screaming. The boys charged into their toilet and bravely liquidated all visible spiders. Later, the boys did the same for the lady's toilet.

We had supper and cleaned the dishes. A group prepared a campfire. Once it had burned down a little, everyone sat around the fire, roasted marshmallows, and sang songs. I was not into singing, but I loved hearing happy people singing and joking. I loved the entire group. They were intelligent and fun to be around. Later, the girls asked me to check their toilet for fuzzes that might be lurking below the toilet seat. I shook out a huge spider and a lizard. Upon seeing this, the girls swore they would hold it in until they returned to Managua in a week or so. Others, who were more practical, marched forward and quickly did what they needed to do.

The next morning, I found my cycle's back tire flat. I had to find a small truck to carry my cycle and me into town, which was less than an hour away. After waiting a couple of hours, I located a truck and loaded my cycle into the back of a truck, and we were off. At the tire repair station, it took an hour for them to make the repair. I paid the gentleman and started back to camp on my cycle. Halfway home my cycle started to wobble on its back tire. Yes, it was going flat again. All I could do was to push it off the road, through the deep ditch, and up on the other side, which was no small task for a heavy cycle with a flat tire. I laid it down to make it more difficult to spot from the road and buried it under dead weeds. I then applied my chain and padlock and started to walk home.

The next day I had to find another truck to take me to find my cycle, which I was worried might not be where I left it. It was. We returned to the same tire repair shop. The man found four more holes in the tire. I begged him to check every inch of the tire to avoid a repeat of the previous day. I paid and started back to camp. I worried constantly if I were going to make it, or if I would find another hole in my back tire.

I Return to the Farm

The next morning, I decided that I should return to Managua to check the farm. I had become accustomed to having meals with the group filled with laughter, but I had the farm to look after.

I hit the road early, even though I was not in a hurry. I let the breeze hit my face at an easy fifty-five miles per hour. I relaxed and enjoyed the ride. As I passed the midway point home, I approached a small clearing on the right. It had three thatched houses with three men working around their houses. The women were either cooking or washing clothes and four or five children and dogs were running around. A new five-barbed-wire fence separated their area from the highway. There was a gate to allow people through the fence, but not animals.

As I approached their houses on the highway, three boys started throwing small rocks at me. One rock hit me in the solar plexus. It hurt. It was like being hit in the chest with a rock hurled at fifty-five miles per hour. I checked ahead of me and behind me. There was no traffic. I laid my cycle on its side and brought it back up on the opposite side of the road having reversed directions. I accelerated rapidly running on my back wheel and turned abruptly from the highway to the offroad next to the houses. I had their attention. The men, women, and children stopped what they were doing and focused on me, not knowing what to expect next. I revved the cycle's engine a couple times and gave a false start so that my back tire could throw sand like a dog on the beach. Now the three children started to scream and run; the fathers stood up, and I prepared to carefully guide my cycle through the narrow gate and into their yards.

Once I had my cycle on their side of the fence, I accelerated behind one kid and then another. The dogs barked and chased me. The men began to try to reach me, but they could not. After a few seconds, I thought that I had made my point. It was time to leave. I took my cycle next to the gate, pointed my cycle sideways, idled it, and shouted that *the next time you throw a rock at a motorcycle; the consequences would be more serious.* I turned toward the adults and shouted, "You should teach your children not to throw rocks at traffic." I passed through the gate, hit the highway, and sped away.

When I had left suddenly on my trip to follow the volunteers to their rural school, I had not made my bed. Therefore, I decided to straighten the sheets before jumping into bed. When I snapped the upper sheet, a large scorpion fell out. I secured him and took him outside. Upon returning to my bed, I noticed that one of my boots had fallen over. I reached down and set it upright. I heard something so I grabbed my boot, walked to the porch, and shook the boot upside down. Out fell another large scorpion. I went to bed hoping that I had not missed anymore.

The next morning, I walked around the farm to check on its status. I saw that the brick layer had finished laying the silo's floor and walls. We could now start cutting silage, even though, we had no roof. I sent Don Luis to find a corn chopper and a motor to power it. He came back with a nice chopper, but the motor was old, and I mean old. I was not convinced that it would even run. Don Luis grabbed a rope and with one try, the motor grunted into action. It sounded like our old John Deere Model A tractor. It gave a puff of life, and then made me wonder if it had died before another puff of life appeared. It took a few cycles of puffs and no puffs before I was confident that it was working.

We had a couple of men in the milo field cutting the milo stalks at their base. We had also hired a pair of oxen and an ox cart to haul the sorghum stalks from the field to the silo. Once at the silo, men unloaded the stalks while one man eased a few stalks at a time into the silage cutter. The motor just kept grunting and groaning, and the cutter kept on cutting. The milo heads had only a smattering of seeds, but we had to take it the way it came from the field.

Seeing that our milo would not be enough to fill the silo, we bought the neighbor's corn field. It had good stalks of corn with respectably large ears, but unfortunately, the stand was very thin. We also took what came from the field. By this time, we had a barrel filled with water that two men pushed up and down the silage in the silo to compact it and drive out as much oxygen as possible. As we finished cutting the silage, the carpenter placed the roof on the silo. We were now ready for the dry season, even if we had not had a wet season.

After a week, the church group returned to the farm and spread out to view how the farm had changed during the last few days. There was again chatter and laughter around the farmhouse. That evening, I took Nancy for a walk around the farm to show her what we had done and explained to her why we had done it. On a usual day on the farm, I spoke little and then, only to farm hands. It became very monotonous and uninteresting.

The next evening, I obtained permission to take Nancy for a motorcycle ride to Lake Managua. We left early evening. I parked the cycle on the edge of the path that vehicles take to the lake. We had to walk an additional fifty yards or so to the water's edge. The shore was dirt and not sand, as I had imagined it. We talked. I was sad because I knew she would be returning to start her first year in nursing at the

University of Vermont in a few days. I would be very alone after the group left. I had become accustomed to their company.

As we talked and walked along the shoreline, I caught a glance of movement near my cycle. I saw one National Guardsman walking around my cycle and examining it closely. I saw a second Guardsman positioning himself in a shadow under a streetlight. This was not good. There had been cases of immoral behavior by Guardsmen when a lone female was involved. I did not like what I saw. I made an excuse that we needed to return to the farmhouse, while I placed my hand in the middle of her back and turned her in the opposite direction; we started walking toward the motorcycle, slowly. I pointed out to her the presence of the Guardsmen. I told her to mount the cycle as soon as she arrived. I started a conversation with the Guardsmen near the cycle. He was asking me questions. I answered them, but I continued to mount the cycle and started it. I put it in gear and left him talking to the air. I had no idea if they had bad intentions toward my cycle, or toward Nancy, but we successfully left them behind and returned to the farmhouse. I never told Nancy about my worries.

The time came for the group to leave. The silence and sadness on the farm without them crushed me. Even the farm workers seemed saddened by their absence.

I Leave the Farm

As time passed, I had sunk into a depression that became worse with time. I missed Nancy. My work on the farm gave me less and less satisfaction. I started to consider leaving Nicaragua. Before I could leave, I needed to look for my replacement. I went to the Peace Corps office and learned that an agricultural volunteer had just enlisted for a third year in Nicaragua. I convinced him and the Peace Corps to allow him to take over for me. I informed my supervisor of my impending departure. I explained that I had found someone to take on the task of managing the farm. They were sad to see me leave but happy that I had found someone to continue my work.

I sold my motorcycle to a Mennonite agricultural volunteer. I would miss my beautiful motorcycle. I bought an airline ticket to

Burlington, Vermont, and said my goodbyes. I was excited because I had never been east of the Missouri River.

I arrived in Burlington at night, a chilly Vermont night. Nancy picked me up and took me to her dormitory. I needed a day or two to find my own place and a few more to find a job. It was a little clumsy at the dormitory, but none of her colleagues seemed shocked to see a man in their dormitory. Much had changed since I had graduated from the University of Nebraska just a couple of years previous, or the change was not due to time but region. Vermont was much more worldly due to so many students arriving from New York City, Boston, and other large urban areas.

I found a room that I rented by the day. It was tiny but adequate. My main problem was transportation. I could not find work without a car. Within days, I was able to buy a Volkswagen Beatle. This would be excellent for the deep snow that would be coming soon. In fact, it was already cold. I needed to buy winter clothes. My clothes were appropriate only for the Nicaraguan heat.

Once I had a room, a car, and clothes, I looked for a job. I found a part-time job in the Natural Resources department at the University of Vermont. I worked for a Mormon professor of economics. I enjoyed my job. Mostly, I was an errand boy, but that was fine. At lunchtime, the professor would kick back in his chair and talk to me about economics. He was conservative, but his logic was impeccable. It was working for him where I learned how important it was to understand statistics.

I wanted to move out of my room and into an apartment, but I did not make enough money for that. I started seeking a second part-time job. I found one at a gas station. I now worked thirty hours a week at the university and thirty hours a week at the gas station. I rented a nice small apartment in a neighboring town where rent was cheaper than in the university town of Burlington.

I was busy. I did my laundry and my shopping on Saturdays plus I worked at the gas station. On Sundays, I only worked at the gas station. That was when I cooked a hot meal that included baked ham, sweet potatoes, and green beans. I always looked forward to that. It was the only hot meal I had during the week. Each morning, I made six ham sandwiches, because I would eat lunch at the university and eat supper while on duty at the gas station. I would arrive home at 10:00 p.m. most nights.

On December 23rd, 1972, while I was working at the gas station, a special news edition appeared on the radio announcing that, earlier that morning, a strong earthquake had rocked Nicaragua, centered on Managua. I was dumbfounded. As I listened to more details from the radio announcement, I wondered about each of my friends living there. I tried to envision the status of their homes and apartments. I knew that Dr. Parajón would be busy caring for those injured by the earthquake, but I wondered about what the others would be doing, but most of all, I worried about if they were safe.

Between customers, I went to a place behind the front desk, sat, held my head in my hands, and tried to understand the gravity of what had happened. I confess that tears formed, and I had to brush them aside, especially when the outside bell rang informing me that a new customer had arrived at the gas station.

The next few days were no better. I received more news from the radio and television stations, but I had no specific news about my friends. I do not remember the estimates of the day as to how many people were killed, injured, or left homeless, but it would have been extremely high numbers. Today, I checked Wikipedia and they estimated that from 4,000 to 11,000 people were killed, 20,000 were injured and 300,000 were left homeless out of a total population of one million.

I wrote a letter to Joan Parajón, the American wife of Dr. Parajón. I had no idea if the letter would ever reach her, given the mess that the earthquake had left Managua in. After a few weeks, I received a letter from Joan bringing me up to date on my friends. They were all unhurt. Finally, I could relax. I resolved to visit Nicaragua at the end of the semester and see for myself what had happened.

Meanwhile, my Mormon supervisor recommended that in January I start to take economics courses. I took his advice and took two courses: farm management and production economics, but I kept working sixty hours a week. I never had a spare moment, but I liked my life. I was learning useful skills and making money.

As my university supervisor became better acquainted with my personality, he recommended that I take courses in the economics department, plus courses in calculus and statistics. Of course, being hard-headed, I rejected his recommendations. I had found my introductory courses in economics very boring and did not want to take more of the same. He then guided me to another department on campus--a new department. I enrolled for a master's degree in Adult Education and prepared for my trip to Nicaragua.

I Return to Nicaragua

Once again, Juan met me at the airport and took me to Dr. Parajon's house. I was very emotional because we had to drive a detour around Managua to reach the house. Where Managua had once been a busy city, it now had a four barbed wire fence around it and only a few buildings stood. Joan told me that she had told another friend, Jimmy, an American church volunteer, that I was coming. He had managed to rent a newly constructed temporary house in a recent development and welcomed me to stay with him while I was in Managua.

Juan drove me there and showed me the place. Jimmy was at work. It was a very adequate one-bedroom apartment with a living room large enough to have a second bedroom available for his guests. Jimmy was the go-to guy to house guests when someone from outside Nicaragua flew in for some reason. Later, I saw Jimmy and it seemed like yesterday that we had last seen each other, yet it seemed like ten years because of all that had happened.

The next day I received a ride to the fence placed around the destroyed center of Managua and took my camera. I carefully swung my legs between two barbed wires and started walking where Managua had once been a vibrant city. These were the streets where I had ridden my motorcycle on the weekends to get away from the farm. The streets had been full of cars, trucks, motorcycles, and people. It was hard to go far without stopping for someone or something that was in my way. And now, I saw a lone stalk of corn growing in the once busiest of streets. I could not see a person or car in any direction.

I looked up at a tall building, at least fifteen stories. During the quake, the first story had collapsed, as it had in many buildings, but on top of this building was a man with a sledgehammer standing on the outside wall chipping away at the structure. Why was he there? What did he hope to accomplish? He had to be the most optimistic man in the world to be chipping away at such a large building, but there he was.

After a week of finding and meeting with my old friends, I felt better. I could breathe again. I said my goodbyes and returned to Vermont.

My time at the University of Vermont had achieved one major thing; it awoke my desire to learn. It gave me a taste of learning useful skills from my classes in agricultural economics, especially farm management. I had a new respect for university learning and looked forward to using all my non-major credit hours on taking the few agricultural economics courses taught in the Department of Natural Resources.

I spent the next year taking my courses, working, and trying to have a social life. I graduated and left the university for my second Peace Corps tour, this time in Brazil—but that is another story.

Living in Brazil

Chapter 13

First Assignment: Cuiabá, Mato Grosso

After an uneventful training period, the Peace Corps sent me to Cuiabá, Mato Grosso—the geographic center of South America. When I stepped off the plane in Cuiabá, I felt like I had been dumped into a pressure cooker. It was ridiculously hot and humid. In the rainy season, it would rain constantly and would be even more humid.

Not only was this the geographical center of South America, but also the continental divide ran through Cuiabá. To the north, the water drained into rivers that found their way into the Amazon River. To the south, the water drained into rivers passing through Argentina and into the ocean.

An implication of being the geographic center of South America was that Cuiabá was located farther from civilization than any other place in Latin America. Anything manufactured was manufactured elsewhere, and elsewhere was always half a world away. They shipped everything in from the industrial south: São Paulo and its surrounding region. The roads for the distance between São Paulo and Cuiabá were poor, almost impassable during the rainy season and filled with potholes during the dry season, making transportation costs high. The cost of living in Cuiabá was the most expensive I had seen anywhere. The only product that was inexpensive was lumber. There was no shortage of lumber because farmers cut trees to clear land.

Farming in southern Brazil was very advanced. After World War II many Germans had decided to move to Brazil and had settled in the southern states. There were cities where people everywhere spoke German; they taught schools in German, until the federal government passed a law requiring all schools and government business to be conducted in Portuguese. The architecture of most buildings in regional cities was German.

In the south, the demand for land was high because everyone wanted to farm and own his own land, but landowners not only did not want to sell any land; they also wanted to buy more land. When the government opened rural Mato Grosso for development, there was a land rush. People aspiring to own large farms, such as small farmers and hired men, rushed north to grab as large a piece of land as was possible. If they had land, they rented it to a neighbor and left their families while they went north to locate suitable land and clear it for farming. Only then would they bring their families north.

This surge north had consequences. The city of Cuiabá and the surrounding region were growing fast. The population now was predominately male. Housing was scarce and expensive. Jobs were difficult to find and low paying. There was much hustle and bustle. Hardware stores were selling axes, spades, chains, chainsaws, and nails. Everyone had a backpack or a mule to carry his provisions into the wilderness.

Problems with My Assignment

When I arrived, the Peace Corps director told me that there were problems with my assignment and that they needed resolution before I could start. Until then, I would be in a holding pattern.

The Peace Corps director told me to find a place to live and wait. This was not easy because our living allowance was minimal relative to the escalating costs of living. A Peace Corps secretary told me of a bunkhouse-style boarding house located on the edge of the city. It consisted of a large room with no room divisions. On each side were rows of narrow beds. There were about thirty or forty beds in all, and rarely were any vacant. In one corner were shower and bathroom stalls. Males rented the beds by the day, week, or month. It was not a secure place, and nothing of value could be left there, including while you slept. I left my billfold inside my pillowcase. At night, it was hot, there was no ventilation, and mosquitoes were a major problem. Everyone who could afford one, bought a rotating fan, and arranged it carefully to blow slightly above their body, sweeping from head to foot. This minimized the risk of catching a cold in the heat yet dissuaded the mosquitoes from landing on our bodies.

I met some men at the bunkhouse who had come from Rio Grande do Sul: a great agricultural state far to the south. They all envisioned that one day they would own large farms that they could bequeath to their children. They spoke very confidently, as if it were a fact that simply had not happened yet. These men were preparing to disappear into the forests and stake their claim, and then they would cut huge trees using their axes and chainsaws. These determined men would try to burn the fallen trees as quickly as possible and throw seeds into the soil, expecting that crops would jump out. They were often disappointed. Forest soils were good for trees, but not so much for crops.

Most of the trees the farmers cut were mahogany. The size of a tree was determined by a measurement where men faced the tree, stretched out their hands, and held the hands of the men standing next to them. The measure was how many men it took to encompass the girth of the tree. It was common for a tree to require three to many more men to embrace it. The farmers burned the trees where they fell. They had no value.

The lack of reasonable roads, even in the dry season, prevented anyone from transporting the trees for processing into planks. Besides, no sawmills capable of milling the large trees were available. Even if they could have processed the wood into planks, it still would have had to travel hundreds of miles to find any market; therefore, the trees had no value. Cuiabá was located at the end of the world—where the wind goes before it stops to rest and turn around. It was like Cuiabá was an island located in the middle of the Pacific Ocean.

The *Erva Matte* Ceremony

The residents from the bunkhouse were friendly. We often sat on our beds and talked about our families and why we were in Mato Grosso. It was from these citizens of Rio Grande do Sul, also known as

Gauchos, that I learned of *erva matte*, or green tea. I learned that it was part of an exquisite social ceremony shared in the most basic situations, but always with great significance. They carried the tea in a bag as one carried tobacco for smoking. The container in which they placed it for drinking was called a *cuia*, from the name of the gourd from which it was made.

The host, the man who suggested that we partake of the *erva*, continued the conversation as he carefully loaded the *cuia* with tea. The *cuia* was always five or six inches deep and two or three inches wide. The host filled it to within one inch of the brim and then tipped it on its side to prepare an open space going from the top of the *cuia* to its base. Then the man produced a long silver straw with a quarter-sized filter at the bottom. He placed the metal straw carefully along the side until it reached the bottom of the *cuia*. He slowly righted the *cuia* and reached for his thermos bottle, which he always filled with recently boiled water. He poured it into the *cuia* along the straw. The first suck from the straw was the hosts. This was because it contained small pieces of leaves, he deemed too unpleasant for his guests. After the host was confident that the tea was no longer filled with leaf fragments, he passed it to the next person, who sipped and passed it to the next and the next, until it was gone. Then the process would start anew. It was wonderful.

A Boil on My Neck

It was at this point that I became aware of the boil on my neck. It was very painful and grew worse each day instead of better. It was especially painful in the hot climate, and my shirt constantly irritated it by rubbing it. The Peace Corps authorized me to have it removed surgically. I had to find my own way to the hospital, which was not easy. I did not have the money to take a taxi. I either had to walk in the heat and sweat like a fool or learn the bus routes. I walked.

Early the next morning, they put me under general anesthesia and removed the boil. I was lonely when I slowly came out of anesthesia. No one visited me, and no one would pick me up. I felt bad from the aftereffects of the surgery, simple as it had been. My family at home had no idea. It would have been nice to have a friend or family member there to talk to me.

It would be a couple of more hours before the doctor would release me. Forced immobility and not feeling well were a recipe for loneliness. I slept as much as possible and had a dream while the effects of the anesthesia were wearing thin. I dreamed two lovely ladies were walking down the corridor, and upon seeing this young man in this huge room all alone, they stopped, looked, and entered my room. They approached my bed. One was the mother, and one was the daughter. They were both beautiful, with bright smiles and huge eyes. One asked, "Are you an American?"

I smiled and replied, "Yes. How did you know?"

The other asked, "Are you here alone?"

"No. You are here with me."

This caused them both to smile even wider. One asked, "Don't you have any friends?"

Understanding that I might be able to gain sympathy, I said, "No. I know no one." I was pressing my luck, I thought, and they might discover my theatrical ploy.

"Oh, that is sad," said one of the ladies. They were a team and could conduct excellent conversation as they alternated questions and answers.

"Miss," I managed to say weakly.

"Yes," answered the daughter as she came closer to hear better.

"Will you marry me?" I pleaded, using my most desperate voice.

I saw the daughter break into a wonderful smile, as did the mother while she grabbed her daughter's shoulder and hurried her out of the room. They looked back at me as they left the room and smiled. I had not yet mastered my technique with the ladies, but I knew I was improving.

Meeting People at the Bar

Day after day, I had nothing to do, especially since I had only enough money to pay for my boarding house, laundry, and basic food. I did manage a couple of Pepsis each night as entertainment, but that was the extent of my crazy money.

For security reasons, I left my suitcases filled with my belongings in the Peace Corps director's office. I used a small duffel bag to take a change of clothes to my bunkhouse each day and then returned with my dirty clothes to the office the next day and exchanged them for clean clothes from my suitcase. Then I went to the center of town to watch the movement, and movement there was. It reminded me of what a boomtown might have looked like during periods of rapid expansion in the old West. People were everywhere, always busy, doing something or going somewhere, buying things, and taking them somewhere. I just stood, watched, and waited. I was frustrated. I was envious of all those who had a purpose in their lives.

Once while I was at a bar in the center of the city, drinking my Pepsi, another American came in, ordered a beer, and sat at a neighboring table. He was about my age, but he had a long, uneven beard and wore a crumpled hat. I started a conversation with him, and he joined me at my table. He was an anthropologist hired by the government organization tasked with protecting the Indigenous communities. He was an official Indian negotiator. When trouble broke out between the ranchers and Indians, they called him in to negotiate a settlement and avoid casualties.

He told me stories of Indians shooting arrows at slow-moving trains passing through their territories. He said that sometimes ranchers would invade the Indians' land, and the Indians would catch them there and pin them down in an untenable situation. Other times the ranchers would catch the Indians in a weak position and pin them down. Someone always ran to find the anthropologist, who hurried to the spot to start negotiations. He said he was busier than I might think.

We met each night and shared stories. It was relaxing and good for me to have someone to speak English with. Then one night, an Indian came running around the corner and was relieved when he saw

145

my friend. He ran over to our table, and they spoke quickly. My friend said he had to run, and he and the Indian ran away into the night.

A Trip North of Cuiabá, deep into the Forest

The Regional Peace Corps director arranged for me to spend a few days with an experienced volunteer, Mike. Mike was twenty-two or twenty-three years old and had married a young, beautiful local girl. The volunteer was in his third year and spoke fluent Portuguese. I envied his language ability. He worked in agriculture, supervising a nursery that produced grafted fruit trees which he gave to the pioneer farmers.

Mike confided in me that he was afraid to return to the United States. He had been immersed in Brazilian culture for so long that he was not sure how he would adapt back to the American culture. He was concerned about how his wife would adjust since she did not speak any English and she was attached to her family. She had seen her mother every day of her life. He told me that he was thinking of going to his state's university and majoring in horticulture and then hurrying back to Mato Grosso to get a job doing what he had been doing.

Mike's Peace Corps duties included supervising a couple of dozen workers, some were agronomists, yet Mike had never gone to a university. This was often the case. Peace Corps volunteers often had responsibilities far beyond what they could obtain in the United States. For me, Peace Corps offered four advantages: first, helping people; second, learning to speak fluently a foreign language; third, learning how to live in and understand a culture different from your own; and fourth, gaining responsibility far above what you would see for one or two decades in the US.

Mike's young wife prepared a very tasty meal: black beans, rice, and a small piece of meat accompanied by local cheese. It was simple but perfect. We had an enjoyable conversation, always in Portuguese since Mike had difficulty with English and his wife spoke no English. He spoke it so seldom that he thought and dreamed in Portuguese. We retired to our rooms to sleep early because we had to be up early to travel the next day. I rested on the sofa, although I could not sleep.

I stood and looked out the window. The darkness was complete. There were no streetlights—none. I could not distinguish any objects outside the window. It was absolute darkness.

Early the next morning, we drank strong coffee and ate French bread. We quietly entered the Jeep and drove to an open gas station. It was still dark outside. We filled five cans with gasoline, five gallons each, and situated them in the back. This was an old-style Jeep with a canvas top, like those used in World War II. Mike pulled a blanket from the Jeep, gave it to me, and ordered me to completely soak it in water. After I soaked it in a tank, I handed it to him. With no explanation, he folded it several times and tucked it tightly around all the gasoline cans from bottom to top.

And then we were off into the dark, north of Cuiabá. Mike lived in Diamantino ("small diamond"), which was a couple of hours north of Cuiabá, and we headed north again from there.

He drove and drove, and eventually, the sun came up. The road was no wider than the Jeep and was full of ruts and large pools of water from the recent rains. His ability to maintain his speed under those conditions was possible only if he knew the route well—and he did.

Wilderness had been around us only an hour before, but now it was almost gone. It too was moving north as the pioneers continued their land clearing. On both sides of the road, we saw huge stumps and the remains of unburned trees intermixed with green corn one or two feet tall, growing among the tree remains. As we continued north, the corn became smaller, and the tree remains were larger and larger. Finally, there was no corn, and the farmers had only felled the trees but had not been burned yet. Somehow, the farmers had missed the opportunity to burn, and the rains had arrived, washing the unprotected dark earth away in great volumes. Gullies of assorted sizes were growing visibly larger each day. My heart ached as I watched the conservation nightmare unfold mile after mile. It was a disaster.

Then I smelled and saw smoke but saw no fires. As we proceeded ever farther north, the smoke became denser and stronger in smell. My eyes were watering, and Mike weaved around invisible dangers in the road. It was obvious that he knew every spot in the road. Then I saw the fire. It was on both sides of the road, burning through huge trees. I could see the fire and hear the crackling.

Mike pulled to the edge of the road and carefully tugged at the corners of the wet blanket to ensure that all the spare gas tanks were covered. He asked me to watch that the blanket did not leave any part of any gas tank exposed. I understood and kept a close eye on the tanks. There were sparks blowing in the breeze and falling on the Jeep. It was hot, and our windows were open, as was the back of the Jeep. Sparks were everywhere. Occasionally, one would escape my eye and land on my pants or sleeve, drawing my attention only when I felt the burning sensation on my leg or arm. This was frightening and painful, and we were driving into it. After five miles, the fires stopped, and the smoke cleared. We had made it through the fire alley.

After another half hour, we continued north, but suddenly, the vehicle lost power and rolled to a stop. We stopped in the middle of a huge pool of water created by the rut that was the road. The road was just a bit wider than the vehicle. We stepped from the vehicle without getting our feet wet because the ground was the same level as the Jeep's floorboards.

I knew nothing of the mechanical mysteries of vehicles. I thought we were doomed. I asked how far we were from a gas station or a mechanic, or from anywhere. "About fifty miles," Mike said, but he showed no concern. I was frantic.

Mike stepped onto the front bumper and threw open the hood, which now rested on the windshield. He checked a couple thingamabobs and ordered me to open the cubbyhole to retrieve a screwdriver, which I immediately did. Mike was the most serious Peace Corps volunteer I had ever encountered. He never wasted a word. I watched as he removed the ignition cap and found a doohickey and separated it from the other thingamabobs. He announced, "This is the problem. It's broken."

I remained unconvinced that the problem was so simple. I asked, "How long will it take us to return to civilization?"

He pulled a huge knife from somewhere and began whittling on something while he asked, "Why?"

I said, "Well, if it's broken, do we not have to go buy a part to repair it?"

He said, "Let's walk up the road. There is a house, and we can see if they have any old radio batteries." Then he answered my question. "No, we don't. I can make the part we need."

I kept my mouth shut and tried to keep up because he already was yards ahead of me. On the left we saw a huge pasture and, next to it, a large plantation of cassava. In one corner of the cassava plantation, there was a home garden and next to it was an old shack. The shack had a grass roof and dirt floor, and they used small tree branches to make the walls. Like most rural houses, it had no door. The house was well ventilated. In the field a dozen people, each with a hat, were bent over hoeing a crop. They were all sizes, genders, and ages.

Mike announced that we would try them. As we approached, he explained to me that they were immigrants from Japan and had accumulated four thousand acres of land, of which they cleared a little each year. They produced everything they needed and had purchased only a radio and batteries, because there was no electricity within forty miles. He also said that they had two thousand head of cattle, and the land and animal assets they owned far surpassed a million dollars in value, yet from age three to one hundred, they worked twelve hours a day, wore homemade sandals, and lived in a hut with a dirt floor and see-through walls. They lived poor despite being wealthy. This was the dream that all people from the south had when they migrated to the north. This was everyone's dream.

Mike led me to the oldest gentleman, where he inquired whether the family had any old batteries. The other family members did not stop to watch or listen. They continued their task, which required them to keep their eyes on their plants to avoid mowing them down along with the weeds that surrounded them. Unfortunately, they had no batteries. Mike graciously thanked the man, and we immediately returned to the rutted road.

Mike never slowed his pace. He said, "There is another house a mile or two down the road." And we continued to walk at his fast pace.

Soon, a hut appeared a short way from the road. I followed him to the house. They made the walls from bamboo, with ample cracks for air circulation. There was a doorway but no door. I was concerned about how he would knock. He walked to within ten feet of the house's entrance and stopped. He clapped his hands and yelled, "*Oh de casa!*"

I learned that *oh de casa* was a polite way of knocking on a nonexistent door. It was not a good idea to walk up to a house without a door and knock on whatever was available to knock on. The house owner might take offense at your looking into his home without his permission.

After a second the owner appeared in the doorway and smiled. He took the two steps down, since the house was built two feet off the ground and shook our hands. He noticed that I continued to stand a step behind Mike. He told me not to worry as he waved his hand in the direction of the steps into his house. I did not know what he was talking about. That was when I saw a small bamboo cage located at the side of his steps and, in it, a sizable snake looking straight at me. I jumped back. That was when he really laughed. He was enjoying himself. He told me that the snake was only ten to twelve feet long and was still a baby. He used him for rat control. I noticed that he also did not have any dogs or cats as pets.

Mike quickly turned the conversation to what mattered. The farmer did have an old battery and was happy to donate it to our worthy cause. The gods were smiling because he had just replaced his radio's batteries and had not yet disposed of the old ones. There were two, and Mike asked if he could use both. Mike offered thanks, and we departed. There were no wasted motions by either the farmer or Mike.

We found the Jeep exactly as we had left it. Mike grabbed the old part and looked at it. It was a piece of graphite. He explained that batteries also had a graphite bar inside them. He took out his super knife, opened the battery, and removed the graphite, which he compared to the failed part. He whittled and compared, whittled, and compared. Within five minutes he tried the newly fashioned part. It fit. He replaced all the thingamabobs, closed the hood, and ordered me inside. I was there instantly. He turned the key. The engine fired, and we continued our travels.

Meeting Another Peace Corps Volunteer

Farther down the road, we stopped to visit another Peace Corps volunteer. This PCV was living near a new city that was only six years old but already had 27,000 inhabitants. We found the PCV in his yard, and we all talked a little. This PCV did not seem to be hyper or particularly busy. He and Mike informed me that this region was a new frontier, and no one living in the region now had been here seven years ago. Everyone had come from somewhere else and for varied reasons, but they all had one reason in common: they appreciated the fact that no law and order existed in the region. In the frontier towns, there was no law; therefore, a certain class of citizens favored living there. Everyone was armed with a pistol or knife and knew how to use both—and had used both.

Both PCVs counseled me to avoid card games and drinking in groups, especially with people I did not know well, and to never inquire into the history of any citizen. People did not take kindly to being asked where they came from. If I asked the question, they might suspect me of representing law and order. They preferred the city without law and order since many of the citizens had, at some time, run afoul of it. People had died or disappeared because a local citizen mistook another citizen for a person representing the law.

All three of us crowded into the Jeep and entered this new city. I was fascinated. The houses were all constructed from mahogany planks, mostly unpainted. They raised the floor on each house a couple of feet from the ground, and the space under the floor was surrounded by a lattice of narrow wood. They separated the wall planks by half an inch. This might have helped ventilate the houses. They made the roofs from tile. The city of 27,000 did not have a paved or cobblestoned street. All the roads were dirt. Along the sides of the streets were vehicles parked in all ways, and farmers tied three or four horses to rails placed next to the roads for that purpose.

My companions selected a restaurant, and we entered. They also constructed the floor from wooden planks with half-inch spaces between them. We sat at a table, and a waitress took our orders. The other PCVs were acquainted with people at other tables and had cross-table conversations. I noticed that the men they spoke with wore cowboy hats and had pistols strapped to their waists.

When the meal arrived, we were quick to start eating. In my excitement, I dropped my knife, and it fell through the crack in the floor. I knelt on the floor and lowered my head to see if I could retrieve the knife. Mike yelled at me not to stick anything between the cracks. I looked down, and my eyes widened as I distinctly saw two eyes looking back at me. The guys ordered me back into my chair and quickly fetched the waitress to replace my knife.

I saw from my companions' facial expressions that they had underestimated my stupidity. They explained that the people placed anaconda snakes under the houses to control pests. They limited the snake's movement to the space under the house by the lattices that surrounded the space between the ground and the floor. This arrangement was convenient because it allowed rats to the area under the houses. The snakes were content to stay under their respective houses because their food came to them, and they were always well-fed.

About this time, a waitress with free time was sweeping the floor. She did not need a dustpan because she guided things into the space between the boards. Sometimes she dumped small pieces of food there. They explained to me that the snakes liked only live food, but the bits of food that the waitress swept between the boards attracted rats, which kept the snakes busy.

We returned the local PCV to his house and chatted more there. He and Mike were remembering their early years as volunteers. Mike told of a trip he had made with another PCV in a dugout canoe on a huge nearby river. As Mike paddled, he kept the canoe away from the edges. The new PCV asked him why he did this. Mike said that when he was recently arrived, he had paddled near the shore and under overhead branches. As he was passing under a branch, an anaconda had dropped down and bitten his thigh. Anacondas' bites were not venomous, but they hurt and could become infected. The snakes did this to secure their prey while they dropped down and coiled around them. Since there were two men in the canoe and they both had knives, they were able to ward off the snake. Since then, Mike had always avoided the river's edges.

On another day, the river was extremely hot and humid, and paddling had made the same new PCV hot. On an impulse, he had asked, "Hey, can we stop for a little and swim?"

Mike said no.

The new PCV asked, "But why not? The river is clear. There is no danger. I only have to be careful when I dive to avoid those logs that are deep in the water."

Mike replied, "Those are not logs," and continued paddling.

After returning Mike's friend to his home, we returned to Diamantino. I thanked Mike for his kindness and caught a bus back to Cuiabá. I went to the Peace Corps office for an update on my job. It was not good. The job had disappeared. The Peace Corps director was arranging for me to be transferred to Natal, Rio Grande do Norte: a city located on the beaches in sunny Northeast Brazil. Even better, my director said that within three months he would be transferring to become the regional Peace Corps director in Recife, a city four hours south of Natal. I liked him and knew that I could trust him. I was excited.

Moving to Natal, Rio Grande do Norte

After thirty days in Cuiabá, my job had disintegrated. The Peace Corps informed me that I would have to accept the position in Natal, Rio Grande do Norte, or return home. I was not ready to return home. I looked at Natal on the map. It was extremely far away, but it was indeed on the beach. I thought it might require adjustments from me since Natal had more than a half-million people, but I was a flexible person.

Our regional Peace Corps office was in Recife, Pernambuco, a city of one million people and located on the beach. I flew into Recife from Cuiabá and received my orientation at the Peace Corps office. It was a huge city, but I liked it. Once the Peace Corps resolved all the bureaucratic problems, I was transported four hours to the north along the coast and introduced to my supervising agency. I would be working in the equivalent of our state agricultural extension office.

At the time, I did not know what I was supposed to do, but now, forty-five years later, I understand perfectly: they expected me to do nothing. They expected nothing from me. They wanted nothing from me. They hoped that I would be quiet, invisible, and undemanding and that I eventually would go away. They had so many major problems to resolve that my idiosyncrasies were not high on their list of priorities. They were kind, and they gave me a desk and a chair and asked nothing from me. In exchange, I had a reason to live in Brazil for two years, to learn the language and the culture and even mature more. Looking back, I had a wonderful deal.

I had to find temporary living quarters, so I rented a room in a cheap hotel in the downtown area until I could manage to locate a permanent place. I had to find a place rapidly since the hotel room rates were consuming my living allowance. The cost of living in Natal was much lower than it had been in Cuiabá, but we received a smaller living allowance.

Since I knew no one, I walked around the downtown region alone. The streets were so busy, so full of people. Residents were walking up and down the street, and if they bumped into me, they never said they were sorry. When I bumped into them, they were surprised when I apologized. They stopped to see who had spoken to them. They knew I was from way out of town. People filled the wide sidewalks. In addition, people were standing on the street selling hot dogs, candy, other food, and lottery tickets and begging. Each stationary person interrupted the flow of people and caused a backup, like a wrecked car on an interstate highway.

I entered a large department store. The stores there were different from our stores. The opening to the street ran the full width of the store. Displays were everywhere, with little room for people to walk. People were constantly bumping into each other, with no one taking offense or even noticing. Bumping into other people was as normal as breathing. Customers must be slightly aggressive, or they would go home without purchases. People often knocked merchandise to the floor and trampled on it, but no one noticed.

It was very warm, and I was sweating profusely after walking only a dozen steps. After walking three or four blocks, I returned to my hotel room at noon and took a shower, but it did no good. I was sweating again within minutes. Not only was it hot; it was humid.

I had my clothes crunched up in my suitcases and needed to find someone to wash them. I had my clothes washed by hand. I had to count each item in each laundry batch to be sure that everything was returned. It took a couple of days, but the wash lady always returned my clothes fresh and perfectly ironed.

During this period, I was living mostly on cookies. My living allowance was not large, and if I had eaten in a lunch place, especially all three meals, I would have had no money left after the first week in the month. I went to supermarkets to study their inventory and prices. I noticed how dirty their floors were compared to our supermarkets. They had so many fresh fruits and vegetables. Grapes fell to the floor, and people stepped on them, leaving stains and wet spots. No one was concerned about the untidy floor or that someone might fall. In Brazil customers did not sue businesses for anything. Customers knew the condition of the floors and took preventive action by sidestepping. The store periodically cleaned its floors, just not as often as in the US.

I soon became acquainted with other Peace Corps volunteers living in the city. There were three who were finishing their term and would be leaving in a couple of weeks. They lived in adjoining houses on the beach. The houses were small, four hundred square feet, and old, but they were no more than a few steps away from the beach, and each volunteer could afford his or her own house, if the volunteer lived prudently. I was doing my best to adapt to all the sacrifices required to be a PCV. If it would allow me to live in my own house on the beach, I would make the sacrifice.

My First Day on the Job

On my first day on the job, a manager took me around and introduced me to the other people in the office building, which was a former two-story house. Rooms were small, and most could barely accommodate two desks. Larger rooms could accommodate three or four small desks. The room's walls to which I was assigned were bare, except for an outdated and crooked calendar. The man with whom I would share the space was not there my first day. He appeared on the second day. He was an American from Kearney, Nebraska, a farm boy who had been brought up using scrapers to level land for irrigation. He was about sixty-five years old. He had married a local lady, and they had adopted a girl. He had fought in World War II and had been a POW for three years in Poland. My upbringing was like his. I too was a farm boy who was brought up using scrapers to level land for irrigation. We had much in common.

Not knowing what to do with my time, I tried to read Portuguese books, but I found my language ability still severely lacking. I continued anyway, since my goal was to learn a new word each day.

There were two new volunteers trying to rent the beach houses as the older PCVs vacated them. I quickly visited with the third volunteer and received her blessing to rent her house after she left.

Finally, the day came, and I moved into my new house. I was so happy. I had to buy a mattress, which I threw on the floor. I bought a fan that had a sweeping motion to help me combat the mosquitoes and stay cool at night. I bought all the kitchen pans and equipment in the house from the exiting PCV. I walked to the supermarket and bought bread, cheese, ham, eggs, rice, and beans—all the essentials to survive.

I grew to dislike my lack of work at the state extension service. It was a long walk from my house on the beach to work, two miles or more. With the heat and humidity, I was always sweaty and miserable. On the plus side, I had many good talks with Emil, my American neighbor at work. The Brazilian employees did not seem busy, nor did they seem concerned that they were not busy. They spent most of their time drinking coffee, reading newspapers, and chatting. They would come late to work and leave early. No one cared.

I always hurried home as soon as I could in the afternoon because I could capture time on the beach. I enjoyed playing Frisbee with myself. When there was a strong sea breeze, I could throw the Frisbee into the breeze, and the breeze would bring it back to me. For more exercise, I could throw it at an angle and then run like the devil to catch it. It was like throwing myself a pass in football.

There were few people on the beach at that time, but a handful of people always congregated to watch me play Frisbee. It was beautiful—the sun was setting, people were sitting together on the beach with the breeze blowing their hair, and the bars were turning on their lights and preparing the tables for their evening guests. That was my signal to head home.

I Meet Dick and Mike

My house was located on a small rock outcropping on the beach. The outcropping was wide enough to maintain a street down the center, no more than two or three hundred feet long, with houses on both sides. My friend Dick had a small house on the street. On one side of his house was another house, and on the other was a corridor used by people to reach the beach. It was only six feet wide. This was the same corridor that passed by my house and separated my house from the wall of the nearby bar. This bar stretched from the street to the beach. There was a small, covered area by the street, but most of the bar was outside. There were coconut trees growing there, surrounded by outdoor tables that people always occupied. The spot offered a gorgeous view of the beach and the city, although guests sat under the coconut trees at their own risk.

Next to Dick's house and heading into the corridor were Mike's house and then my house. My house consisted of two bedrooms, each big enough for a small bed and dresser. It also had a small kitchen and living room. The living room was wide enough and long enough to hang a couple of hammocks. I used it for a small picnic table, a hammock, and a couple of easy chairs. Behind the kitchen was an accessible area where the maid did the laundry. There sat a tank, three by four feet and at least three feet deep, that I used to bathe at night under the stars. I had a *cuia*, a half of a gourd, that I used to pour water onto my body. At night, it was cold, but on a sweltering day, it was refreshing.

On Saturday mornings, around nine or ten o'clock, Dick, Mike, and I, along with any other volunteers visiting from other rural sites, would meet at a bar just across the street on the highway that followed the beach. It was already hot, and a cold beer tasted sweet.

The bar's lot was deep and went up a very steep hill. Only the first thirty feet from the street were useful for a business. After that, the hill's slope was too steep. Both sides of the bar consisted of vacant lots filled with weeds, small and large. The bar's owners built a four-foot-high adobe wall to surround their property. As the waiter brought each beer, he would remove the cap and toss it over the wall into the neighbor's lot. Each time he did it, he scared the rats. They would scatter in all directions. We loved watching the weeds part as they ran through them. We always speculated about how large they must have been.

By eleven o'clock the beaches started filling up, and by one o'clock they were full of people. By three o'clock only a dozen people remained. That was when I liked to go to the beach. Once, I was walking along the beach, minding my own business, when a bunch of young ladies lying on the beach started whistling at me and calling me over to them. They scared me, and I ran away. I was not used to that. Brazilian ladies were very forward, and I had not yet become accustomed to that.

I was to learn that the entire northeastern region of Brazil had more women than men. Periodic droughts caused the destruction of the agriculture and livestock production and related employment. This lack of production fed into other industries and led to further unemployment. To find employment, the working-age men moved to São Paulo to find jobs and never returned. Women could not migrate because they had to stay behind with their families. This resulted in more women in the Northeast than men.

David

David was a force of nature. Everyone in the state of Rio Grande do Norte knew David or wanted to know David. He was famous, and everyone loved him. When I had met him during my training in Belo Horizonte, he had presented himself as a quiet, timid man. He had come to our training, given his serious and succinct presentation on horticulture, and left. In Rio Grande do Norte, his image was different.

David was from a New York farm. He had graduated from Cornell University with a master's degree in horticulture and had been one of the first people to join the Peace Corps after its formation. The Peace Corps sent him to Rio Grande do Norte, and after he finished his two-year tour, he had stayed in-country with only a few coins rattling in his pockets. He had begun working for several agro-related companies. For one job, he traveled the countryside buying corn from farmers, which Purina used to manufacture animal feed. He became intimately acquainted with the geography of the state and discovered the best place to farm. He soon had found the perfect little farm with an absentee owner; first, he rented it, and later, he bought it. It was next to the Açu River and three hours' travel by car from Natal. Until David arrived, no one had considered that the river water could be used for irrigation.

David started producing vegetables, and as he produced them, he developed different technological packages for each vegetable. He could not go to the extension service for help because—and I am ashamed to say so—they did not know how to give that help. The technical advice given by the extension system was for states located far away from Rio Grande do Norte, which had quite different soils and climate. David was innovative, optimistic, and self-reliant. He did not attempt any project before he knew it would work. He conducted small test trials to find the optimal technological package for each crop he wanted to produce before he applied it to his farm on a larger scale.

Once he had mastered the technological packages, he sought special markets to obtain the highest price. He found that the offshore oil platforms located off the coast of Natal were perfect. They demanded high-quality food and would pay for it. David could produce it. He secured the contracts and went about producing. All he needed to do was buy an old VW van to make the three-hour trip from his farm to the point of delivery. This was not easy since he had no capital to start his farm. He continued working his jobs during the day and worked the farm at night and on weekends.

David lived in a small, old, three-sided machine shed, where he slept in a hammock slung from two posts. He bathed in the river and ate his meals in bars in town. The town was a half mile from his farm. He ate mostly rice and beans, chased down with ice-cold beer. David loved his beer. His work uniform consisted of a pair of shorts, a light

159

shirt, a pair of sandals, and a floppy hat to keep the sun off his neck and face. His needs were minimal. David was a complex man, but one with simple needs.

He himself grabbed the oxen and ran them up and down the fields to make plow furrows that he used for planting. He threw the harness over his shoulder and grabbed onto the handles attached to the long, sharpened log used to make the furrow. The scene was reminiscent of mid-nineteenth-century Nebraska.

There were days when I heard a knock at my door and was surprised upon opening it to see David. The first thing he asked for was an ice-cold beer. Nothing tasted worse than a moderately cold beer. Brazil's beer always tasted good if it was served ice-cold. My refrigerator was too old and broken-down to keep beer cold; however, I did have a bar next door. All I had to do was open my door, take two steps until I was facing the six-foot-plus wall surrounding the bar, and yell, "*Oh, José, passe duas geladinhas por cima!*" I would hear José grunt a confirmation, and within a minute, two beers would appear on a tray over the wall. I took the beer, placed the money on the tray, and held the tray above the wall until José secured it. David and I could then get down to business.

David always talked about the farm—his crops or his small machinery or new things he was thinking about doing. He always had a new market he wanted to produce for. He dreamed of sending his produce straight to Paris, France. I enjoyed listening to him. David had no concept of time. He might arrive at any time and stay for hours. Indeed, there were times I had to cast him into the night because I needed to sleep to be productive the next day. David could drink until 3:00 a.m. in Natal, make the three-hour drive to his farm, hitch the oxen, and spend all day in the hot sun, making furrows. David had a source of energy that I envied.

One Sunday David knocked loudly on my door. As soon as he knocked, I knew who it was. He knocked aggressively and with purpose. When I opened the door, there was David, except he was wearing a pair of old 1960s-style glasses with thick black plastic rims. A string secured the glasses by a string tied around his neck and attached to the nose part of the glasses frame. He had on a T-shirt, a pair of swimming shorts, and a silly smile. I also noticed seaweed hanging from his ear and his glasses. He entered my house and asked for a beer. I stepped outside and yelled for José, and two cold beers appeared on top of the wall.

David told me that he had been partying on the other side of the river with friends, but they had wanted to take a nap after drinking and eating. David had wanted action, so he had swum across the river where it flowed into the ocean. Depending on what part of the cycle the tide was in, this could be extremely dangerous due to the undertow. David did not seem to mind. David drank a few beers and then disappeared as quickly as he had appeared. He apparently had other places to go.

Making Pizzas

I found an old recipe book lying in a corner of the house, left by the previous PCV, and within it I found a recipe for pizza. I decided to try it and made a trip to the supermarket. The sacks of ingredients were heavy to carry home since they included flour, a small ham, and tomato paste and sauce, but I powered through the walk. When I reached my house, I needed a cold beer to start, so I did the "one cold one over the wall" routine, and José obliged.

I struggled with the dough, but I blindly followed the directions. While I waited for the dough to rise, I mixed the sauce ingredients and cut the ham into small pieces. The ham was the most expensive ingredient and nearly broke my bank. It put me in emergency mode for the rest of the month. When the dough was right, I stretched it into the pan and spread the sauce over it, and into the oven it went.

I made my first pizza in secret. I did not want to have guests over and have nothing to feed them if my experiment failed, but it did not fail. When I took the pizza out of the oven, it was beautiful and exuding wonderful smells. I ran to see if Dick and Mike were home. I wanted to share my good fortune and a cold beer with them.

Alecrim on Market Day

Alecrim was an old town that Natal had grown up around and absorbed. It was at least three hundred years old. Its streets were all narrow, constructed from uneven cobblestone that required people to look down as they walked to avoid stumbling. The sidewalks were narrow, often insufficiently wide for a person to walk. The houses were narrow as well and shared walls on the sides. Most houses were just wider than was needed to stretch a hammock, but they went deep into the block. On any day of the week, the streets were alive with people, but one day a week, the streets were jammed: that was market day in Alecrim.

In larger cities, each small town inside the city had its own market day. Each market had its own specialties, such as fabrics or cooking utensils or spices, but all markets had the basics. I loved going to Alecrim on its market day, especially if I was feeling lonely or depressed. The colors of Alecrim were astonishing. So many people walked through the streets, and they dressed in bright colors. In addition to the people, there was the merchandise: clothing, fabrics, plastic materials, fruits, vegetables, and spices. It was a color festival that would elevate anyone's spirit.

Each store spread its wares outside its narrow store space. Those wares tumbled onto the sidewalk and even spilled into the street itself. There was a sound fest as well. The store workers yelled and waved their arms, trying to attract the attention of people walking by. The scraping of cartwheels and the clank of shoed horse feet against the cobblestones interrupted the screaming of street hawkers.

People walking in the streets constantly bumped into other people while trying to find what they were looking for. They had to dodge other people doing the same. Porters were scurrying back and forth while carrying large loads on their backs. Other porters were bringing merchandise to the stores to be sold yet that day. It was chaos. I would usually buy mangoes or papaya or cashew fruits or pineapples to take home with me. The fruits were all soft from ripeness and emitting their fragrances. I never wanted to go home, but my legs and arms eventually tired, and I had to find a bus.

Learning to Dance the Samba in Brazil

Upon my return, I decided to apply my new knowledge of dancing the samba. On the first Saturday night, I took a bus to the nightclub and waited for the partying to start. People did not start to enter the club until around 11:00 p.m. The dancing was great after 1:00 a.m. I noticed a shapely blonde enter with two companions whom I deduced to be her sister and brother. After watching them for ten minutes, I was convinced I was right. I stood and approached her table. I gathered all my courage and asked her to dance. She seemed happy to accept. She had a wonderful smile that revealed her soul—it was a happy soul.

I discovered immediately that she was a motivated dancer. She placed her arms around my neck. I was not sure what to do, so I grabbed her waist. She was already into the beat of the music, and her hips were moving around like a washing machine in the middle of a spin cycle, only she was going up and down as well as around and around. I was not so much dancing as hanging on. As she tossed me around the dance floor, I tried to relax and enjoy it, but my main concern was not being thrown into other people or a wall. Her hips were moving in ways I could only imagine because I was too close to see what she was doing. I tried to look around to determine if anyone was laughing, but no. To other people, everything we were doing seemed natural. I had no chance of showing her my moves.

After three or four dances, she invited me to her table. Since people had taken over my table, I decided to accept. I explained to her that I did not know how to dance but wanted to learn. I am sure that she was already aware of that, but she was not concerned. She was happy that she had an opportunity to dance and that I was capable of hanging on or following. She asked a few questions: Who was I? What was I doing in Brazil? Did I miss my family? And then we returned to the floor to dance again.

Later, we agreed to meet again the following Saturday at 11:00 p.m. And so, it came to be that we met every Saturday night at 11:00 p.m. There was no way that I could apply the samba that I had learned in my private lessons in the US. Once, when I tried, my partner asked me what I was doing. I told her that I had learned to do the samba while I was in the US. She told me to stop it. She advised me to feel the music and follow the rhythm. The problem was that I had no rhythm. In the end, I clung to her waist and tried not to lose her on the dance floor. She was fun to dance with and nice to look at.

One day when the four of us (her sister and brother were always present) were sitting at the table, she started asking me personal questions. Did I have a girlfriend in the US? Did I like Brazilian women? After more questions, I realized that she wanted to take our relationship to the next level. That was not in my game plan. She next asked what my religion was. I said that I was a *macumbeiro* (a voodoo priest). Her face tightened in surprise. She had not expected that, not from an American. Her smile became forced. She was very trusting of people, so it never occurred to her to ask me if I was telling the truth. She could never imagine otherwise. Then, stupidly, I added for emphasis, "And if you ask any more questions, I will turn you into a frog." I smiled, thinking I was funny. She did not smile. Her enthusiasm quickly diminished, and we soon parted ways.

The next week, I was at the nightclub by 10:00 p.m. and claimed a small table. When 11:00 p.m. came, I started to look for my dance partner, but she did not appear. By midnight, I wanted to dance. I could not just get up and dance without losing my table. Also, it was customary for men to carry purses, or *capangas*, in which they stored their money, photographs, car keys, cigarettes, passport, and other official documents. I had one and had become dependent on it. I could not dance with it; it was too large. I could not leave it on the table, or I would lose both the table and the *capanga*. I was stuck.

I Meet Katia and Vania

I started looking around to see if I knew anyone so that I could join their table. This way, I could leave my *capanga* on their table for them to watch, and I could find someone to dance with. I strained to survey the club for anyone I might recognize. There, across the room, was a guy I knew. He was with two girls. He was a good guy, but I did not like him much because he was always talking about women as his conquests, and he used foul language to do it. I thought that the two girls he was with were ladies of the night or at least had loose morals, and I only wanted to dance.

I grabbed my *capanga* and headed toward his table. To avoid meeting the ladies, I greeted the guy, asked permission to place my *capanga* on his table, nodded toward the ladies, and kept walking. I went to another side of the room and stood against the wall, trying to spot a suitable lady with whom I could dance. Yards away, I saw a pretty girl also standing against the wall and not dancing. After a short wait, I decided it was safe to approach her. I needed to make sure that she was not accompanied. Her partner might have been taking a bathroom break. When Brazilian men took a bathroom break and returned to find someone hitting on their woman, they could become very volatile. It was always better to be extra cautious than get into a fight.

I approached the young lady and asked if she was accompanied. She was not. I asked if she would like to dance. She said no. I thought, *what are you doing in a nightclub if you do not want to dance?* I asked her why she did not want to dance. She replied that she did not know how. I had thought all Brazilian women knew how to dance. *What is this?* I wondered. I asked her again. She said she could not dance because she was working. I did not understand and insisted she try to dance. She agreed. Unfortunately, she truly did not know how to dance. That was when I started to understand what she had meant when she had said she was "working." For you innocents, like I was, she was a lady of the night advertising her charms in a nightclub filled with drunken men.

Embarrassed, I made my way back to my friend's table with my tail between my legs. I asked for permission to join them and pulled up a chair. They were laughing because they had seen my performance as I tried to find a dance partner. Conversation was difficult because I had not made a good impression on the two young ladies. In fact, later I learned that they considered me rude, crude, and arrogant, but they were willing to smile at me and conduct a small amount of pleasant conversation, out of respect for social etiquette, which did not allow them to speak their mind or be disrespectful in any way.

I learned that the two girls were sisters. The younger one was still studying at the University of João Pessoa, located in the neighboring state. She was majoring in psychology and was home on vacation. All I could manage to learn was that their names were Katia and Vania, and they lived just off the town square by the city auditorium, where the city held concerts. In fact, the next week there was to be a concert there by a pop star known all over Brazil. The two sisters showed no interest in further contact with me. I had really made a bad first impression.

During the next week, I pondered what I should do. I decided to venture up to their neighborhood and try to locate their house. I walked down the street at night, trying to remain in the shadows because I did not want anyone to see me. I looked into the open-doored houses until I spotted one of them. I wanted to go say hi, but I was very shy and returned home, angry at myself for being such a weakling.

I had an idea. I could prepare a nice pizza sauce and take it to their house. We could make the crust there, and everyone could enjoy a nice slice of pizza. For me, this was an expensive endeavor because the sauce ingredients were costly, especially the pork, but I would do it. The next day, when I left work, I swung by the supermarket, bought the ingredients, and happily lugged them home.

On Saturday, I hailed a taxi to help me carry my cooking pot and all my ingredients to Katia and Vania's house. I had the taxi drive a little past the house. Their father was rocking in a chair on the front porch, like a sentry determined to protect his daughters, and I needed to exit the taxi and collect my things and myself before facing the sentry.

Struggling with the weight in the huge pan, I approached the porch and tried to smile, though I do not think it showed. I asked if Katia and Vania were home. The man yelled for his wife to come out and take care of the inconvenience. A short, happy woman appeared while drying her hands on an apron. I tried to explain how I had met her daughters and that I had brought ingredients for a pizza, which I had hoped to make with Katia and Vania. She smiled and motioned for me to enter the house. She guided me into the kitchen area and asked me to sit down. She relieved me of the pizza ingredient pan and set it on a table.

The mother's name was Naide. I called her Dona Naide as a sign of respect. We liked each other immediately. I asked for Katia and Vania, and she informed me that regrettably, they were attending the Rita Lee concert and would be back in an hour or so.

I explained how I normally made pizza. She nodded and reached for a cutting board and a knife, both of which she pushed toward me. I started cutting the peppers, onions, garlic, pork, and other ingredients. She was busy doing something else, and then suddenly, there was a sizzle from a pan that had appeared on the stove burner. She took the sauce ingredients, pushed them around in the pan, and stirred a little before turning the stove off.

She reached for the flour, and without the benefit of any cookbook, including the one I had brought for my guidance; Dona Naide produced the most beautiful crust I had ever seen. Now we just needed the girls to bring the crust and sauce together for twenty minutes in the oven.

To say that Katia and Vania were surprised to see me in their house would be an understatement. Seeing me in the kitchen and on good terms with Dona Naide was more shocking. We talked and ate the most delicious pizza I had ever tasted. Dona Naide was an expert chef. I was able to break down a few barriers that my behavior in the nightclub had raised. My interest was in the younger daughter, Katia. Yet, she showed no special interest in me, but when I asked if I could visit again, Dona Naide replied that I should come anytime I wanted. I felt a little better. I had won over the mother; now I just had to worry about Katia and her father, José. Out of respect, I must call him Seu (Mr.) José.

Seu José was going to be a tough nut to crack. I learned that he was retired military. He was regimented in everything he did. He had served through the communist rebellion in the late 1950s and early 1960s, and he was not a fan of anyone wearing a beard. The sight caused him flashbacks to the revolution, especially in the case of foreigners with beards because they were the ones who had instigated the revolution. Unfortunately, I had a beard. Katia let this information about her father leak in one of our private conversations because she still wished that I would stop stalking her. But she could not just tell me that because her mother liked me. I had a powerful ally. There was no bond more powerful between a daughter's mother and suitor than that formed over making a pizza from raw ingredients.

I started visiting Katia two and then three times a week. We would go for short walks around three or four city blocks. She lived in the downtown area, so there was always much to see. We also stayed at her house and talked. Dona Naide constantly served me orange juice or an avocado milkshake or cashew juice. I loved all of them, but cashew juice was the best. Katia had two older sisters. Vania was a couple of years older than Katia, and Tania was a couple of years older than Vania. Tania was a journalist and worked for the government. Vania was a teacher but worked in community development for the government. During this time Seu José remained on the periphery, acting like he was indifferent, but he was not. He heard, or was told, everything that happened or was said. As the head of the household, he was in charge. Luckily for me, Dona Naide was his trusted consultant.

Carnival

Carnival was approaching. Carnival, to my mind, is not the equivalent of Mardi Gras. After I experienced my first Carnival, I realized that the Brazilians were professional partiers. The New Orleans Mardi Gras celebrators were amateurs. Carnival was a period of six days (Friday to Wednesday) of absolute debauchery. The entire country stockpiled beer to avoid running out during Carnival, but they always ran out near the end anyway. Married men could go on escapades with anyone they chose, as could women, although only a small group took advantage. You could dress anyway you wanted. If you wore a mask, then no one would know who you were, and your silly and obnoxious behavior could not be associated with you. You were free to be stupid for six days. There were many hookups and instances of micro-dating during Carnival.

Friends formed groups to celebrate Carnival together. Party goers called these groups blocks. Everyone in the block dressed alike, for the purpose of helping each member recognize other members of the group. When Carnival was in full bloom, people were known to become intoxicated, in some cases very intoxicated. It was important that when members saw another member falling, they give that person a shoulder to lean on. They could not leave a fallen comrade behind. If one block member lost his or her sense of direction and started to wander off to follow the beat of a different drum, another block member should catch the wanderer by the belt and redirect him or her back to the block.

To help themselves stay together, members of a block often tied a rope to form a large enough circle for all the members to hold onto the rope as they danced to the music. If any member fell by the wayside, his or her neighbors should notice and reattach the member to the rope. The block also discouraged nonmembers from attaching themselves to the rope.

There were small groups of drummers who wandered the streets, beating samba music with a rhythm that attracted people to dance. Each musical group attracted its own following as it meandered through the streets. When people tired of that music, they pulled aside to drink and wait for another group to come by.

There were trucks that they had converted into large, mobile sound systems. They positioned all the speakers on the first story. These could be six or more feet high and were located on the two sides and back of the truck. People herd the sound they produced many blocks, even a mile. There was a platform on top of the speakers, a second story. This was where the musicians and the control for the speakers were located. There were also very bright lights in all directions that blinked to attract people and encourage them to follow the trucks as they wandered slowly through the city.

The crowds that followed these trucks were densely packed. Everyone was drinking. People sometimes stopped briefly to drink a beer, or they might have hard liquor placed in a flask strapped around their neck, and then they would return to their jumping and screaming.

The trouble with dancing in the streets was that anyone could do it. Poor people from the barrios were there, and some were intent on robbing whatever they could. Revelers simply had to be aware. Since people spent hours jumping up and down, they minimized everything they carried with them. Usually, they carried a little money in a secure pocket and their native drink flask. That was all.

People "jumped" Carnival only in clubs. People used the term "jump" because that was mostly what the Carnival dance was: jumping up and down for six days. It was not for the weak. That was why our city of Natal had a warm-up in September with a long weekend. Everyone drank and danced to start to get into shape for Carnival. Then in December there was a longer period in which people started to build up their resistance for both jumping and drinking. Again, Carnival was and is not for the weak. It requires physical and mental strength to have a good Carnival.

Katia, Vania, four or five other people, and I formed our own block. We bought fabric and decorated it so we could easily recognize each other. Our block rested in the early afternoons at Katia's house. Dona Naide served us energy drinks made from mangoes, oranges, avocados, cashews, watermelon, cantaloupe, and a host of other fruit. I know that each day she went to the market early to stock up on fresh fruit for us. She was enjoying the experience as much as we were. These were happy moments. The group laughed, joked, and talked while we consumed the fruit juices. Then in early afternoon we wandered into the streets and jumped a little to warm up for the evening's ordeal. People were everywhere, and all with happy faces—not one sourpuss in the bunch. That was Carnival: happy times.

We separated from dark until about 10:00 p.m. to try to nap and eat something. I seldom could do more than close my eyes. I had no appetite for anything other than sodas or juices. We reconvened at Katia's house at 10:00 p.m., and from there we all went to the nightclub and started our jumping, which continued until the sun came up. Exhausted, we each went to our own home and tried to nap until about noon. Napping was no easy task because Carnival never stopped. Music played constantly and everywhere, and people were always dancing and drinking and shouting. Rest was only a dream. The beat of Carnival was in the air and could not be escaped.

At sunup on Ash Wednesday, the band led everyone out of the nightclub where we were celebrating and into the dawn. We went to our cars and on to the beach, where we all dived into the waves. It was a tradition to mark the end of Carnival. I was ready for it to be over.

A Nightclub in João Pessoa

Although Carnival ended Wednesday morning, Brazil did not start to move until the following Monday, and then just barely. Katia had returned to her university in João Pessoa, the capital city of the state of Paraiba, about two hours south of Natal. I was lost without being able to visit her.

On Friday night after Carnival, I took a bus and traveled to João Pessoa to visit her. She found a place for me to stay that night, and we spent the next day together. On Saturday night, she and I accompanied a friend of hers and the friend's fiancé to a nice nightclub, where we found a small table. Since we were two couples, one couple could maintain the table while the other couple danced. The dance floor was crowded, which had the advantage of facilitating close dancing. It was a night that I could not have imagined even in my best dreams. It was perfect, and Katia did not seem to remember our clumsy first meeting.

The Engagement

After knowing Katia for no more than thirty days, I proposed to her. She took a week to decide, and then we had to break her acceptance to her parents. Her mother was incredibly happy, but Seu José would be no pushover. I was nervous and had done much rehearsing. He had made no attempt to lessen the strain in our relationship over the few weeks that I had known Katia. He had kept his distance and not joined in any of the fun we were having.

On the night of the deed, I grabbed another rocking chair that Dona Naide had inside the door, carried it out to the porch, and parked it next to Seu José's chair. I placed it parallel to his chair but at a respectful distance. I synchronized my rocking to his gait. He gave a "good evening" to me, and I returned the greeting to him. After four or five minutes of silence, I just blurted my question, asking him for permission to marry Katia. He remained silent for a couple of minutes and continued to stare forward, as did I, although my heart was in my throat. He asked if I had asked Katia and, if so, what she had said. I told him that yes; I had asked her and that she had agreed. He asked if I had told Dona Naide. I told him that I had and that she approved. Then, he said, he also would approve. I stood, shook his hand, thanked him profusely, and then shook his hand again and ran into the house. He must have thought that Katia was marrying an idiot. The ladies were sitting close enough to the porch to have heard, but far enough away to be discreet. They were already smiling and hugging each other. What a day! Seu José continued rocking and staring straight ahead. He was adjusting.

It was late February, and I would leave for the US for graduate school in May. We had to be married before then. Her parents needed time to prepare for a wedding—to obtain a date in a church, to rent a reception hall, and to save the money to pay for it all. After much work and calling in of favors, the date was set for May 8, 1976.

To square things with the church, the priest had to collect data from us. For Katia, that was easy, but for me, not so much. The first question was difficult: what was my address? I did not know. I did not receive mail at my house. So, I returned home and found someone walking on the outcropping on which my house was located. I asked what it was called. The person said Bat's Point. *Okay, that is a start*, I thought. I went to the six-foot-wide corridor that led from the center of the outcropping into the sea. I asked someone what that was, and he told me, "Corridor of the Sexual Perverts." *Okay*, I thought again. My house was the third house in the corridor. I returned to the padre and told him that I had discovered my address. He perked up, smiled, and looked at his secretary, who prepared to type my response. I announced that I lived on "Bat's Point, Corridor of the Sexual Perverts," and that I was pervert number three. The secretary tried to contain a smile and looked at the padre for guidance. He gave a holy smile and said that he would fill that in later.

I had one good friend at CEPA (in English, the State Commission for Agricultural Planning), where I now worked. He was a young economist, married with a baby. He agreed to be my best man. He invited Katia and me to his house so that I could call my family and tell them of my engagement. That would be his gift to us since these calls were expensive. I remember that Katia and I sat on a long sofa, with Eduardo and his wife sitting in chairs to my right. They had served us coffee and had completed the required small talk when Eduardo handed me the phone and told me to dial away. I did.

After a short wait, Mom answered. She was shocked because we had never spoken on the phone while I was in Brazil, although I had been home only six weeks before. I told Mom that I was engaged. She was speechless. I had not had a girlfriend six weeks earlier. Suddenly, I felt strange and looked to my left, where Katia used to be, and she was at the far end of the sofa, looking at me like I was from Mars. This was the first time she had heard me speaking English, and it was like I was another person, one she did not know.

I had no suit. Katia and Vania drove me to a store that sold suits, especially those needed for marriages. They introduced me to a couple of clerks and left me so that they could do some serious shopping themselves. First, the clerks offered me a *batida*, a strong drink of fruit juice mixed with a native alcoholic drink made from sugar cane. Who was I to be discourteous? I accepted. Popular additions to the firewater included lemons, cashew fruit, and mango. The clerks offered me a peanut *batida*. It was so cold with small pieces of ice. It was delicious. The clerks brought so many suits for me to see. I hated trying on clothes, but as long as they kept serving me *batidas*, I would look at them. An hour later, Katia and Vania returned. They were surprised that I was having trouble standing, but I was incredibly happy. They asked if I had found a suit. I had. They asked to see it. They were not happy. Katia had not envisioned me in a blue, black, and white checkered suit. I had to start all over, and this time Katia and her sister stayed to stand guard.

The Yacht Trip

Natal had a yacht club located where the ocean met the river. The club itself was located on the river. Once yachts found the river, all they had to do was go upstream a little and dock. It was a small club because not many yachts were around, but one day a huge two-masted yacht came up the river and docked. My memory of its dimensions is foggy, but it could have been twelve feet by sixty feet. Its owner, a thirty-year-old Canadian who had his hair tied neatly in a long ponytail, never smiled.

We PCVs eventually met everyone who sailed into port. First, we were always traveling down the beach toward the yacht club, and second, the yacht captains and their crews were always seeking a pleasant beach located close to their yacht: that was our beach. It was inevitable that we would meet.

It did not take long for the yacht's captain and us to meet and end up in a bar trading stories. The Canadian captain had already spent a couple of years traveling around the world from port to port. He had just arrived from South Africa. He was going to Fortaleza and then on up Brazil's coast and eventually into the Caribbean Sea. After that, he had no idea.

He mentioned that he was one man short on his journey from Natal to Fortaleza and asked if any of us were interested. I was, but I had to get permission from my supervising agency. My supervisors happened to be okay with it since they did not want to be bothered with me anyway. I was going to Fortaleza by yacht.

We sailed out of port late in the afternoon, with dark clouds covering the skyline over the water. We were sailing into rain. The captain took the first watch at the helm. It was his job to take us out to sea and set the course toward our destination. Another crew member was at the stove making supper. I was hungry. Yet another crew member was checking things on deck.

The captain told me that everyone had to take a turn at the helm and at cooking. The shifts were four hours long. There were eight bunks below where we could retire to wait for our shift, but I did not spend much time there initially. The motion of the yacht made me queasy and uneasy. I spent most of my time on deck, where I had the benefit of the sea breeze.

Sometime during the night, the captain called me for my turn at the helm. My orientation consisted of the captain pointing to a six-inch-long thick thread tied ten feet up onto a rope. The sea breeze kept it horizontal on the left side of the rope. The captain told me to keep it flying on the left. He added emphatically, "Never allow it to drop," and went below deck.

I did not feel confident, but I did what he told me for four hours. There was a full moon, and it was enjoyable to watch it and its reflection on the water. I loved hearing the yacht pound against the waves as it plowed its way north to Fortaleza. I was in heaven, even if I could not be certain that I may be about to send us all into a pile of rocks on the coast.

When it came to my turn at cooking, the orientation was equally as brief. The captain showed me the stove, the pans, and the store of food and condiments. Not being an experienced cook, I decided on scrambled eggs and rice. The stove had a wire guard around it about one inch from the stove's surface. I learned that was to keep the pans from sliding onto the floor as the stovetop moved up and down and sideways with the motion of the yacht. I used a larger-than-normal pan for the rice, so I did not have to fill it beyond half full, which allowed the water inside the pan to move about with the motion of the yacht without overflowing.

As for the eggs, I reasoned that if I heated the pan fully before pouring in the beaten eggs, they would stick to the pan before they had a chance to roll out of the pan and onto the floor. I was worried that the crew would complain because I was not a particularly good cook, but they did not. They ate quickly and quietly and even complimented me. They were simply happy they had not had to cook.

After a couple of days, we sailed into port at Fortaleza. I shook hands with everyone, caught a taxi to the bus depot, and waited for a bus to leave for the eight-hour trip to Natal. I stayed seated while waiting because whenever I stood, the ground moved in a wavy motion that made it difficult for me to stand without putting my hands out to stabilize myself against invisible walls. People stared at me, so I sat down.

The trip back to Natal was not as enjoyable as the trip up. It was extremely hot and slow. I just wanted to be back at my little house, where I could go into my backyard and use the *cuia* to take a wonderful bath from the water tank and then sleep.

The Marriage

The day arrived. I awoke midmorning and showered. I put on my suit, but instead of dressing in my good shoes, I put on a pair of old, dirty tennis shoes. My best man came by to pick me up and drove me to Katia's house, where I intended to play a practical joke on her. Her house was long and narrow. On one side was the living room, kitchen, and an area to wash clothes and dry them on a line. On the other side, without the benefit of any corridor, were the bedrooms. The bedrooms were all connected, which reduced privacy, but it was the way they constructed the houses at that time.

The house was bursting with people and activity. The bride needed a huge support system. All I had to do was to exit my best man's car, and I immediately heard the gasp when one girl noticed my shoes. Her gasp spread to the next girl and the next until the sound went deep into the house. Then the gasps came back through the bedrooms until they reached the bedroom next to the street, whereupon I heard Katia shout, "Lyyyyynnnnn, take those shoes off this minute! Where are your dress shoes?" I responded that they did not fit, and all I had were my tennis shoes. Katia was starting to have a fit when I heard Dona Naide say, "Now what is important? Is it the shoes he wears or the act of getting married? He can get married barefoot. No one cares." I loved Dona Naide. She was my favorite person in the world.

My job was done. I returned to the car and exchanged my tennis shoes for my dress shoes, and we went to the church to wait for the bride.

Once we were at the church, I took my place near the altar. People were arriving and being seated. Soon, Dona Naide was standing near me. The padre appeared and reminded me that the bride had to arrive on time because there was another wedding after ours. We could have no delays. I smiled and shrugged my shoulders.

As the time approached, my best man and I were in position, as were the bridesmaids. The padre again looked at his watch. Dona Naide noticed this and told him that Katia would be arriving immediately. The padre said he could wait only twenty minutes before he would have to cancel the wedding. I told the padre that he was more than generous; I could wait only ten minutes. Then I would cross the street and have a cold beer at a nice outdoor bar located under huge shade trees. The padre shrugged his shoulders and announced that he would join me. Dona Naide pleaded with us to be patient. I felt guilty for pushing Dona Naide's buttons. She did not deserve that, but it was so easy.

Katia was ten minutes late. The wedding proceeded without a hitch until they told me that I could kiss the bride. The photographer was there, ready to capture that important moment. We leaned in for the kiss, but at the last moment I pulled back and extended my right hand. When Katia saw my hand, she instinctively reached out to grab it, and we shook hands. Katia was a bit confused. The photographer took his photograph and spent his flashbulb. We then kissed, and the photographer swore loudly because he had not been able to replace his flashbulb fast enough to take the picture. He had no photograph of the kiss. But that moment of levity served to break all the tension that had surrounded the wedding. People started talking and laughing, and the fun began.

Chapter 14

I returned to the USA and worked three years on a PhD when Katia became pregnant. She informed me that she wanted to have the baby with her family in Brazil. We moved to Brazil, and I started to look for a job. I eventually found one with CEPA (The State Commission for Agricultural Planning).

Becoming Sick

It was Christmastime, 1980. Every year CEPA had a party at Christmas. We were all expected to attend. Even though I was never sociable, Katia and I had to go.

I had been tired for a week, but that night I was even more tired than usual. I was exhausted. Midway through the party, I had to beg forgiveness from our host. I was not feeling well. I had to go home to rest. I felt myself wanting to lie on the floor. I felt like my body weighed a ton. I nearly turned the driving over to Katia, but she still had a grudge against the van.

When we arrived home, I pulled off my clothes and lay face down on the bed with my arms and legs stretched out. I felt dead. The next morning, I did not want to get up. I did not feel rested, and I had a severe headache. When I walked, I had to take tiny steps to minimize body movement and migraine pain. I could no longer lie down because it caused a throbbing pain in my head. I could rest only by sitting up in the bed. I was miserable. That was Saturday morning.

On Monday I called in sick to work and managed to get a doctor's appointment. Seu José drove, and Dona Naide balanced me on her shoulder. The doctor found that I had hepatitis. He ordered thirty days of absolute rest and said my diet needed to consist of only sweets. I could eat all the candy I wanted, and piles of pancakes soaked in syrup, plus ice cream. I thought that the doctor must be crazy, but he was the doctor, right?

What a wonderful disease to have, at least once we controlled the headache. The only problem was that I was at the peak of contagiousness, and in addition to our having eleven-month-old Kevin, Katia was eight months pregnant with Nick. Happily, Katia's family jumped in to take care of me and keep me separate from Katia and Kevin. The doctor believed that I had contracted hepatitis from conducting my milk study. I had to suspend it.

Part-Time Consulting

David, the American farmer in Rio Grande do Norte, had thrived while I was in the US working on my doctorate. He had teamed up with the Algodoeira São Miguel to produce cottonseed for them. An English firm owned the Algodoeira. It was the world's largest producer of sewing thread. The company was fond of long-fiber cotton, which Egypt and Northeast Brazil produced. Most Brazilian production of this cotton occurred several states north of Rio Grande do Norte, but Rio Grande do Norte had the perfect soil and climate to produce the seed required for large-scale long-fiber cotton production.

David had access to large areas of irrigated soil located next to the Açu River. He also had the expertise to manage the large quantity of resources needed to produce a good crop every time. The Algodoeira and David made an agreement: The Algodoeira would finance the production and provide the land, and David would manage the resources and produce the crop. They had already been doing this for a year or so and were in the process of expanding the production area. David needed to know his costs and control his costs. For cash-flow purposes, he needed to know how much he had spent week by week. The Algodoeira was holding him accountable for the money they were advancing to finance the production, and he had to show the company where every dollar went and when he spent it.

I agreed to collect the data David needed. I created all the data forms necessary for such reports, and David allowed me to interview a dozen employees to find some who were sufficiently literate and willing for me to train them to collect data.

I taught David's new record-keepers to fill in the forms each day. We needed to know what tractors and implements the employees used and how long they used them. We needed the same information on all labor. We needed to know about fertilizer, insecticides, and other chemicals. Cotton production was labor-intensive, so this was no small task. The employees were not accustomed to writing anything down; most were illiterate and had no idea how important each detail was. Obtaining reliable numbers was going to be a large task.

Each Friday night, I traveled the three hours to David's farm, where I checked the records and collaborated with the employees who were collecting the data. It took more than a month before we were collecting data that was accurate. After a couple of weeks, I started taking preliminary reports to David. I checked the quality of the new data collected and returned on Sundays to Natal. On Mondays, I was back at CEPA.

This routine was very exhausting but necessary. Even my job at CEPA did not generate enough income for us to save any money. Our growing family required more cash. Brazil's inflation did not help. Inflation that had started out at seven percent per month turned into eight percent, then nine and then ten percent. Even seven percent inflation monthly turned into 225 percent annually. Goods costing one hundred dollars at the beginning of the year would cost 225 dollars by the end of the year. Our salaries increased only four times a year. During the last months of the year, we had to be on a tight budget.

David still did not have a house on the farm. He and I slept in hammocks strung up in a three-sided machine shed. The mosquitoes were horrible, but it was nice to sleep outside, even if it was hot. One Saturday night we got into our swimming trunks and went to the river to bathe. There was a gentle current. It was relaxing to stand with the water up to my lower chest. I allowed myself to float slowly downstream. It was heaven.

We put on clean clothes and went to David's usual bar in town, where he ordered beers. I was starving. After a couple of hours had passed and David had drained several beers, I decided I would not wait for David any longer, and I ordered food. I had consumed only one beer but already had a severe migraine headache from lack of food and from spending the day in the hot sun. I should not have waited so long to order. I had been waiting for David's lead, but it had not ever come. I learned to fend for myself.

The most difficult part of cotton production was the harvest. It was done by hand, and David had hundreds of acres ready for harvest. That year he contracted 1,100 people to pick cotton. They came from all over the region, and many were not upstanding citizens. My problem was this: I had to formulate a method for tracking how many kilograms of cotton each person picked each day. At noon on Saturdays, all picking stopped, and the 1,100 people would line up and expect immediate payment, in cash, and with exact change. Their goal was to hurry to the Açu market before all the sellers sold all the good fruits and vegetables. Before we could pay them, we needed to sum each employee's dumps of cotton, which we had only just obtained, into the wagon. It all took time, making the waiting employees restless.

To organize the labor, David selected twenty to thirty bosses, with fifty or so workers reporting to each boss. When David hired the workers, he gave them a sequential number from one to 1,100. I printed these numbers on thick paper using my computers and then had each number plasticized. We punched a hole through each ID and a chain strung through the hole to hang around the picker's neck, like dog tags in the army. Each time the workers dumped their cotton, they showed their number to their boss, witnessed the weighing, and initialed beside the record that they agreed with the assigned weight. We could not have discussions or disagreements about how much cotton each worker had picked on payday. Payday had to run smoothly, every time.

I needed to provide David with a list of how many bills and coins of each denomination he would need each Saturday. He needed this information by Wednesday. I had to find a way to estimate these numbers. For an added level of security, I needed to increase the number of smaller bills and coins to guarantee that no matter what a worker's final wage, we could immediately provide payment in exact change.

To obtain this quantity of cash, David would go to all the banks in Natal and take all the cash they could spare. His bank would then send a request to São Paulo to have the remainder sent on the next day's flight. This was a massive operation. Very few operations in Natal used 1,100 employees, and they could pay their employees by check. The cash payroll for 1,100 people was gigantic. It could also be a target for thieves.

On-site, David opened multiple tents to service the enormous number of pickers more quickly. Each tent managed a range of ID numbers. David had two men with machine guns guarding the money in each tent. We could not underestimate how juicy a target for theft his operation was. A full week's payroll for 1,100 men could entice many people to try to steal the money. On Saturday, there might have been more cash on that farm than in all of Natal's banks.

Having the correct change under those conditions was difficult. After one Saturday, I convinced David to revise the next payday to include work done from Monday to Friday night. That would give me Friday night and Saturday morning to tally how much each worker was to receive on Saturday. It was not enough time to improve our early estimate for the quantity of bills and coins ordered from São Paulo, but we at least would know how much each person was to receive earlier.

The following week, we change the pay week to run from Saturday to Thursday night. And then the next week, the pay week would be from Friday to Wednesday night. This gave us the chance to obtain exact change from the banks. In future years, the business would implement this procedure from the start of the picking season.

This project was a large one, with much money invested and flowing through David's hands. As soon as David finished the harvest and his workers had collected the data, I presented David with his final report. I broke his operation into a dozen major categories and one hundred subcategories. To avoid a massive report, I summarized costs into two-week periods from the beginning until the workers had picked the last cotton boll. It was beautiful. I was immensely proud.

Eventually, David had to present this report to the Algodoeira. He was nervous, but he presented the same report I had given him, and they loved it. I was not aware at the time, but the Algodoeira had other producers like David in other states. All future years' contracts would require the producers to generate a report like mine for the Algodoeira. For me, that was the Good Housekeeping Seal of Approval.

David versus Goliath

David was a man of vision. He was a man who thought. I am sure that much of his best thinking occurred while he was lying in his hammock in his three-sided machine shed.

The state was in its second or third year of a drought. During years of drought, the state's population consumed more black beans than the farmers produced. People ate black beans once or twice a day, yet during a drought, production was far below normal. The state's inventory of black beans decreased during every year of a drought.

The government did not plan much, even if it had an organization called the State Commission for Agricultural Planning. We did only what the federal government told us to do. We did not spend time thinking. No one cared enough to think.

Every new agricultural year, farmers needed black bean seed to plant. They always expected to have a good harvest, but in a drought they did not. The state's inventory of black beans decreased. One thing we could count on was that for each additional year of drought, the lower the state's inventory of black beans would be.

David knew that no one in the government was monitoring the inventory of black beans as it dropped more. David dusted off his technological package for producing black beans and planted all his irrigated land and all the irrigated land he could rent with black beans. He stored the beans and did this repeatedly until David was sitting on a gigantic inventory of black beans, far more than the state of Rio Grande do Norte had.

Finally, the rains returned, and everyone in Rio Grande do Norte and neighboring states wanted to plant black beans, but these states had far too few beans to sell to the farmers. David made it known that he had an abundant inventory of black beans. He offered to sell his beans at a price favorable to him, but the state of Rio Grande do Norte refused to pay. That was when a neighboring state came in and offered to pay his price and buy his entire inventory.

David would have made a huge profit in addition to saving the day for an entire state, except for one thing. The state of Rio Grande do Norte called an emergency session of its legislature and passed a law stating that in times of state emergencies, farmers could export agricultural products only with the state's permission. The government forced David to sell his beans to the state for a ridiculously low price. What a way to reward someone who just saved your population from a shortage of black beans!

The House of Representatives and the Men's Club

In one of Wolden's editorials, he revealed information about the end of the year's legislative session. The legislators rented two luxury buses, and after they ended their arduous work, the entire legislative body went to the city's best whorehouse to relax. What is more, there was no public outcry of immorality. No one cared.

Nicholas Becomes III

Nicholas was a small and fragile child, born at the beginning of the dry season. During his first months of life, it was extremely hot, and many babies were becoming sick and dehydrated. Soon, Nicky joined their ranks. We bought remedies at the pharmacy, and he seemed to get better, but then he would relapse. Sick babies filled all the hospitals. Newspaper articles announced that a baby had died while in the care of the state hospital, which had to accept anyone who appeared at its door. It was where the poor people went for medical care.

There were other stories of babies suffering from neglect at this hospital. This might have been because the staff was insufficient to care for all the babies who needed treatment. The administrators might have failed to increase staffing enough to deal with the increased demand. Or the staff might not have empathy for the babies. In Brazil, doctors were well known for having a God complex. They did what they wanted, when they wanted, if they wanted. The nurses and other staff might have copied this attitude.

One morning at 3:00 a.m., Katia woke me and told me that Nicholas was much worse. I looked at him; his breathing was very shallow, and he had a high fever. We called Dona Naide and told her. She woke Seu José, and they came in an instant to care for Kevin. Katia and I dressed and headed toward the private hospital where Nicholas's pediatrician worked. The hospital turned us away because the hospital was full. We went to the state hospital, where the staff told us we first had to drive across town to obtain a document from another office in the state's medical system. Begging did not help. We returned to our car and drove rapidly across town to obtain the required document and then returned to the state hospital.

When a nurse came to meet me, he motioned for me to turn Nicholas over to him. I made it clear that I wanted to accompany Nicholas into the hospital and stay by his side. The nurse said emphatically that this was not allowed. Hesitantly, I handed Nicholas to him. Before I let go, I told him that if Nicholas were not treated as he needed to be treated, I would find the nurse and punish him appropriately. This I promised him. I wanted him to know that he needed to take care of Nicholas, or I would hold him personally liable. No excuses. It was exceedingly difficult to turn and walk away after seeing Nicholas disappear into the darkness of that cold hospital.

The next morning, we contacted our pediatrician. He found a spot in his private hospital, and we went directly to the state hospital and recovered Nicholas. He had been in its care for only six hours. It had seemed like a lifetime to me.

Gas Stations Closed for the Weekend

When I arrived in Brazil, it was a time of economic growth. The government was trying to manage the economy, to make it do what the government wanted it to do. A very scarce resource was dollars, or foreign exchange. The government needed dollars to import machines for manufacturing, the driving force behind the economic expansion. The largest competitor for foreign exchange was the importation of petroleum. The government tried to force people to economize petroleum because everyone was driving around and buying gasoline, which squandered the country's precious foreign exchange.

To encourage its citizens to minimize their consumption of gasoline, the government set the price of gas at the pump at two or three times the price for which it was sold in the US. When the high prices did not encourage Brazilian citizens to reduce gasoline consumption enough, the government had to find another way. One morning we awoke to find that the government had passed a law forcing gas stations to close at 6:00 p.m. on Friday night and prohibiting them from reopening before 6:00 a.m. on Monday morning. The government hoped to keep people home over the weekends, with their cars in their garages.

This new law immediately created long lines at the gas pumps on Friday afternoons since drivers wanted to top their tanks off before the pumps closed. Monday mornings were also impossible since hundreds of people were running on empty, and long lines did not thin out until midmorning. The Brazilian people did not like this new law. They would need to apply *jeito*.

This did not bother me since I did not drive much on the weekends, unless I had a trip to David's farm scheduled. When I did travel to his farm, it was his responsibility to fill my tank so that I could return home. All he had to do was set aside a couple of five-gallon cans of gas.

On my first trip to David's farm after the state legislature had passed this law, Sunday afternoon arrived, and I mentioned to David that I needed gas to get home. He told me not to worry and climbed into my VW van's passenger seat. He guided me into Açu, and after several turns, we came upon a lengthy line of vehicles. He directed me to enter the line. The line behind me quickly grew as we inched forward. I saw police cars both ahead of me and behind me. Eventually, we came to a wide gate in an eight-foot-high wall that surrounded a property encompassing an entire city block. I could already smell gasoline. I hoped that no one working there or anyone in the cars would be smoking.

Inside the walls I saw hundreds and hundreds of five-gallon cans filled with gasoline. There was an army of workers using funnels to fill cars with workers attending five or six vehicles at any one time, including the police cars. Even the police were buying black-market gasoline.

This was another example of *jeito* in action. Anytime someone placed an obstacle in a Brazilian's path, the first thing the Brazilian did was to look for a *jeito*, a way around the obstacle. A citizen could not undo laws passed, but he could find a place that sold gasoline illicitly. After a few months, the government desisted, and life returned to normal. The government had not considered the "*jeito* effect." Brazilians always found a way around an obstacle, like water found a way downhill.

Trip to Paraiba for Consulting

David connected me to another small-scale American farmer, Mike, who had a small, irrigated farm just inside the neighboring state of Paraiba, at the far end of Rio Grande do Norte. He produced milk, beef, pork, vegetables, rice, black beans, and fruit, all on a small plot of land. He wanted to know which enterprises were not making him a profit. He wanted to focus his scarce resources only on profit-making enterprises and remove the others.

I thought about what I needed to do. I created some forms that he would need to collect the data that I required to answer his question. When I was ready, I called him, and we agreed on a weekend for me to visit. Since it would be at least a six-hour drive, and since I had never traveled this route before, I left early Saturday morning rather than Friday night. This would allow me to drive exclusively during daylight hours.

Through three-fourths of Rio Grande do Norte, I had nice asphalt highways on which I made suitable time. It was hot and dry, and I had to stop frequently to drink water. After a while I spotted a narrow bridge ahead. On the left side, just three feet from the road, were a couple of *bodegas* with four bicycles parked outside, like horses tied to a hitching post.

As I approached the bridge, I slowed and pulled into the center of the road. I looked in my mirror and, in the distance, saw another car following me. I slowed more as I approached the one-lane bridge. Then I saw something on the left side of my field of vision. I heard crashing sounds, and then an object flew ahead of me on the edge of the road. I was entering the bridge, so I dared not look back. As soon as I had crossed the bridge, I looked back to see the car that had been way behind me stopped on the side of the road, just short of the bridge, with its front grill smashed and the bicycles strewn about. There were four big-boned men standing beside the car and shaking their fists at me, as well as men exiting the *bodegas*, shaking their fists at everyone as they tried to locate their bicycles. The car had to have been traveling at a very high speed.

Luckily for me, the pavement stopped at the bridge. The dirt road beyond the bridge was wide because people used the flat ditches as additional lanes. There were numerous potholes left from the previous rainy season. These had hardened into concrete-like surfaces, preserving the potholes until the next rainy season. Large rocks emerged from the road, by up to a foot. The rocks were scattered about and embedded in the road. If a vehicle were to hit any of the rocks, the impact would destroy the bottom of their car.

The men had reentered their car and had started their pursuit of my VW van. To my advantage, the van had high road clearance, making it easier for me to go over the rough road. Their Chevet had a low clearance and given that there were four big-boned men sitting inside the car, the car had no chance of gathering speed on that road. I, on the other hand, put my accelerator to the floor and lowered my head to prevent it from banging into the ceiling as I sped on at top speed. They quickly disappeared in my rearview mirror. They were still shaking their fists at me. Had the road been paved, they would have caught me.

When I finally reached Mike's farm, he greeted me warmly. As I drank first a cup of cold water and then a cold beer, I told him about my experience on the road, and then we got down to business. I explained what I had in mind and showed him the forms that I had previously created. We made changes as we reviewed them.

I discussed an elaborate experiment that we would need to properly determine whether producing milk could be profitable. It involved modifying the cows' diet and would take three months to execute. Mike agreed. I did not want to ask him to eliminate his dairy herd if I could not be certain that it was the correct decision.

I returned after a couple of weeks to check on the collection of data and to answer any questions that Mike had. I was extremely cautious as I reached the narrow bridge and the dirt road that followed. I kept my eyes glued to the rearview mirror for any cars traveling at high speed.

In the end, I advised Mike to eliminate the dairy cows, the beef herd, and the pork production. The grain, vegetable, and fruit production enterprises were all profitable. Mike seemed happy. I think he had already known that this would be the case. I returned home. My job with Mike was done.

Consulting for the Algodoeira

The Algodoeira São Miguel had been operating in Brazil for 150 years. During this time, the company's people had collected seeds from all the different native cotton varieties they could find. They took meticulous notes on the characteristics of each variety and each year crossed different varieties, attempting to find new varieties with improved characteristics.

As time passed, this work grew increasingly complicated and expensive because they had to find ways to safely store the seed so as not to lose any of the varieties. Finally, in 1981, they had to discard some of the varieties. It was too expensive to maintain all of them. Normally, this job would have gone to the company's in-house statistician located in the Algodoeira's head office in England, but she had a backlog of projects that she could not complete for a year or more.

This was when the Algodoeira contacted me. I explained that I did not have a Ph.D. in statistics and might not be able to complete the task. They wanted me to try. They handed over all the data to me. Luckily for me, during my doctoral training, I had taken numerous statistics courses. One was a course normally not studied in the field of economics, but I was interested in agricultural experimentation, so I took the course. During the last week, the professor introduced a methodology that someone had just developed. In fact, he had just read about it in a publication. He had copied the table needed for us to apply the methodology and handed it out to all students. I had saved it.

Applying this methodology, I tested all the seeds and made my selections for seeds to be retained and seeds the Algodoeira should abandoned. I explained the methodology to the Algodoeira and gave them my findings. Later, the Algodoeira informed me that their statistician in England had unexpectedly found time and had examined the data. She had applied a methodology like what I had used, and her selections were remarkably close to mine. I did not mind having my work checked. I felt the pressure of making a mistake and causing the dumping of a 150-year-old seed that might result in it disappearing from this earth forever. I was happy to share the blame if we were wrong.

Opening a Computer Store

My consulting clients needed a quick turnaround for reports. As soon as they turned over the last piece of data, they wanted their final report. This required me to have my computers and printers working all the time. In 1981, both computers and printers were prone to not work. The computer that I used had a stolen reverse-engineered version of Radio Shack's TRS-II, or something like that. It had two weak points: its hard drive (five-inch floppy disks) and its keys. The drive constantly needed alignment, and it was common to have two or three keys not working on the keyboard. I needed in-house computer repair.

I had already opened a business for my consulting: ECONSULT. If I rented a space and hired a repair technician, I would have my in-house technician, but he would be expensive as he waited for my computer to break down. I decided that I might as well sell computers and—why not? —offer programming classes. Computers were just starting to be used, and more people wanted to learn how to program.

I rented a large house near the city center. I bricked over the garage door opening, repaired the inside, and added an air conditioner plus a sturdy eighteen-inch bench around the walls to hold the small computers and TV monitors. Beside the computer programming classroom was an old room previously used to store tools. I remodeled it, added an air conditioner, and called it my office. We arranged the large living room to display computers, printers, calculators, and accessories. I used another room to store spare parts and for the technician to make repairs. An accountant used another room. I allowed him to use his room for his outside business in exchange for his free service for my company.

I advertised for a programming class to start on Monday morning and flew to São Paulo on Wednesday afternoon to acquire the right to sell the most popular brand of computer produced in Brazil. I bought one unit of the company's large computers and one unit of its medium computers. Then I bought twelve units of a tiny computer that I would use in the beginning computer programming class.

When I returned home on Friday night, all I knew how to do was turn on the computers. I had no software for any of the computers. The computer company had included, for free, the game of hangman. I parked the large and medium computers and grabbed one of the small computers which I would use on Monday for the programming class. I had bought a book explaining how to use the BASIC programming language. By Sunday afternoon I was beginning to get the hang of it and started preparing my first lesson.

I was ready for the first class on Monday morning. I was relieved when that class went well. In fact, the rest of the course went smoothly too. New courses formed quickly, and I had to hire professional programmers to teach them. We gained a reputation for being honest and offering high-quality courses. It helped when Brazil's gigantic petroleum company started sending its employees to us for training.

The professional programmers organized a course in COBOL using our midsize computers. This was also a success. Companies had an increasing demand for data-entry workers. I created a course to train students in data entry. It was a self-taught course where people could come in anytime if they had scheduled time on the computer and follow the directions. I mapped the lesson plan; all the students had to do was follow it. When they completed the lesson, they would take a timed test. Afterward, we provided them with a document showing they had trained with us and showing their typing speed and the percent of correct numbers entered during their timed test.

Over time, our courses were what maintained ECONSULT and allowed us to pay our bills. Computer sales were nonexistent. I blamed myself because I was not a salesperson and did not know how to hire or supervise salespeople. I was a teacher. I should have focused on my strong suit instead of my weak points.

Our third source of income should have been equipment repair, but no revenue was forthcoming there either, in part because we had to sell the service and our sales department was ineffective. Eventually, I learned of another reason there were no repair sales: People often contacted my technician, but he had the clients pay him directly rather than include me. For parts, he asked me for computer boards that he said were needed for the maintenance of our computers and then robbed parts from them to keep his side business going.

When I discovered what was going on, I fired him and found a young man who had just graduated from technical school. I hired him and, at great expense, sent him to São Paulo to become accredited in the repair of our computer brand products. I could trust this young man, but the previous technician had already done excessive damage. I had him go through our inventory of computer boards to determine how many the previous technician had robbed of parts. To repair these boards, I had to pay more than two thousand dollars.

Tarantula Mating Season

At home, I usually spent each evening in my office. I studied computer programming, calculus, or other topics that had caught my fancy. One such night, Katia came to the doorway but said nothing. When I looked up and saw her, she was pointing toward the ceiling. I looked up and saw on the ceiling directly above my head a tarantula that had to be six to eight inches across.

I ran for the broom, knocked it to the floor, and attacked it. Katia grabbed the dustpan. I swept it into the dustpan and ran it outside, where I dumped it on a concrete slab. Katia handed me the cigarette lighter fluid and matches. She pointed at the tarantula blob and then at the lighter fluid and matches. That was the Brazilian way. I obliged her.

Katia informed me that January (it was January) was the month that tarantulas chose for mating. She told me to check our outside wall. She gave me the lighter fluid and matches to take with me. I put on sandals and started to check our perimeter. Before finishing, I had found six or eight tarantulas climbing down the inside portion of our outside wall into our property. I should remind people that our house was the only house standing on three or four city blocks. It might have been for that reason that we had so many tarantulas invading our property. Even so, after a week, mating season must have ended because the invasion of the tarantulas stopped.

Large Rats Invade Our House

The area around our house was flat, and our house was the only house on four square blocks. There was much unoccupied ground nearby. The city had not even marked off the streets. There was no need until people started to occupy the area, and the city did not have the budget to provide services before citizens needed them.

Natal had thousands of homeless people. They usually banded together in an area and created a shantytown with homes made from cardboard or scraps of wood, with bits of tin serving as roofs. The houses were tiny and fragile, but they offered protection for their inhabitants. Normally, these people avoided property lots because the lots' owners were very protective and would sue the city to have the squatters removed. The streets around the blocks, however, were another thing. The city owned the streets occupied by the homeless, and the city never knew what was going on. These shantytowns tended to follow the streets. It was very unlikely that anyone working for the city would care enough to create a fuss and have a shantytown removed.

Such a shantytown appeared on a street one block from our house. It grew a little each day and became a significant hideaway for homeless people. One day the city placed signs throughout the cardboard homes, stating that the residents had to leave by a certain date. Some inhabitants left, but others did not believe the warning and stayed. On the stated day, bulldozers appeared, and within an hour the town no longer existed. It was gone.

That night Katia kissed the heads of Kevin and Nicholas, both of whom were still sleeping in cribs, and went to bed. Later, I came out from my office and went to bed. During the night, something woke me. I sat upright in bed and listened. I heard nothing, but something was not right. I crept over to the bedroom door and turned on the light. Just above my head, walking along the ledge of a slatted area above the door, was a giant rat. I do not exaggerate—from nose to tip of tail, he was no less than two feet.

Katia turned and sleepily asked me why the light was on. I told her to look at the door. She screamed. The rat dropped to the floor and disappeared down the hallway. Katia yelled for me to close the door to the boys' room. I hurriedly closed their door and the door to the third bedroom. I collected the large glass cover from a coffee table and placed it across our bedroom door opening, impeding the rat from reentering our bedroom, where Katia had taken refuge and from where she yelled encouragement. Then I went to the kitchen to grab a broom and made sure that the bathroom door was open. I was ready for battle.

I found the rat in my office and herded him from there, through the living room and into the hallway leading to the bedrooms. I beat the broom against the floor to rattle the rat. He picked up speed as he headed toward our room. He hit the invisible glass table cover that I had placed in the doorway. He lost his senses just long enough for me to catch him and force him into the small bathroom between the bedrooms. I jumped in behind him and closed the door. It was him and me, *mano a mano*, in a tiny bathroom. Katia yelled encouragement from a safe distance. The broom was too long for me to swing it properly, but I was able to use it effectively enough to doom the rat. I got the dustpan and threw him over the wall. I would deal with him tomorrow.

Katia and I thought the rat had come from the destroyed shantytown. Now the rats that had lived there also were homeless. The next night, I had to deal with two more rats, and each night thereafter for a week or so, I had to fight it out with more rats—and then it stopped. The rats had moved on and found new housing elsewhere. Our lives returned to normal.

Voodoo versus White Table Spiritism

Anyone who lived in Brazil needed to be aware of voodoo because most people practiced it. Before I moved to Brazil, the only thing I had known about voodoo was what I had seen in the movies—not much. In Brazil, voodoo was called *Macumba,* and the *Macumba* priest was called a *macumbeiro.* People used *Macumba* to communicate with spirits, usually to bring about bad outcomes to one or more people. The *macumbeiro* did not care. Whether he or she was asked to do good or evil, the *macumbeiro* just did it—for a price. The client always had to pay for the *macumbeiro*'s services.

There was another form of Spiritism as well—White Table. This branch of Spiritism was vastly different from *Macumba.* First, people called it White Table because the host sat at a small table covered in a white cloth with a Bible on one side. White Table priests never would do anything that could bring harm or distress to any person, and they never charged for their services. They believed that their gift of communication with the spirits was a God-given one; therefore, it should be shared for free with anyone who needed it.

In Brazil, Spiritism (White Table) was an official religion. In fact, even though ninety-two percent of Brazilians were Catholic, forty-four percent were Spiritists. You may ask how that was possible. I asked a person who claimed to be a member of both religions, and he said, "Clearly, I am a Catholic, but what if my time comes and I am at the pearly gates only to discover that God is not a Catholic but a Spiritist? That is why I am also a Spiritist—for insurance, because surely God is one or the other."

When I was having problems with ECONSULT, Vania, Katia's sister, suggested that we accompany her to a White Table session. I was reluctant but curious. I agreed to go. Vania, from previous experience, knew that we needed to take with us a bottle of *aguardiente* (firewater) and a vile, cheap cigar. We went to the practitioner's home with our purchases. A white-haired lady in her mid-sixties met us at the door. Her house was neat, with many religious symbols displayed on her furniture and walls. She led us into her office, where she had a card table set up. She covered the table in a white tablecloth, with a Bible placed neatly at one corner.

Vania introduced Katia and me to the woman. She was very gracious. After learning that this was our first White Table experience, she explained what was about to happen. She explained that the spirit communicated through her, but when the session ended, she would have no recollection of what we had discussed.

We held hands while she prayed. After her prayer, she lowered her head and muttered words I could not hear. She was calling the spirit with whom she preferred talking. He was an old African slave from the early 1800s. When he appeared, he always asked for strong "firewater" alcohol made from sugar cane and cigars made from the strongest and most vile tobacco every produced. When he lived as a slave, these would have been the best he could have hoped for. The spirit's name was Preto Velho (meaning "old Black man").

When his spirit came, our host's body jumped like someone had hit her hard on her back or like she had received a large electrical shock. She continued to look down with her eyes closed. At this point, she had no idea what was happening. We knew that Preto Velho's spirit was in control when our host gave the belly laugh of a happy old man who was about to receive a gift. Occupying our host's body, the spirit immediately asked for his firewater and cigar. He took big swigs of firewater and smacked his lips and inhaled a large drag from the cigar. Within a couple of minutes, he filled the room with smoke. We opened all the windows. I should note that our host never smoked or consumed alcohol—ever.

After Vania had discussed her business with Preto Velho, he paused, and then stated knowingly that I had questions that I wanted to ask him. He told me not to be afraid, to ask him anything I wanted. His answers were often funny but spot-on. He was a gregarious man;

one I would have loved to meet in the physical world and call my friend.

Suddenly, he said someone else was calling him and he needed to go. Within a couple of seconds, our host's body snapped back and forth, and he was gone. The woman would need three or four minutes to collect her thoughts and become her normal self. Meanwhile, we had to empty and hide the ashtray and the firewater bottle. We had to try to disperse the smoke. She had no idea that she consumed alcohol and smoked a vile cigar each time Preto Velho came.

When she was able to reorient herself, she asked us what had transpired. She showed no sign of having consumed such a large amount of powerful alcohol, and she was not aware of the smoke residual that should have been in her mouth but was not. We waited and let Vania speak because we did not know what we could and could not say. After our host said another prayer, we thanked her for her generosity and disbanded.

Getting Things Done in Northeast Brazil

Brazilians, or at least *nordestinos* (people from Northeast Brazil), never did business with a stranger. That was me, the stranger. They always did business with family or friends, even if the price offered by the stranger was more favorable. In northeastern Brazil, you could trust family and friends—and no one else. One did not make friends overnight. It took years, decades, to establish friendships, and a few marriages somewhere along the line also could help.

Economists, especially marketing people, would not understand the *nordestino* economy, where people would pay more for something even when another company offered it for less. Most economists would find the *nordestino* an irrational being. But after living in this strange environment for years, I came to understand it.

Once I visited a business and found it receptive to buying a computer. The owners asked me to present them with a proposal and said we could talk. I returned to my office and prepared the proposal, which I left on top of my desk because I expected to return to the business to present my proposal yet that afternoon.

As soon as I printed the proposal, a young man entered my office and sat on the corner of my desk and started fidgeting with the proposal. I had seen him around Natal. He made money doing favors for friends, but he had no job. His family was middle-class, even though he presented himself as being from the upper class. He looked like he had just left the tennis courts at the country club. I should have reached out and removed the proposal from his hand. It was evident that he was reading the proposal. He suddenly told me to pay him a commission of ten percent and he would close the deal. I denied his request, telling him that he was not an employee and could not represent my company without being an employee. He said that he would speak with the firm's owner and "put dirt on the deal" so that I could never sell anything there. This irritated me, so I told him to do what he must. He did. I was never again able to get beyond the front desk at that business. I do not know what he told them, but he made good on his promise. I never again allowed him into my office.

Doing business in Natal was complicated in ways that an American could never imagine. For example, when I needed to obtain a driver's license, they told me to go to a government office between the hours of 10:00 a.m. and noon and wait in line, and this was only on Tuesdays and Thursdays. I arrived at 10:00 a.m. to find a lengthy line. At noon, I was still three people from the counter, but at exactly twelve noon, the counter employee slammed a "closed" sign onto the counter. Without any explanation, he turned and left, leaving unhappy people in the line.

I learned to arrive before 8:00 a.m. so that I could reach the counter before noon. I was elated when I reached the front of the line before closing time. But the counter agent told me that I needed to fill out a form before I could apply for the driver's license. He explained, with great remorse, that they did not have the form at this office and that I could find it in a bookstore. I went to three bookstores before they informed me that there was only one bookstore in the city that carried the form. It was completely across town. When I found this store, its clerk informed me that the store was out of the form, but next week they should have more available. He showed great compassion before he turned to help another person.

I returned to the bookstore twice the next week, but they did not have the necessary form either time. On my third trip, I found that the form had arrived, but unfortunately, I could not pay for a government form there. I had to pay for it at a specific bank branch located in another part of the city. With great difficulty, I found the location. I was surprised that all I had to do was stand in line, pay, and obtain my receipt, which I did without difficulty. I returned to the bookstore to discover that the receipt had to be stamped by someone at yet another office located in another corner of the city. That stamp took only one more day to obtain. With the proper receipt, I received the form with ease. On the next Tuesday, I was in line at 8:00 a.m. When I reached the counter, just before noon, they informed me that unfortunately, the director had had to leave unexpectedly, and only he could sign a document that I needed. The counter agent suggested, with obvious satisfaction, that I return at a more appropriate time. He reached for the "closed" sign, slammed it onto the counter, and disappeared through a door.

It was then that I mentioned my problems to Seu José. He offered to drive me to the office after lunch. I reminded him that they were open only between 10:00 a.m. and noon on Tuesdays and Thursdays. He smiled and told me not to worry. He might find a *jeito* to resolve my problem. *Jeito* was important. You had to have it to get things done, yet one could not purchase it. It was more important than money, and much harder to obtain.

Seu José confidently led me into the government agency that Tuesday afternoon. He smiled and spoke familiarly to everyone as he walked straight to the counter, although there was still a line for something else. He looked through an open door into the director's office. The director saw him and waved him in. We went around and behind the counter and through the director's door and shook hands all around. The director asked what Seu José needed. He told the director I needed a driver's license but had encountered problems along the way. The director was deeply sorry for all my difficulties and called to an employee to come and bring the form with him. The employee appeared in the doorway with a form. The director handed me the form and requested that I fill it out. He even gave me his personal pen to use. In five minutes, I had my driver's license.

That was *jeito*. Seu José had it because he had carefully cultivated many friendships during his decades living in Natal. He had helped many people with problems and never asked for any payment for his services. Payment would come later, when he needed a favor, like now. That was how a *nordestino* survived. He made friends and kept them by doing favors when requested. Never should one request a favor for minor things. That was wasteful. Seu José had just cashed in one of his favors for my driver's license. No one kept score verbally, but everyone knew the score. You never discussed it, but people always understood when a new favor was owed and when people cashed in an old one. Seu Jose did this for me because I was his son-in-law. I was family.

Despite my personal lack of *jeito*, I made a modest living by helping large farmers calculate their production costs and by preparing budgets for them. Most of my revenue came from my series of computer classes. We were always finishing a class and starting others. They were always filled to near capacity.

No one else in the city yet offered computer classes. Life was good for a few months, and then one day, a class ended, and no one signed up for another class. Then another class finished, and again, no one signed up for another one. Finally, all classes were over, and I had no income and no cash reserves, since by this time, I had left the employment of CEPA, and I was in trouble.

I had been living on the edge for years. The problem with living on the edge is that sometimes you fall off. I was worried and did not know what to do. The transition from surviving to not surviving was quick and painful. I had never contemplated that this could happen to me. I did not understand. I was living in a foreign country and had no one I could turn to for financial support. My father-in-law had a small amount of *jeito*, but he was a simple man with limited financial resources. He could not save me with money. It was a critical point in my life. I had to find a way out—and fast. I could not involve Katia's family in a problem that was not theirs.

In Nebraska, life had been easier. My banker there was the son of my father's banker and the grandson of my grandfather's banker. There was equity in this relationship. When the banker loaned me money, he knew that my father and my grandfather had never failed to repay a loan; therefore, it was easier for him to extend a loan to me. In Natal, I was a foreigner with no capital and no equity, and even my father-in-law's reputation did little to help me obtain loans. Furthermore, short-term loans cost from twenty to twenty-four percent a month while inflation was between ten and fifteen percent per month. Interest was not your friend.

One night, it was late, and I had closed the store. I had been in my office, trying to find a solution, but I finally decided to go home. At the same time, my night security guard was arriving for his watch. We needed a night security guard because we could not leave our computers and electronic goods exposed to thieves. Instead of going to his room, he approached me. He was a simple man who came from a rural village. He was not comfortable speaking with people outside his social class, but I had always been good to him and always spoke kindly to him. He directed his eyes toward his feet when he spoke. He said, "Pardon me, Mr. Lynn, but I noticed that there are no more classes. Are you not offering any more computer classes?"

I explained to him what had occurred. He listened, but I felt that he had already known what was happening before he came to me. He looked at his feet again and paused before he suggested that this might be a "work." I had no idea what he meant. My Portuguese was excellent, so I understood the literal words he had said but not his meaning. I asked him to explain. He said it had to be a "work," a spell, a curse placed on me by someone who did not like me or was envious of me.

How to Counteract a Macumba Spell

The night security guard told me that he knew someone in the country who could remove the spell. I told him that we knew someone from the White Table who could manage this. He begged forgiveness but adamantly claimed that White Table magic was not strong enough to overpower *Macumba* magic. He said, "Sir, you can't fight fair in an unfair fight and expect to win." He continued, "It takes a mighty powerful *macumbeira* to overpower *Macumba* magic." He told me that the priestess he knew was enormously powerful and could handle the job. I told him to make the appointment. I could not sustain another week without computer classes.

The next day the night security guard, Katia, and I drove two hours to a small village located off the highway. We turned off the highway onto a steeply downward-sloped cobblestone road. The holes filled the road from the rain washing away the cobblestones during heavy rains. We headed downhill and into the village, advancing slowly to keep from smashing the bottom of our Chevet, a car I had recently purchased, on cobblestones each time a tire dropped into a hole. After a couple of blocks, the cobblestone stopped, and dry clay continued, also with deep potholes left from the last rains. At the end of the village, we turned left. There were no houses on our right. Mid-block, there was a large open entrance into an area enclosed by a six-foot-high wall of adobe bricks.

We stopped near the entrance and continued on foot. No one was inside. There was a large open area covered with a roof made of palm branches. On two sides there were benches for people to sit on, as in an auditorium. Later, the priestess arrived and assured us that people were preparing. A couple of men walked in with small drums and set them up near one bench. Ladies started appearing. They dressed as Bahianas: Black women from the state of Bahia dressed as the women would have dressed 150 years ago. Each woman had a scarf wrapped around her hair and wore a white blouse and a skirt with many layers, like the skirts used in US square dancing.

The drums started beating a very infectious rhythm. One by one, the women fell into a line and started dancing in a large circle. They twisted and turned as they went about in a wide circle and held their arms up. Inside the circle were chalk markings on the concrete floor. Suddenly, one woman dropped to the ground and started flopping around like a fish on dry land. A couple of other women stayed with her to keep her from hurting herself, and then another woman dropped to the ground, and others stayed with her. The priestess went to each woman and spoke quietly with her until she could stand and dance again.

Our night security guard explained that dark spirits had come uninvited and occupied the dancers. The priestess sent these unwanted visitors on their way as quickly as possible, but they did not always want to leave. The women continued their dancing until they could attract the spirit they wanted for this task. After more than a half hour, the night security guard told Katia and I that he thought they had contacted the spirit they wanted.

At this point, someone appeared with two or three black chickens. The priestess cut their throats, and drained their blood into a bowl and sprinkled it about, forming designs on the concrete. While the priestess was busy doing her stuff, the other women continued dancing in a circle and singing. Katia and I were shocked. We had had no idea this was going to happen. We were extremely uncomfortable. Suddenly, the ceremony finished.

The priestess came to us. She said that her work had been successful. She told us that we needed to "sweep [our] roof, every day." Our night security guard assured us that he knew what to do. She told us that somewhere in our house, in the far-right corner, we would find five coins buried vertically. We needed to find them and carefully extract them without touching them. We had to place the coins in a glass jar and cover them in frog urine. We had to cover the jar and bury it in a special manner. Our night security guard assured us that he knew what was needed. I should state that this simple priestess had never been to Natal and had no idea what business we were in or what our store looked like.

We paid her and headed home. Once we were back in Natal, I drove to ECONSULT. We started looking in the kitchen, located in the far-right part of the house. Under the sink there was a concrete floor, but the concrete was of two shades. Someone had broken a part of the concrete and then replaced, although this had occurred some time ago since the concrete was not fresh. I grabbed a hammer and started pounding. I found five coins, each placed in a vertical position. The night security guard took over and disposed of these coins as asked by the priestess. I have no idea how he found the frog urine. I prefer not to think about that.

The next morning, early, I climbed onto the roof and found at least six small packages wrapped in plastic. Inside the plastic were chicken heads and other bird bones. We burned them. Someone had placed these on the roof over the main entrance to ECONSULT and over the door leading into our computer programming classroom. The night security guard, our interpreter, informed us that my enemies had done this to produce the strongest effect at the door to keep people out of ECONSULT.

By that same afternoon, people started calling about when our next class would start. Within a couple of weeks, our programming classes were back to normal. I had to continue sweeping the roof and found new spells there on an almost daily basis, but none had any impact on our business. This did not mean that my enemy was not determined. The rainy season was upon us, and one day when it was raining very heavily, a leak developed in my office, falling from the ceiling onto my computer. I had to move my desk to protect it. I got a ladder and climbed onto the roof, taking a spare clay tile with me. I found the broken tile and removed it. Before I had a chance to replace it, my eyes caught sight of something inside the roof. It was another chicken head. My opponent had climbed on top of my office, removed a tile, and inserted a chicken-head package inside my roof. Had he noticed that he had broken a tile, I might not have caught him. After three or four weeks, the frequency of spells dropped until they stopped.

On Using Candy for Money at the Supermarket

Whenever I went to the supermarket, they never gave me the correct change. If the difference between the cash I paid and the bill was less than a dollar, instead of giving me my exact change, the cashier would take a sack of individually wrapped candies, pour a few onto the counter, and call it even. All Brazilians played along and accepted this. I did not. This irritated me. The cashiers did not even ask me if I liked that candy or if there was another candy, I might like better. They never asked me if I accepted the exchange between candies and money. I was supposed to accept it and move on. The supermarket was a big business that should have a way to give exact change. It could easily serve several thousand customers a day. It made money from that play.

The next day after one of these occurrences, I bought a bag of individually wrapped candies elsewhere and filled all my pockets with them. I reentered the supermarket and grabbed a can of Coca-Cola. I headed to the line to await my turn with the cashier. When it was my turn, I placed the Coke on the table, pulled a couple of dozen candies from my pockets and threw them onto the counter, grabbed my Coke, and started to walk out. The checkout lady at first did not understand and was speechless. Then she understood and yelled. Everyone started to watch us. She asked me what I was doing. I told her that I had just paid for my Coke with candies. She said that was ridiculous because candies were not money. By this time, a couple of security guards were watching, and people behind me were joining in by defending the supermarket and swinging their fists at me for delaying their checkout. I asked the cashier if she gave out candies when she did not have exact change. She agreed that she did. I told her that candies were in fact money then because the store itself was using them as such. Now the upper management had arrived, and I repeated my argument to him. He seemed perplexed and did not know what to do. I was enjoying myself because I was making sense to everyone except my fellow shoppers.

Finally, to avoid the other supermarket shoppers from hanging me from the rafters, I grabbed my candies and paid in cash. The cashier had to borrow money from a neighboring cashier so that she could return my exact change. She did not want to push her luck and give me candies in lieu of change. I left. My job was done. I had needed to do that. It was so easy to create good drama.

Another White Table Visit

Katia and I were feeling down. We decided that we needed a visit with Preto Velho. We made the appointment and bought the required vile cigar and a flask of firewater.

After Preto Velho appeared, we lit the cigar for him and opened the flask of firewater. After he had had a couple of draws on the cigar and a couple of sips of firewater, he was open for business. He asked me what I wanted. I told him that I missed my family and wondered what they were doing. He told me to select one person and focus my mind on that person. I thought about my mother. After seconds of silence, he told me that she was in the kitchen and might have a headache. She was seated at a funny table (our table had a large lazy Susan in the middle), and she had a cup of something, which she was stirring with a spoon (Mom was a tea drinker). With her other hand, she was holding her head, like it hurt. Preto Velho said he was leaving there because he could not understand anything the people said. He said they talked funny (English).

Preto Velho volunteered to me that in an earlier life, I had been a farmer in Ireland. Well, I had not seen that coming. As usual, he had to suddenly dart off to address another caller, but I felt better.

Chased by a Motor Scooter

I always returned home for lunch. On this rainy day I turned onto the main street that passed in view of my home. The street was very wide because it was a main street, and it had no effective ditches. People used the flat ditch areas like they were extra lanes. There could have been three lanes in each direction, except it was a dirt road with many potholes. People did not drive in a straight line; sometimes they could swerve suddenly to dodge a pothole. For this reason, it was not wise to pass close to any vehicle. It was always best to give other vehicles a wide berth.

I was traveling at a normal speed when my front right tire hit a pothole filled with water. A jet of water shot out from the hole. By coincidence, a man on a scooter was feet away from that tire and was absolutely covered in water and almost knocked from his scooter. He blamed me. In fact, once he regained control of his scooter, he started chasing me while waving his fist at me. With an angry man chasing me, I could not turn toward my house. I had to lose him first, so I drove on. I was in the city, so I had to be careful, or I would hit another vehicle or a pedestrian. With those limitations, I could not lose him. In fact, he was tiny, but he could pick me out of a crowd several blocks away because I was driving a VW van. It stuck out.

All I could do was avoid streets with streetlights and keep driving, hoping that he would tire. When I looked in my rearview mirror and no longer saw an angry little wet man on a scooter shaking his fist at me, I turned my van toward home.

My Friend Killed Outside a Nightclub

Katia's family was close friends with another family who had a daughter near my age. This family was very prominent and was friends with everyone, even those with politically opposing views. Most people had to pick a political party and hope that it won in the elections, but this family did not have to worry. They had friends in all political parties. It did not matter who won the election; the members of this family would still have excellent jobs and could obtain financial loans. Their lives would continue normally, and they would flourish. There were not many people in the state who could enjoy those benefits.

The daughter had also been my boss at CEPA. Besides working at CEPA, she owned and operated a large ranch. She had obtained a significant financial loan at a negative interest rate (i.e., monthly inflation was higher than the interest rate). On paper such loans were available to everyone, but in reality, they were not. Only a select few had any chance of obtaining one, and she was one of them. She had barbecues with the governor and with Brazil's president and vice president. She was connected.

She and her husband liked to unwind from their busy schedules. One night they went to a nightclub, the same one where Katia and I had met. She and her husband were drinking. As they drank increasingly, they danced more aggressively and sometimes bumped into other people. Because people were full of drink, they exchanged words. She and her husband did not slow down or apologize because they never had to do that. They annoyed many people who just wanted a nice night of dancing.

Upon leaving the club, they entered their car and started for home. Another vehicle blocked their vehicle. Men exited with guns and shot both the woman and her husband several times. She died at the scene, and her husband needed years of physical therapy, after which he could walk only with the use of a cane. Her murder and his assault were crimes that were never solved.

In Brazil, you must assume that everyone is armed and can seek revenge. They are, and they do.

Chapter 15

Move to São Paulo

I tired of not selling computers. I tired of not repairing computers. I tired of trying to push water uphill. I worked long hours and never saw my children except on weekends. I always left for work before they awoke and arrived home at night after they had gone to sleep. I had to deal with increased employee problems, and I was aware of how fast we could go from just surviving financially to dire straits. I had added the computer enterprise to ECONSULT to lend support to my consulting. Now I had no time for consulting because I was busy solving computer-related problems.

I confided this to my friend who managed the Algodoeira São Miguel. He invited me to a party that he was hosting. It involved whiskey and sandwiches. They had also invited David. The manager told me that in attendance would be a man from a company in São Paulo that created agricultural software. There would be other men present as well, but I no longer remember who they were. I met at least a dozen men at the party and enjoyed our conversations. I appreciated the Algodoeira manager trying to help me, but I did not see myself getting any closer to a solution that would allow me to move to a market more open to my services.

I saw no future in Natal. It was a region where one's future depended entirely on who your friends were. Your individual capability played no part. Natal was a city of a million people, but it was owned and operated by one or two dozen families. If you were not connected to those families, you were on your own. I was on my own.

My experience was that when one person started to get ahead, there were one hundred people there to drag him back down again. There were many ways this could happen. They could spread rumors, and they spread very quickly. Deals that were certain one day were impossible the next day because someone had reached out and killed the deal in an unknown way. The teachers I hired were stealing my class materials and starting their own classes on the side. Let us not forget the role of "spells." I was exhausted from fighting these wars. I just wanted to go back to my consulting without anyone interfering in my results.

Katia and I were uncomfortable. We did not want to leave our friends and family in Natal, but we knew that there was no future for us there. We decided to say hello to our friend Preto Velho. We always felt better after talking with him.

As usual, he was not serious until he had had his puffs on the cigar and a few swallows of firewater. I explained our situation to him. He asked if I had met any new people recently. I told him that I had. He asked me to concentrate on one of them. I made my concentration face to show him that I was concentrating. He said, "No, not that one, the one behind him."

I moved my focus to the man I had met from São Paulo. Preto Velho confirmed, "Yes, that's the man! He will offer you a job in São Paulo within a few days."

I must admit that I felt better, but I did not believe it. Four days later, the man from São Paulo offered me a job. As part of the offer, the firm would pay for our move in its entirety. I accepted.

Finding a House in São Paulo

My first task was to fly to São Paulo and find a house. My new boss gave me directions to his business, and I took a taxi there. He showed me my new desk and a map of São Paulo. It was so much larger than anything I was used to that I almost wet my pants when I thought of the task at hand. Within a couple of days, I had to find a suitable place for my family to live; it had to be a home that we could afford and in a location that would allow me to get to work in a reasonable time.

My boss showed me the communities that were too expensive for my salary. He ran his finger around the map, showing me how far out I should start looking because the farther I went out from the city center, the more rents would drop. Anywhere closer than he was advising, I could not afford the housing. I made a mental note of how far out I had to go on the subway before I could get off to look for housing. I thanked him and started my journey.

I found one leg of the subway and rode way out before stepping off. It looked like it could rain at any moment. Great! Now what should I do? I walked and walked, looking for houses for rent. I wrote down numbers, and then I searched for a phone booth. Once I found a phone booth, it was usually impossible to reach anyone at the numbers listed on the signs, and if I did, the homes were not available until much later, and that did not help me.

I kept looking. I stopped at another subway station and started to make a small circle around it, looking for "for rent" signs. I decided I would keep making the circle larger until I found a house. After an hour or two, I found one. The sign pointed down a steep dead-end street, an offshoot from a street with moderate traffic. That was perfect because there would be no traffic by this house. There were cobblestones missing from the street. They looked like the rain had washed them out during heavy rains.

The stubby street had only two or three nice houses on it before it dead-ended. At the end of the street was a six-foot adobe wall built across the street, with a door in the wall. Behind that door was a completely different neighborhood. It looked like it had started out as a neighborhood of squatters and had eventually become legitimized. There was no vehicular traffic because there were no streets, only narrow sidewalks. They had built houses next to each other with no space in between. Five feet outside one resident's front door, across a narrow sidewalk, was someone else's front door. Sometimes the roofs from the houses on the two sides of the street nearly touched each other. Since these poor people had no cars, they did not need to leave space for cars to occupy. There was no wasted space.

The last house on the right before the wall was the house for rent, and the owners lived next door. The house was new. It had a two-car garage surrounded by thick metal bars. The enclosed garage area could become a nice, safe place for the kids to play. The house was narrow, less than fifteen feet wide. Inside, the living room and the dining room had nice hardwood floors. Between the living and dining rooms was a half bathroom. Past the dining room was a kitchen. It was not large, nor was it small. Behind the kitchen was a space for the maid to live and to wash clothes by hand. Between the kitchen and the maid's room was an open space designed for clotheslines to dry clothes. Upstairs there were three bedrooms and a bathroom with a shower. Outside the room that would be our bedroom was an exceptionally large open patio from which we could view São Paulo. All floors were tile, except for the living and dining rooms.

I wasted no time. I had the owner fill in the contract, and I signed it and paid the first month's rent. I felt good. I took the subway back to the airport and caught a flight home yet that night. I was so relieved. To find a house in such a large city was a monumental task.

Christmas was approaching. In early December I announced to our employees that we were closing shop. I told them that I would pay them through the end of December. I sold off the inventory and assets. I was happy but nervous.

We packed our house's belongings into a truck. The truck driver agreed to meet us at our hotel in São Paulo at 10:00 a.m. on December 28. We flew out of Natal on December 27. Kevin was days from turning four years old, Nicholas was days from being three years old, and Christianne was three months shy of one year old. It was not an easy trip.

We arrived at the hotel and spent the night. The next morning, we checked out and waited in the lobby. At 10:00 a.m. the truck driver walked in. I had never believed he would meet me on time. Given my experience of people always being late in Latin America, I would have been surprised if he had even showed up, much less showed up on time. This was a good beginning to a new life.

I caught a taxi and gave the driver our address. The truck driver followed us. It took a while for us to reach the house because we had to make sure that we did not become separated in the heavy traffic or at traffic lights. When we reached the final turnoff to the dead-end street, I had the taxi stop, and I showed the house to the truck driver. He would have to back down the street. I grabbed our suitcases and led

Katia and the kids to the house while the movers started unloading the boxes. I had to stand at the door and direct them to the correct rooms.

Soon, the movers were gone. I took Katia around the house and showed it to her. I had hoped she would be as excited as I was. She was not. I hoped that time would change her opinion. It did not.

I started work right away. My first assignment was to do a quality check on a large agricultural investment software that they had created to aid large businesses in making huge investments in agriculture. For example, VW had a farm with hundreds of thousands of acres. Banco Safra had a ranch with over three hundred thousand acres. And there were many more.

The government was sponsoring such projects. Brazil had a program wherein if a company bought undeveloped land, the company either could pay millions of dollars in its normal taxes or could pay no taxes and invest in the company's ranch the money that it otherwise would have paid to the government in taxes. So instead of paying taxes, the companies owned land. This was a program that entirely favored the rich. There were dozens of such projects around Brazil. Each project was worth millions of dollars. This software program targeted these companies.

My boss had brought a young Englishman to Brazil for a year to develop the software program. The business had then deemed the program ready and sent him home. The program was phenomenal. When I arrived, I asked to check it for defects before they released it for sale. My boss reluctantly allowed me to evaluate it. I told him that it was an expensive program destined for only a few companies. If one such company bought the program and discovered problems, it would share that knowledge with everyone else that might purchase the program, and our company would make no more software sales.

On the first day of testing, I discovered a major problem. Under an extremely specific set of circumstances, the program blew up and gave ridiculous answers. After a week's work, I isolated the problem to within two or three lines of programming. The lines seemed perfect, yet they did not yield the correct answer.

The company brought the Englishman back to São Paulo to solve the problem. In the end, it was an idiosyncrasy in the BASIC language in Apple computers. One line placed in the middle of the program had created a problem. Once I moved the line to within the first few lines of programming, the program worked perfectly. That was all. I just copied, deleted, and pasted one line of code. It cost the company ten thousand dollars to discover and correct the problem. Now the company had an expensive product ready to market.

I immediately learned that working in this office was not going to be easy. There was a female computer programmer and a female office manager. They were both young and loved to gossip. One problem was that the office manager was the mistress of one of the partners. The two ladies spent much time together gossiping. I was in the next cubicle, trying to work. Their gossip included things about me. I never understood whether they did not care that I heard what they were saying or believed that I could not hear them. It was unpleasant, and I did not think that complaining would help.

Two Weeks at a Convention in Rio de Janeiro

A two-week agriculture convention was coming up at the convention center in Rio de Janeiro. Every business even remotely connected to agriculture had bought space at the convention center, including my bosses. People involved in agriculture from all over Brazil would be there. It would be an excellent chance for our firm to snag some business. The company elected to send me and contracted another person from outside the firm to go with me.

My bosses had friends who lived in Copacabana in a two-bedroom apartment. The friends were willing to sublet the apartment to my bosses during those two weeks because they would be out of the country. I was not happy about being away from home for two weeks, but I had no choice. I was excited, though, about the contacts I might make and the things I might see.

The convention center opened at 10:00 a.m. and closed at 9:00 p.m., and we had to be there during the entire fourteen days. The routine quickly became monotonous. Only a half dozen people stopped at our booth. We tried to sell them our expensive computer program, but 99.9 percent of the visitors did not need it. I tried to sell them consulting with cost-control software, which we would develop, but no one was interested. People did not see the need for these services. They thought they could operate their farms or ranches without outside help.

My partner and I traded off maintaining the booth. One sat and tried not to look bored while the other explored the other booths. There were dozens interesting booths. I learned that our company was not prepared for this expo. We needed to have more things ready to show. We needed posters showing the benefits of rotational grazing or showing the advantages of knowing the cost of production. The producers needed ways to make forecasts of their costs and revenues. I was frustrated. I felt the company must have become aware of the expo just a couple of days before deciding to send us there. They had done no planning or preparation.

I obtained a half dozen business cards, but no one showed any viable interest in our services. At the end, I only wanted to go home. I did not look forward to reporting to the two owners that our efforts had not been fruitful. I had the feeling that they would think our lack of sales was my fault.

Leaving the Company

When I returned to the office and had to listen to gossip again and feel like they would blame me for the lack of sales, I found myself unhappy in my work. This company was like ECONSULT in that it had many problems, one of which was that it had no sales force. That was why they hired me—to sell things—but if they would have clearly stated that to me, I could have told them that it was not going to happen. I did not have sales expertise. I detected that they did not have enough revenue to sustain their workforce, and this was the reason they were on edge all the time.

One of the bosses ran around the world doing consulting for the World Bank. After being gone for a month, he would drop into the office to finish his reports. He worked day and night. He could have lived a good life had he used his income just for himself. Instead, he sank his earnings into a company that had no chance at generating revenue because no one was making sales or supervising the workforce.

The other boss spent his time on his farms, supervising work there. This left our office unsupervised and in the hands of the office manager. The company was doomed to fail for the same reasons that ECONSULT had failed as a computer-based company.

One day, a person I had met at the expo asked me if I would be interested in collaborating with him. Most ranch owners lived in the city and had other business interests. They looked at their ranches like an occasional hobby. They would only visit their ranches from time to time and had full-time in-house ranch managers to take responsibility for the day-to-day activities. My client was not like this. He was a rancher who lived on one of his five ranches, and he made his living from ranching. I decided to leave the software company and collaborate directly with this rancher.

He wanted me to look at his pastures and his operation to give him advice. I suggested he divide his large pastures into smaller paddocks and use rotational grazing. He was overgrazing all his pastures. This was bad because it caused his grass to slowly degrade. His future revenue depended on the quality of this year's pastures. I showed him where he needed to place electric fences for cross fencing. The rancher had to place water at strategic locations to keep the cattle close to water yet dispersed on the grass.

I created data-collection forms designed to document how the rancher moved his cattle herd from pasture to pasture and paddock to paddock. From this I could determine how hard the cows were grazing each paddock. Sometimes he might need to remove animals to lessen the grazing pressure on certain paddocks. As the grass entered the dry season, he needed to leave all paddocks with considerable leaf growth because root growth depended on leaf growth. Grass without a good root system was less likely to survive the dry season.

This rancher was genuinely nice. He told me the problems that he was having. There were dozens, even hundreds, of landless peasants encamped along the road that passed by his pasture and into town. During the dry season, they would often try to set his pasture on fire, although usually they caused insignificant damage because he had overgrazed his grass, leaving nothing to burn. They would also cut his fences, allowing his cattle to escape onto the highway. They were trying to drive him off the land so that they could split it up among themselves.

Once when I went to visit him, his wife told me that he was gone. I reminded his wife that we had made an appointment for that day. His wife said, "Yes, but the peasants tried to kill him the other day when he was driving into town. They fired shots at his pickup. They left holes in his rear window." She assured me that he would be back in three or four days, after things cooled down.

The Chicken Ranch

One person with whom I had spoken at the Rio expo was part-owner of an operation that produced eggs, among other things. He had given me his card. I called him and asked for a meeting to explain what I could do for him. He invited me to his ranch so that I could meet the other three owners and visit their business enterprises.

Their story was complicated. Two sisters had gained ownership of this large operation when their parents died tragically in an automotive accident. One sister, age twenty-four and single at the time, was a veterinarian. The other sister, age twenty-two and single at the time, was an economist. Together they owned 160,000 laying hens, 2,000 head of cattle, a small system of pork production, a transportation company, and five ranches producing coffee, corn, black beans, and soybeans. Within a year of receiving these assets, they had found husbands. Surprise! One had been a veterinary product salesman, and the other had been a beer salesman.

As I made the four-hour trip, I tried to think of how I could help them. Without seeing the group of enterprises, I had no idea. But I knew that they would want me to explain how I could help them within minutes of arriving. I would have to deflect that question until later.

When I arrived, they led me into their office. It was an exceptionally large room with no partitions, and it housed six to eight office employees. I learned they had up to two hundred employees total. They offered me a tiny cup of sweet coffee, and each took one themselves. Before I could finish my coffee, they were already asking how I could help them. I asked if I could refrain from answering that question until I had seen the entire operation.

The egg operation consisted of eighteen batches of 10,000 birds, 160,000 of which were laying eggs. Every batch of hens arrived together as chicks and stayed together until they were shipped out to soup factories. I saw that the business had no individual production records. What production records they had were always for the combined 160,000 laying hens. I made a mental note of this.

They used their transportation company to distribute eggs to their egg buyers and to bring back truckloads of corn that Brazil had imported from the US. I watched a couple of men grinding corn with other ingredients to make feed rations. They had a total of five or six different feed rations to accommodate all the ages of chicks and chickens.

The cattle operation was in good condition. Their pastures were not overgrazed, and their herdsmen knew what they were doing. The same went for the business's coffee and grain production.

We met again late in the afternoon. My plan included the following: count the eggs by size for each of the sixteen lots and create a spreadsheet that would allow the owners to predict how much cash and revenue the eggs would generate month by month during the life of each lot. To do this, I would need to create data-collection forms and train people to fill them out correctly.

The chickens laid eggs that the egg processers classified into one of five or six assorted sizes, ranging from small to jumbo. Each egg size had its own price. To predict cash flow, we had to predict the distribution of egg sizes. Fortunately, egg sizes depended on the hens' age and breed and were predictable. Since each of the eighteen lots had a different hen age, each lot had a different expected distribution of egg size and a different expected flow of revenue.

The people on the farm who received the eggs from each lot were overwhelmed when the eggs started coming in from all eighteen lots. Usually, they just piled them up and processed them as they came in.

Now management was asking the egg processors to pile the eggs from each of the sixteen lots separately. They were more than unhappy—they were near revolt—but with time they learned to manage easily enough.

The office manager recorded the data into a spreadsheet each day. After I showed the office manager how it worked, he could easily spot an error in data if, for example, one case of eggs that belonged to lot sixteen was placed in lot ten by mistake. That ability to quickly spot an inconsistency was a management tool.

One week the office manager noticed another inconsistency. One lot of hens was producing only half what they normally produced—of all egg sizes. He brought this to the attention of the veterinarian. She visited the building to investigate and learned that the chickens were producing half their eggs without a shell, and these eggs broke as they hit the wire mesh at the bottom of the cages. The egg collectors had never mentioned this because no one had ever cared when it happened before. It had happened many times before.

The veterinarian collected feed samples as the feed left the feed-grinding operation and again when it arrived at the affected hens' housing. This lot of hens was housed about a mile away from the main operation. The dirt road that connected the two locations had potholes. The veterinarian found that the feed was fine when it left the feed mill but was deficient in micronutrients when it arrived at the hens' housing. She concluded that the rough road shook all the micronutrients to the bottom of the feed wagon, and the augers used to empty the wagon did not pick them up. She started having the micronutrients added at the destination, which solved the problem.

Each day that the hens laid eggs without shells cost the company from 250 to 500 dollars or more. Before, the loss of 5,000 eggs out of 160,000 eggs from all the lots was undetectable. But now the loss of 5,000 eggs out of 10,000 eggs from that specific lot demanded attention. It was possible that the company had suffered tens of thousands of dollars in undetected losses over the years. This simple system was a powerful management tool.

Over the next couple of weeks, I worked on the spreadsheet that would estimate the feed needed and the cost of producing each lot of chickens. If printed, the spreadsheet would have taken twenty pages. It was very sophisticated. I was proud of myself.

The German Pig Farmer

I do not remember how, but I met a young German pig farmer whose name was Gerd. He was in his early forties, and he was handsome, rich, and friendly. He worked as an oil broker during the week, and on the weekend, he was a gentleman farmer. His father was on the board of directors of some exceptionally large bank in Germany. The father was very wealthy, and Gerd had many valuable investments in Germany. He confided in me that he lived off his German income and played with what he earned as an oil broker.

Gerd was married to a beautiful younger woman with dark skin and jet-black hair. She was allegedly an Indian princess. They had six children together and lived on an entire city block in São Paulo, where real estate was expensive. As a couple they were very dedicated to each other. I enjoyed watching them together.

Gerd had a farm about three or four hours outside of São Paulo. On his farm, he had a beautiful house with four bedrooms, a beautiful kitchen, and an enviable living room, which featured a cozy fireplace and a sunken area whose built-in sofa could accommodate a dozen or more people. Gerd liked to host parties for his friends on his farm. He was very sociable.

Gerd showed me his livestock operation. He had a couple hundred cows and a capable herd manager, although he overgrazed his pastures. His main enterprise was not cattle but pork production. He had already built six housing units for his sows. As soon as he weaned the sows' piglets, they were moved on to another housing unit, where there were introduced to a growing and fattening regime.

Each month, he added more production units. I do not remember how many sows he had at the time, but his production could no longer be considered small. His goal was to become a large producer of pork. He was increasing his production capacity slowly but steadily. Gerd needed to keep track of how much money he was investing in each housing unit, and he needed to know his costs of production. I recommended that he start collecting data so that he could manage his investment. I would create the forms needed.

Gerd was a member of an exclusive local cooperative. Not all farmers could join. He explained to me that only farmers of German, Swiss, or Austrian blood could join. The group excluded Brazilians because, he said, they had difficulty keeping their word. When the co-op agreed to invest money in a new structure for the co-op, members agreed to put up money. They had discovered that Brazilians often made promises they could not or would not keep, whereas the German farmers did exactly what they had said they would do. For the co-op to make progress, they could not waste time with people who did not keep their word; therefore, they excluded Brazilians.

Once in São Paulo, Gerd invited me to lunch at an expensive restaurant. I could not imagine why we needed to meet there. Worse, I had to wear a suit. I went because he asked me, and I could not refuse him anything. I met him and his wife at the restaurant. Gerd always dressed in a suit, but previously I had seen his wife only at the farm, where she dressed for lazy weekends. On this day, she wore in an exquisite dress and indeed looked like an Indian princess.

We sat at a table in the middle of the restaurant. I did not feel at ease or at home. As we received our menus, Gerd and his wife were busy identifying who else was at the restaurant. Gerd pointed out three or four men who oversaw multimillion-dollar agricultural projects. Some projects I had read about in the newspapers. The restaurant had a balcony, and Gerd kept squinting at a table located in its far corner. Finally, he recognized the man as the head of a company starting an agricultural project worth more than ten million dollars. He was thrilled. He had not yet opened the menu.

In the end, we never talked about business. I figured out that I was an adornment that they needed. They had not wanted people to think that they had come to the restaurant only to see who else was there, so they had brought me. If anyone asked them, they could say they were meeting with their agricultural consultant.

I found just watching Gerd and his wife in that scenario interesting. I could see that Gerd wanted to be that man at the corner

221

table on the balcony more than anything in the world. Each time he added a new pork production facility, he was one step closer to realizing that dream.

Six months after we started working together, Gerd invited me to his house for relaxation. He told me that he was killing a yearling or two and having a barbecue. He had invited the members of their cooperative over. I thought that was an excellent idea. Cold beer and barbecue always made for an enjoyable afternoon.

When the day came, I was sitting in a chair next to Gerd, drinking beer as the yearlings roasted on a grill. The smell was enticing. Then the people started arriving. Not two or three, but twenty or thirty. They were all German, Swiss, or Austrian farmers. Most were in their sixties or even seventies. One elder gentleman rode in on his horse. He wore a riding outfit with flared legs between the hips and knees and black riding boots up to his knees. As he walked toward us, he slapped his riding stick against his boots. I looked at his head, expecting to see an SS hat with a Nazi insignia.

The guests spoke German among themselves. I felt out of place and outnumbered. Many people spoke Portuguese, but it was the first time I had heard Portuguese spoken with a German accent.

Later in the evening, after darkness had crept in, the conversation turned to World War II. I stayed silent. They talked about what had happened to their fathers and uncles. Some had been killed in the war. Others had been wounded, and still others had psychological problems. Some of the older gentlemen had themselves been in the war. They were mostly silent.

Many Germans had decided to leave Germany and go to Brazil toward the end of the war. Some fled from the Allies to escape war crime allegations. Anyway, I stayed silent, but even if I felt out of place, I did not want to leave either. I wanted to hear whatever they had to say. It was a unique opportunity to gain experience about people by listening to their stories while they were completely at ease. They did not realize that I was an American. These stories were worth the long trip to the farm.

Surprise—All Prices Are Frozen

Despite all the government's best efforts to contain inflation, it steadily increased. If my memory is correct, it was between fifteen and eighteen percent each month. At fifteen percent, goods costing one hundred dollars at the beginning of the year would cost 535 dollars at the end of the year. The government was worried because the effects of high inflation were devastating for working people, unemployed people, and retired people. Businesses were fine because they just raised their prices as inflation increased. Working and retired people could not just raise their wages and pensions.

One problem with such inflation was the difficulty in making large purchases. Let us assume you wanted to buy a new car. You visited one store, and its price was 24,000 dollars. You wanted to make sure you had the best deal out there, so you visited another store but found that it was charging 28,000 dollars for the same car. You ran back to the first store, only to find that while you were out searching for a better deal, it had raised its price to 32,000 dollars. The problem was that when you were making a purchase, you had to be in tune with the market so that when the market gave you a fantastic price, you could recognize it and jump on it. If you waited, you would lose. Yet this mentality helped feed more inflation: buy now no matter what the price; otherwise, the purchase might be more expensive later.

One fine morning, Brazil awoke to the news that the government had declared all prices frozen as of three days previous. Whatever price businesses were charging three days ago was the maximum price they could charge now and in the future. Some people had just adjusted their prices for inflation a few days earlier. They would be in good stead because they always added a little extra to the price for unexpected inflation. The problem was that the retailers that had not adjusted their prices for a while and that had been preparing to increase their prices, by as much as twenty-five to thirty-five percent, were caught in an unsustainable situation. Their selling price was frozen at a level insufficient to cover their costs, much less give any profit.

Those businesses caught with an unfavorable price had little choice. Their only protection against bankruptcy was to stop the manufacture or marketing of their items. Each week there was more empty shelf space in stores. Shopping lists for the supermarket were useless. You bought what you found on the shelves. If you found toilet paper, even if you did not need it, you bought it because it might disappear and not reappear for months. Within weeks, at least half of grocery store shelf space was empty.

It was true that common workers saw benefits from this government action. Their money went further than it ever had before. Their standard of living improved. They had never been able to eat meat before, so living in an economy now without meat did not impact them.

The biggest fight broke out between the government and ranchers. Beef was a product that happened to have an exceptionally low price when the government froze prices. Ranchers could not sell their beef without incurring a monetary loss. They were steadfast against this. Beef disappeared from the butchers' shelves and was not replaced. People shifted consumption from beef to pork and chicken until those meats too became difficult to find.

During a six-month period, we never ate beef or pork. We sometimes found chicken, but more often we found only eggs, and there were times when we could not find even eggs, but we were fine. Rice and beans were a meal, or when we had eggs, rice and eggs were a complete meal. We did not suffer. We always had enough to eat.

In Brazil, farmers and ranchers depended completely on loans from the government. These loans always involved large piles of paperwork, but even so, they were worth the effort. The government offered these loans with negative interest rates. For example, if inflation was 535 percent annually, a loan might have a twenty percent annual interest rate. That was a huge advantage for the rancher. Large agricultural enterprises often had one employee whose job it was to obtain all these loans that the company could obtain. The loans were not just critical to ranchers; they were necessary. No farmer could survive if he were forced to go to a regular bank for a commercial loan and pay interest rates greater than the rate of inflation.

The government had grown tired of these ungrateful ranchers refusing to cooperate. They decreed those ranchers must start selling their herds of fat cattle, or the government would ban for life from receiving any more government loans. This was harsh, but the ranchers defiantly shook their fists and shouted insults at the government. The government was not happy.

After a couple of weeks, the government raised the stakes. It decreed that for every rancher who failed to deliver beef animals of appropriate weight to the butcher, the government would have a representative fly over the herds in a helicopter to determine if the animals were at marketable weight; if so, the representative would radio to a fleet of cattle trucks waiting nearby. Those cattle trucks would have a driver, a helper, and two to four soldiers with machine guns. They would enter the ranch and load the cattle. The government would not pay the rancher anything for his beef animals. That was the price for defying the government.

One day during this confusion, I made an on-site visit to my rancher client who had been shot at. We were standing in a pasture, observing the cattle and the grass's condition, when a helicopter appeared low out of nowhere. It flew slowly over the cattle, scattering the animals, and then kept flying. We looked down at the end of the driveway and saw two cattle trucks and, behind the cabs, four men with machine guns. They backed up and moved on.

There was pushback over the government's brutish behavior. After a couple of weeks, the government backed off. The government eventually paid for cattle taken from owners.

There were side effects of the frozen-price escapade. One was that you could find expensive machines that were unusable because they needed a five-dollar replacement part that was unavailable. The government, in trying to control inflation, killed the economy. Eventually, the government removed price controls, and that caused a spike in inflation because everyone raised their prices just in case the government should decide to reinstate the price controls. The government was unpredictable, except in its ability to make a dire situation even worse.

Our Worker and the Street Thieves

A Swiss company located in the center of São Paulo contacted me to do contract work for them. Like all offices, we had an office boy. His job was to run errands. He always carried a beat-up briefcase that contained bank deposits and office bills that needed paying. In Brazil, you never sent money in an envelope. It would never arrive. Sometimes he carried only bills to pay, and sometimes he carried ten thousand dollars in cash.

Our office was on the fourth floor in an office building. The city had closed the street below to vehicle traffic. They filled it in and covered it with nice, small black and white blocks that formed interesting designs. The street was at least forty feet, if not fifty feet, wide and people filled it.

Once I was tired and decided to look out the window for a few minutes. I saw a businessman in an expensive suit carrying an expensive briefcase. I looked ten or twenty yards behind him and saw that a young boy had started to sprint toward the businessman. The businessman was still unaware that thieves had targeted him. The boy snatched the briefcase and continued his sprint. Before the businessman knew what had happened, the boy was around the corner, where he passed the briefcase off to a confederate, who placed it inside a shopping bag and headed in a different direction. Friends told me that there usually was a third member of the gang nearby with a weapon. If someone would have attacked the thief with the stolen briefcase, the third member would shoot the person fighting with the gang member.

Safety experts discouraged people from wearing earrings, bracelets, necklaces, or even watches. These made people prime targets. They also discouraged women from using purses with long straps because the thieves could cut the strap in a split second.

One day, our business owner tasked our office boy with delivering ten thousand dollars to someone. Just outside our building, thieves attacked him. He fought and managed to get away and immediately returned to our building and came up to our office. He had a couple of cuts on his face and was scared, but he was safe, as was the money. That was a good day at the office.

Going to the Bank on Payday

In Brazil, going to the bank was an experience. Even small banks had ten to twelve cashiers working at any given time. People could not pay bills by mailing checks through the post office because their someone would steal their checks. Everyone had to go to banks to make utility payments, as well as car payments and house payments. Banks were remarkably busy places.

In São Paulo, businesses paid workers twice a month. Thieves knew this and waited for payday to rob banks. Sometimes thieves would rob one bank, walk down the street, and rob another bank, continuing the process until they were satisfied. With São Paulo traffic, it was impossible for the police to reach a bank in time to intercede in a robbery.

We never went to the bank on payday. We always managed to conduct business before or after those days.

Driving the Beltway

The beltway was the road system around the outer edge of São Paulo. People said it was faster than trying to drive inside São Paulo. The beltway had four to six lanes going in each direction, with the two sides separated by a concrete barrier to keep drivers from changing their minds as to which direction they wanted to go. Sometimes traffic flowed quickly, but usually it was slow and even included periodic stoppage time.

Thieves were quick to figure out that when the cars were stopped, they were trapped. They could not move in any direction until the traffic started to flow again. Groups of thieves with machine guns strapped to their arms and with masks covering their faces would wait for traffic to stop. They then walked out into the beltway. Each thief had an assigned lane and walked from car to car, asking for donations of money and jewelry. Sometimes one group of thieves walked downstream, and another group walked upstream. The thieves even yelled at drivers down the line to have their things ready, to save the thieves' time.

Even when they had a loaded weapon in their car, gun-owning drivers did not mess with multiple machine guns. When traffic started to flow, the thieves walked to the edge of the beltway and waited for the next traffic jam. Police had no way of reaching these spots. This was in the mid-1980s, before cell phones, so people had no way of calling for help.

Banco Safra

My consulting business was not growing, and inflation was hurting me. I wanted to ask my clients for more money, but because agricultural prices did not accompany inflation, I did not think it wise to ask. Farmers and ranchers had to watch their expenses. If I asked for more money, they might decide to save money by releasing me from my contract. They were already paying me what they could afford.

My solution was to look for a full-time job. While combing newspaper advertisements, I saw a wonderful opportunity with Banco Safra, the fifth-largest bank in Brazil. Even at fifth place, it was a big bank and owned by one individual. This owner participated in the government's project to entice large businesses into investing in agricultural projects that would turn wilderness into productive enterprises. For example, if Banco Safra had a ten-million-dollar tax bill, instead of paying the government that money, it could invest the money in developing new agricultural land and, in the end, owning that land.

Banco Safra's project of this sort had started out at over 400,000 acres divided into three large parcels of land—the total acres being the equivalent of an area twenty-five miles by twenty-five miles. The land was in the state of Goias, next to Mato Grosso in the center of Brazil. Squatters had overrun one parcel of more than 100,000 acres. Faced with the prospect of sending in a militia to reclaim the land, the bank walked away and allowed the squatters to keep the land; however, the bank doubled the number of security personnel guarding the other two land parcels. They would not give up any more land.

The company's goal was to develop 15,000 acres of land each year. The land was like a savanna. The team in charge of clearing the land braided three two-inch-thick cables together and connected a 200-yard-long piece between two large bulldozers. These dozers took off through the savanna about fifty to seventy-five yards apart. The cable clotheslined the trees and knocked them over. If the workers found exceptionally large trees, they went around them. Larger dozers would individually knock them down later.

Once the large dozers had knocked down the large trees, they brought in large rubber-tired tractors with huge blades with teeth at the bottom to windrow the trees. With one tractor on each side, the workers created rows of piled trees like raked alfalfa. After they windrowed the trees, the tractors turned in the other direction and forced the rows into piles as large as was feasible. After they made the piles, they were set afire. After they burned the piles, they were re-piled and burned again.

As soon as they cleaned up the trees, the workers spread lime and built fences around each area. Each paddock was about eighty acres. They disked the area twice and planted it to grass. The tractors operated twenty-four hours a day, in two shifts of twelve hours each, and seven days a week. It would take a couple of years before the grass could support cattle.

Each year a cattle buyer bought a few thousand cows and associated bulls to occupy the pastures that were coming into grazing. Within five years, they would be buying five thousand head per year. After that, they would not need to buy more cows because they could add enough new cows from their own inventory of heifers. Their goal was to build the cattle population to at least fifty thousand cows.

In São Paulo, there was a group of ten or twelve employees whose job was to do the planning for this project for the next twenty years. I obtained a job with Banco Safra as the assistant manager of this group. The manager was a young man of Italian descent. He was very competent and all business. Along with me, they hired two other agricultural technical people. One was a cattle specialist, and the other was a grass specialist. We had a competent team.

I had to develop a spreadsheet to project the number of cattle by age (unweaned calves, weaned calves, yearlings, etc.). I had to consider mortality and calving rate (number of calves from one hundred cows) and other variables.

I also had to calculate the number of tractors we needed to buy, by size, for the next twenty years. Along with the cost of buying new tractors and selling used-up tractors, I had to include operating expenses, including overhauls for all tractors. Once they had converted all the savanna, we could sell all the dozers and tractors that had been used to clear the land. I loved this work. I developed incredibly detailed spreadsheets.

The problem with this job was my commuting time. It took me twenty minutes to walk to the subway, and I spent another twenty-five minutes on the subway before I had to catch a bus. I spent thirty minutes on the bus and another fifteen minutes walking from the bus to the building. Once, when it was raining heavily, it took me more than three hours to return home. Each day I spent a minimum of three-plus hours commuting. Because my boss was a driven man, it was not possible to spend fewer than ten hours at work. I was tired all the time and did not have much of a family life. And I had to wear a suit every day.

I liked working at the bank, however. My boss was in charge, and he actively supervised. Everyone knew what the bank expected and was doing it. There was no gossiping allowed and no backstabbing. Everyone worked hard and was nice to each other. The boss set the tone. The difference between working here and in Natal was night and day. Yes, I loved Banco Safra.

Visiting the Ranch

One day our boss told us that we had to fly to the ranch and check its inventory of parts. I liked the idea of visiting the ranch, but not the idea of checking inventory. We flew from São Paulo to Brasilia on Sunday. From Brasilia we chartered a two-prop plane to fly us to the ranch, since it had its own landing strip. There were four of us traveling: the grass man, the cow man, the boss, and me. A Jeep met us and took us to a large guesthouse, where we had dinner, then they showed us to our rooms. The accommodations were excellent, as was the cook.

On Monday morning we had breakfast early and set off to the ranch headquarters, where we met the project manager. He never was in a good mood, although being responsible for a project whose annual budget was more than ten million dollars could take the smile from a person's face.

I did not understand what we had to do with the inventory. The ranch had so many items in inventory, especially if we considered tractor parts, fence-building materials, and all the other things—were we really going to count all that stuff? The project manager and our boss engaged in some straight talk for an hour, and then we no longer needed to count anything. I had no idea what had just happened or why four of us had traveled here, except that it was important for us to see the actual ranch for which we were doing all the planning.

We drove around and saw each stage of work, including the clotheslining of the trees, the windrowing, the bunching, and the burning. The fences were new, and the cattle were gigantic. They were all Zebu breed, huge animals with a hump on their shoulders, and they were ill-tempered.

During a group meeting, our grass man said he thought that they could establish the grass quicker if a thin mulch protected the seed. The project manager declared that they would plant two thousand acres of rye as an experiment. His people put in an order for two John Deere combines. They would sell the rye seed and then bale the straw, which they would use as mulch. If that worked, they would expand the enterprise.

After lunch we went to participate in vaccinating cows and weaning calves. When around their calves, Zebu cows were more than ill-tempered—they were nasty and dangerous. Thus, the ranch had wooden corrals that were at least six feet high. The ranch workers drove the cows and calves through a narrow but tall chute. On the outside of the chute, there was a ledge about five feet from the ground. We stood on this ledge with our knees braced against the top fence board and with syringes in our hands. We each had a different vaccination. As the cow came through the chute at forty miles an hour, we leaned forward and gave the cow a dose of whatever vaccination we had been assigned. The calf always followed at the cow's heels. Ahead of me a man controlled a gate. He sent the cow to the left and the calf to the right. As soon as the cow discovered this, she went berserk. She cried, mooed, threw dirt with her front feet, and complained for all to hear.

Behind us were several empty pens. Once I turned around from my task and saw a mad cow pawing the dirt, her eyes focused on my backside. I yelled to the others, and we all jumped to the other side of the chute. She attacked the spot where I had been. She was an unhappy mama and had managed to jump two six-foot fences to reach a spot where she envisioned taking her revenge on us. Cowboys took her back to the pen she was supposed to be in.

There was time for us to talk to people who worked on the ranch. One man told us of the river that ran through the land. It was a huge river. He said that people there had caught fish as large as a man. He said that the ranch had trouble with the Indians coming up the river and stealing the ranch's boats. A couple Indians had walked into the bank's home base, put a canoe on their heads, and walked out. They had done this during the day with no attempt to hide what they were doing. They had bows and arrows slung on their shoulders. The ranch just marked this down as an expense. The company did not want to start a war with the Indians.

Inflation continued increasing a little each month. After I had worked at Banco Safra three months, inflation had reached thirty to thirty-five percent a month and was still increasing. The bank had to do something to keep its employees from revolting. It gave automatic salary increases of twenty-two percent per month for two months, and on the third month, it gave a double increase, which amounted to a forty-nine percent increase. That combination of salary increases averaged out to be thirty percent per month. That helped, but my problem was that my property owner would increase the rent payment for my house in December. My best estimate was that it would be ten times greater. If I paid one hundred dollars per month now, it would increase to 1,000 dollars a month. I did not see how I could afford that. My only solution was to move farther from work, and that was not a viable option as far as I was concerned. We were at an impasse.

Katia and I had conversations about our future. Kevin was going to school, and they taught in Portuguese. Nick was going to preschool, and Christianne was four years old. Finally, we decided that we would return to the US, after living eight years in Brazil. The children would start school in the US without speaking any English, but that is another story.